INVISIBLE EAGLE
The History of Nazi Occultism

INVISIBLE EAGLE

The History of Nazi Occultism

Alan Baker

First published in Great Britain in 2000 by

Virgin Publishing Ltd
Thames Wharf Studios
Rainville Road
London W6 9HA

A catalogue record for this book is available
from the British Library.

ISBN 1 85227 863 3

Cover design by Splash
Typeset by TW Typesetting, Plymouth, Devon
Printed and bound by CPD, Wales

This book is dedicated to Ian Fairweather,
old friend and fellow slacker.

Contents

The historian may be rational, but history is not.

Louis Pauwels and Jacques Bergier

'I'm a sceptic.'
'No, you're only incredulous, a doubter, and that's different.'

Umberto Eco, *Foucault's Pendulum*

Acknowledgements

Grateful acknowledgement is given for permission to quote from the following previously published material:

The Coming Race by E. G. E. Bulwer Lytton, published by Sutton Publishing, Stroud, Gloucestershire, 1995.

Arktos: The Polar Myth in Science, Symbolism, and Nazi Survival by Joscelyn Godwin, published by Thames and Hudson, London, 1993.

The Occult Roots of Nazism by Nicholas Goodrick-Clarke, published by I. B. Tauris & Co., London, 1985.

Extract from *PROJEKT UFO* © 1995 W. A. Harbinson. First published by Boxtree Ltd and reprinted with permission from the author.

Trevor Ravenscroft: *The Spear of Destiny* (York Beach, ME: Samuel Weiser, 1982). Material used by permission.

The Secret Doctrine by Helena Petrovna Blavatsky, published by Theosophical University Press, Pasadena, California, 1999.

Psychic Dictatorship in the USA by Alex Constantine, published by Feral House, 2532 Lincoln Blvd. #359, Venice, CA 90291.

The Making of Adolf Hitler: The Birth and Rise of Nazism by Eugene Davidson, published by University of Missouri Press, 1997.

Casebook on Alternative 3 by Jim Keith, published by IllumiNet Press, Lilburn, Georgia, 1994.

Shambhala by Nicholas Roerich, published by the Nicholas Roerich Museum, New York, 1978.
The Last Days of Hitler by Hugh Trevor-Roper, published by Macmillan, London, 1995.
Explaining Hitler: The Search For the Origins of His Evil by Ron Rosenbaum, published by Papermac, London, 1999.
The Face of the Third Reich by Joachim C. Fest, first published by Weidenfeld and Nicolson, 1970.
Hitler and the Occult by Ken Anderson, published by Prometheus Books, Amherst, New York, 1995.

While every effort has been made to contact copyright holders for permission to use other lengthy quotes, this has not proved possible in all cases. Should these copyright holders wish to contact the publisher, appropriate credit will be given in future editions.

Many thanks also to my agent, Julian Alexander, for his indispensable help and advice over the past two and a half years; and to my editors at Virgin Publishing, Lorna Russell, who got the book commissioned, and Kerri Sharp, who made its journey to publication a pleasure.

Introduction: search for a map of hell

THIS BOOK IS CONCERNED with one of the most controversial notions of the late twentieth century, one that is so bizarre and appalling in its implications that serious historians have consistently dismissed it as the worst kind of nonsense. Put simply, the notion is this: that the shocking nightmare of Nazism and the destruction it wrought throughout the world were the result of an attempt by Hitler and his cohorts to contact and enlist the aid of supernatural forces in their bid for domination of the planet. Upon reading this, older readers may be put in mind of the lurid but enjoyable occult thrillers of Dennis Wheatley, such as *Strange Conflict*, which deals with Nazi magical practices in a highly sensational way, and may dismiss the idea for that reason. Other readers may well pause to consider the hideous excesses practised by the Nazis and be dismayed that the defining tragedy of the twentieth century should be trivialised by such an idea.

There is no doubt that the subject of the Third Reich inspires a deep and abiding fascination to this day, with the origin of the awful cruelties perpetrated in its name still the subject of intense debate. Ever since Hitler's death in the *Führerbunker* in 1945, historians, psychologists and theologians have attempted to understand and explain the frightful aberration that was Nazism. One of the foci around which discussion of Hitler moves is the question of where he stands in the spectrum of human nature. As the journalist Ron

Rosenbaum notes, the very existence of this spectrum suggests an extremely uncomfortable question: 'is Hitler on a continuum with previous and successive mass murderers, explicable within the same framework, on the extreme end of the same spectrum of the human nature we supposedly share with Jeffrey Dahmer and Mahatma Gandhi?'[1] Or is he something else entirely, existing outside the continuum of humanity, evil in some absolute, ultimate way? The theologian Emil Fackenheim believes that such was the magnitude of Hitler's crimes that we must consider him as representing a 'radical evil', an 'eruption of demonism into history'.[2] Hitler's evil is seen by thinkers like Fackenheim as existing beyond the bounds of ordinary human behaviour (however appalling). Indeed, to them it is so extreme that it transcends the field of behavioural science and enters the realm of theology: in other words, Hitler's ultimate nature can only be completely understood by God.

The industrialised mass murder perpetrated by the Nazis resonated irresistibly through the latter half of the twentieth century, and is certainly the principal contributing factor to what the British historian Norman Davies calls 'a demonological fascination with Germany'. In summarising the historiography of the Western Powers, Davies states: 'Germany stands condemned as the prime source both of the malignant imperialism which produced the First World War, and of the virulent brand of fascism which provoked the Second.'[3] In the post-war years, this contributed to the 'Allied scheme of history' in which the West presented (and still presents) itself as the pinnacle of civilisation, morality and altruism. While the numerous reasons why this is far from the truth lie beyond the scope of this book, the attitudes that have accompanied the Allied scheme are of extreme importance with regard to our continuing fascination with the Nazis. Davies writes of 'The ideology of "anti-fascism", in which the Second World War of 1939–45 is perceived as "the War against Fascism" and as the defining event in the triumph of Good over Evil.'[4] It is easy to understand, therefore, how such defining events (particularly those separated from us by a mere 55 years) can tenaciously maintain themselves in the public consciousness.

While historians have tended to concentrate on the many important economic, social and historical factors that influenced Nazi ideology, somewhat less attention has been paid to the Nazis' fascination with arcane and esoteric belief systems, in spite of their undeniable influence upon Hitler and the architects of National Socialism in the years leading up to and including the Second World War. The purpose of this book, therefore, is to attempt to make some sense of the irrational and benighted realms of Nazi occultism and pseudo-science, and to attempt an explanation of the strange attraction they held for their proponents.

Given the human capacity for myth-making, it is perhaps unsurprising that the known history of the Third Reich should have given rise, in subsequent decades, to the assertion that the Nazis were, quite literally, in contact with an evil, transhuman intelligence that chose to exert its influence over humanity through the living conduits of Hitler and other high-ranking members of the Reich. In the course of this book, we shall see that the intellectual fathers of National Socialism, aggressively anti-Semitic Pan-German and *völkisch* nationalists like Guido von List, Jörg Lanz von Liebenfels and Rudolf von Sebottendorff, cultivated an undeniable and profound interest in occultism, theosophy, the idea of Atlantis as a lost Aryan civilisation, and the magical powers inherent in the very blood of racially pure Germans. That Hitler's immediate subordinates themselves dabbled in occult sciences such as astrology is also beyond doubt. Occultism played a significant role in the formation and rituals of the SS; and it is also a matter of historical record that the Nazis embraced cock-eyed cosmological theories such as Hörbiger's World Ice concept (which provided them with an opportunity to denounce the ideas of the Jewish Albert Einstein).

In the decades since the end of the war, some historians have seen Nazi occultism as evidence of the essential irrationality underlying the Third Reich, and as a salutary lesson regarding the power that myth can exercise over the human mind. This point of view is, of course, based on the fact that occultism (however important it may be in the history of the human quest for understanding) is *not* an accurate way of describing the nature of the Universe. The concepts, beliefs, attitudes and actions we shall encounter in this book, however, are based on the opposite notion, that occultism is a genuine and useful system with which to apprehend and influence the workings of Nature.

If we take Fackenheim's belief that Hitler represents an 'eruption of demonism into history', which can only truly be understood by God, and apply it to the subject of Nazi occultism, it becomes clear that the various claims for the reality of genuine Nazi occult power were inevitable. One can easily imagine the thought processes of the writers who have made these claims: the Third Reich was an atrocious aberration in the history of humanity, an utter catastrophe even by our usual bloody standards. How could it have come about? If Hitler was uniquely evil, *why* was he so? What was it in his mind, his nature, his essential attributes and the actions to which they gave rise that took him beyond the continuum of human behaviour and placed him at the level of the absolute, comprehensible only to the creator of the Universe? If his evil extended beyond the human, is it possible that its *origin* lay beyond the human?

In view of the extreme nature of Nazi crimes, the idea that an evil external to humanity (a *cosmic* evil) exists and that leading Nazis actually attempted to make contact with trans-human entities in their pursuit of world domination and the creation of an Aryan super-race may be seen by many as distasteful in the extreme, and demeaning to the memory of those who suffered and died under Hitler's tyranny. It is an uncomfortable notion, to be sure, and one that, as the British writer Joscelyn Godwin notes, occupies 'that twilight zone between fact and fiction: the most fertile territory for the nurturing of mythological images and their installation in the collective imagination'.[5] However, it is for this very reason that the idea of genuine Nazi occult power demands our attention: it has become an important (if unwelcome) aspect of the history of the Second World War and the second half of the twentieth century.

At this point, I should clarify my reasons for and intentions in writing this book. The prevalence of the Nazi-occultism idea is such that I considered it worthwhile to attempt an evaluation of it – especially in view of the fact that humanity stands on the threshold of a new millennium more or less intact. With the arrival of the year 2000, human culture finds itself in an intriguing position, the nature of which might best be captured by the British writer Thomas De Quincey's statement that the present is the confluence of two eternities, the past and the future. As we look with curiosity, hope and some trepidation to the new century and the new millennium before us, we will also, of necessity, look back at the thousand years we have just left behind, and in particular at the century that has just ended – without doubt the bloodiest and most violent, but also the century that saw more and greater scientific advances than any other in the history of our species. And yet, despite the myriad scientific and technological advances that have carried us to this point in our history, it cannot be said with any confidence that science itself has triumphed over mythology. In some ways, this is by no means a bad thing: human beings are not machines, and a worldwide culture based exclusively on hard scientific principles would be intolerable to human nature, which is fascinated by spirituality, mythology and mystery.

However, this inherent need in human beings to mythologise can seriously hinder the quest for truth, particularly historical truth. As the British historian Hugh Trevor-Roper put it, 'reason is powerless against the obstinate love of fiction'. When he wrote this, Trevor-Roper was referring to the so-called 'Hitler survival myth', the idea that the Führer did not die in the Berlin bunker in 1945, but somehow managed to escape – according to various versions, to South America, to Antarctica, and even to a monastery in Tibet. As a historian and British intelligence officer, Trevor-Roper was given the task of establishing Hitler's fate by the then-head of Counter-Intelligence in the British Zone of Germany, Sir Dick White. He made his report to the Four-Power Intelligence Committee in Berlin on 1 November 1945, and the report inspired one of the finest history books ever published, *The Last Days of Hitler* (1947). In this book, Trevor-Roper calmly establishes beyond all reasonable doubt that Hitler did not survive the end of the Second World War. Nevertheless, the Hitler survival myth continued to circulate, particularly in far-right and neo-Nazi circles, and can still be encountered occasionally to this day.

This mythopoeic capacity is brought to bear in the absence of verifiable data. In the case of the Hitler survival myth, in September 1945 no one knew for certain what had happened to the Führer: he had simply disappeared. This gave rise to numerous speculations, particularly from journalists, that he had somehow managed to escape from the ruins of Berlin as his Thousand-Year Reich imploded to the dimensions of his bunker. When Trevor-Roper's final report was delivered, stating that Hitler had died by his own hand and that all other theories were 'contrary to the only positive evidence and supported by no evidence at all', it drew criticism from some quarters. 'The critics did not indeed deny the evidence that was produced, but they maintained that there was still a possibility of escaping so final a conclusion; they maintained that the body that had been burnt was that not of Hitler but of a "double" introduced at the last minute . . .'[6]

Trevor-Roper's use of the phrase 'a possibility of escaping' is interesting and very significant with regard to the present book, since the idea of escaping from a final conclusion to the horror of Hitler resonates powerfully with the fact that Hitler himself managed to escape human justice through suicide. Indeed, as more than one commentator has suggested, Hitler managed a twofold escape: not only did he elude punishment for his crimes but he has also eluded explanation, as noted earlier. This inability on our part to arrive at a satisfactory explanation for Hitler has been called 'evidentiary despair' by Ron Rosenbaum, who illustrates the concept with comments from historians such as Trevor-Roper, Alan Bullock and the Jewish-studies scholar Alvin Rosenfeld. Trevor-Roper still considers Hitler a 'frightening mystery', while Bullock states that the more he learns about Hitler, the harder he finds him to explain. Rosenfeld sums up the problem best: 'No representation of Adolf Hitler has seemed able to present the man or satisfactorily explain him.'[7]

Of course, there have been many attempts to explain the mind of Hitler, to chart the process that took him from unprepossessing Viennese down-and-out to the assassin of European Jewry. Surprisingly (indeed, shockingly), the debate that has continued for more than half a century concentrates partly on the question of whether or not Hitler can accurately be described as 'evil'. Our first reaction to this might be that it is the easiest question to answer that has ever been posed, to echo Alan Bullock's 'If *he* isn't evil, who is?' Nevertheless, the ease with which we seem to be able to answer this question is illusory and, in addressing ourselves to it, we find ourselves grappling with one of the oldest problems of humanity: the problem of the nature of evil itself. As Rosenbaum reminds us, 'it doesn't matter what *word* we choose to apply to Hitler', it does not alter the number of people who suffered and died. 'How we think about Hitler and evil and the nature of Hitler's choice is a reflection of important cultural assumptions and divisive schisms about individual consciousness and historical causation, the never-ending conflict over free will, determinism, and personal responsibility.'[8] It is important to emphasise that to question the use of the word 'evil' as applied to Hitler is not to minimise in any way the enormity of his crimes (which were inarguably horrific). However, our intuitive sense of the existence of evil and the certainty with which we perceive its presence in Hitler is little help in our search for a definition of it. Rosenbaum informs us that during the course of interviews with many historians, conducted as part of the research for his remarkable book *Explaining Hitler: The Search For the Origins of His Evil*, he discovered to his surprise that many were reluctant to call Adolf Hitler evil.

Rosenbaum is instructive on the problems of defining evil in terms sufficiently accurate to allow a serious and rigorous discussion of the primary motivating factors in Hitler's crimes:

[I]n the realm of scholarship, it's remarkable to discover how many sophisticated thinkers of all stripes find themselves unwilling to find a principled rationale for calling Hitler evil, at least in the strict sense of doing wrong *knowingly*. The philosophical literature that takes these questions seriously makes a distinction between obviously evil *deeds* such as mass murder and the not-always-obvious nature of the *intent* of the doer, preferring the stricter term 'wickedness' to describe wrongdoers who do evil deeds *knowing* they are doing wrong. I was drawn to the philosophical literature on the problem of wickedness ... by another defining moment in my encounters with Hitler explainers: my conversation in London with H. R. Trevor-Roper, former Regius Professor of Modern History at Oxford, one of the first and most widely respected postwar Hitler explainers. I'd asked him the deceptively simple question I'd begun asking a number of Hitler explainers: 'Do you consider Hitler consciously evil? Did he know what he was doing was wrong?'[9] [Original emphasis]

Trevor-Roper's answer was an emphatic No: Hitler was convinced of his own rectitude. Although his *deeds* reached an extreme of awfulness, he committed them in the deluded belief that they were right. Rosenbaum also points out that the assumption that Jewish people themselves might be expected to be the first to reject this 'rectitude argument' is also flawed, as evidenced by the statement of Efraim Zuroff, director of the Simon Wiesenthal Centre's Jerusalem headquarters, and the chief Nazi-hunter in Israel. When asked if he thought Hitler was conscious he was doing wrong, Zuroff almost shouted: 'Of course not! Hitler thought he was a doctor! Killing germs! That's all Jews were to him! He believed he was doing *good*, not evil!'[10] (Original emphasis.)

The acceptance by many historians of the rectitude argument leads Rosenbaum to a tentative and very interesting conclusion: 'that beneath the Socratic logic of the position might be an understandably human, even emotional, rejection – as simply *unbearable* – of the idea that someone could commit mass murder *without* a sense of rectitude, however delusional. That Hitler could have done it out of pure personal hatred, knowing exactly what he was doing and how wrong it was.'[11] (Original emphasis.) Allied to this is the so-called Great Abstraction Theory of history, which places emphasis on profound and inevitable trends at the expense of the activities of single personalities as formulated in the now-unfashionable Great Man Theory. According to the Great Abstraction Theory: 'Nothing could have prevented the Holocaust. No one's to blame for the failure to halt Hitler's rise. If it hadn't been Hitler, it would have been "someone like Hitler" serving as an instrument of those inexorable larger forces.'[12] The alternative, which is considered unthinkable by many historians and philosophers, is that a single human being *wanted* to bring about the Holocaust – a human being . . . a member of our species. (The reader may detect a similarity between this notion and the reluctance by some to allow Hitler to be placed within the continuum of human behaviour mentioned earlier.)

While the implications of the Great Abstraction Theory may serve as a form of consolation (nothing could have prevented the Holocaust from happening: it was the result of uncontrollable historical forces), it has been rightly criticised in some quarters for its implicit removal of Hitler from the position of sole creator of the Final Solution. In the last analysis, he remains the greatest enigma: any attempt to explain seriously the origin and nature of the evil of the Third Reich must centre on Adolf Hitler – not as a pawn of larger forces, but as the prime mover of Nazism.

All of which brings us back to the central question, phrased memorably by Rosenbaum: what made Hitler *Hitler*? What turned him from an apparently ordinary, undistinguished human being into the very embodiment of wickedness, the destroyer of more than six million innocent people? According to Yehuda Bauer, a founder of the discipline of Holocaust Studies, while it is possible in theory to explain Hitler, it may well be too late. The deaths of crucial witnesses and the loss of important documents may have resulted in our eternal separation from the means to answer the question, to draw an accurate map of the hell Hitler created on Earth.

Of course, there have been numerous theories put forward, including the suggestion that Hitler's anti-Semitism derived from the unproven seduction and impregnation of his paternal grandmother, Maria Schicklgruber, by a Jew, resulting in the birth of his father, Alois Hitler. According to this theory, Hitler exterminated the Jews in order to exterminate what he perceived as the poison in his own blood. Another conjecture has it that Hitler discovered an affair between his half-niece, Geli Raubal, and a Jewish music teacher, and that he either drove her to suicide or had her murdered. This resulted in a desire for murderous vengeance against the Jews. Yet another theory suggests that the death of Hitler's mother in 1907 was in some way made more painful by the malpractice of her Jewish doctor, Eduard Bloch, for which Hitler, once again, exacted terrible vengeance.[13]

As we have just seen, the desperate search for an adequate explanation of Hitler has resulted in a number of contradictory theories, many of which are built on flimsy evidence. Interestingly, this search has also generated a mythology of its own, revolving around what Rosenbaum calls 'the lost safe-deposit box. A place where allegedly revelatory documents – ones that might provide the missing link, the lost key to the Hitler psyche, the true source of his metamorphosis – seem to disappear beyond recovery.'[14] This mythology was inspired by real events in Munich in 1933, when Fritz Gerlich, the last anti-Hitler journalist in that city, made a desperate attempt to alert the world to the true nature of Hitler by means of a report of an unspecified scandal. On 9 March, just as Gerlich's newspaper, *Der Gerade Weg*, was about to go to press, SA storm troopers entered the premises and ripped it from the presses.

Although no copy of the Gerlich report has ever been found, rumours have been circulating for many years about the ultimate fate of the information with which Gerlich hoped to warn the world of the danger of Hitler, one of which involves a secret copy of the report that was smuggled out of the premises (along with supporting documentary material) by one Count Waldburg-Zeil. Waldburg-Zeil allegedly took the report and its supporting documents to his estate north of Munich, where he buried them somewhere in the grounds. According to Gerlich's biographer Erwin von Aretin, however, Waldburg-Zeil destroyed them during the war, fearful of what might happen should they be discovered by the Nazi authorities.

Rosenbaum informs us of an alternative version of these events, involving documents proving that Geli Raubal was indeed killed on the orders of Adolf Hitler. According to von Aretin's son, the historian Professor Karl-Ottmar Freiherr von Aretin, his father gave the documents to his cousin, Karl Ludwig Freiherr von Guttenberg, co-owner of the *Münchener Neueste Nachrichten*, who put them in a safe-deposit box in Switzerland. Guttenberg was killed following his involvement in the attempted coup against Hitler on 20 July 1944. For the sake of security, he had not told anyone the number of the safe-deposit-box account.

The idea that somewhere in Switzerland there lies a set of documents containing information that might be of some help in explaining the transformation of Adolf Hitler from man to monster is a powerful one, and has generated more than one subsequent controversial claim. There is, for instance, the account given by a German novelist named Ernst Weiss, according to which the voice Hitler claimed to have heard while recovering from war injuries in a hospital at Pasewalk summoning him to a mission to avenge Germany following her surrender in 1918, was actually that of Dr Edmund Forster, a staff psychiatrist at the hospital. Forster 'sought to cure Hitler's hysterical blindness by putting him in a hypnotic trance and implanting the post-hypnotic suggestion that Hitler had to recover his sight to fulfil a mission to redeem Germany's lost honor'.[15]

Weiss, who apparently befriended Forster, claimed that the psychiatrist discovered a dreadful secret during the course of Hitler's treatment, a secret with the potential to unlock the future Führer's psyche and which Forster took with him when he fled Germany in 1933. Shortly before his suicide (to which he was driven by the Gestapo), Forster took his Pasewalk case notes to Switzerland and placed them in a safe-deposit box in a bank in Basel. As an added security measure, Forster rewrote the notes in a cipher of his own devising, the key to which he took to his grave.

As Rosenbaum notes, the unreadable cipher in the lost safe-deposit box is a powerful metaphor for the elusive explanation of Hitler:

These lost-safe-deposit-box stories clearly serve as expressions of anxiety about – and talismans against – an otherwise apparently inexplicable malignant evil. In fact, despite the despairing tone of the safe-deposit-box myths, they represent a kind of epistemological *optimism*, a faith in an explicable world. Yes, something is missing, but if we don't have the missing piece in hand, at least it exists somewhere. At least somewhere there's the lost key that *could* make sense of the apparently motiveless malignancy of Hitler's psyche . . . A missing piece, however mundane or bizarre . . . but something here on earth, something we can contain in our imagination, something safely containable within the reassuring confines of a box in a Swiss bank. Something not beyond our ken, just beyond our reach, something less unbearably frightening than inexplicable evil. [Original emphasis.][16]

If I have relied rather heavily on Rosenbaum's work in the last few pages, it is because it is of considerable relevance to our concerns in the present book. When I began to think about writing *Invisible Eagle*, my intention was to attempt an evaluation of the evidence for Nazi involvement with occultism and black magic. In the course of my preliminary reading, however, it became clear to me that, while early racist organisations like the *völkisch* movement and the Pan-Germans were most certainly influenced by occultist notions, the evidence for Adolf Hitler and other leading Nazis as practising black magicians was decidedly weak. Nevertheless, in the decades since the end of the Second World War, an elaborate mythology has developed around this very concept, the details of which (as lurid as they are unsubstantiated) have been presented in a number of popular books, mainly in the 1960s and early 1970s.

The reason for this, it seems to me, has a great deal to do with what we have been discussing in this Introduction: the need – desperate and perhaps doomed to failure – to arrive at an adequate explanation for the catastrophic wickedness of Hitler and the Nazis. Indeed, this notion first arose during the actual war years and was adhered to at first principally by members of the Spiritualist community, and later by many others (it is estimated that by 1941 as much as 25 per cent of the British population had some belief in the paranormal). An interest in occultism and Spiritualism became a great comfort to those who had lost loved ones either overseas or in the Blitz, since it held the potential to establish for them the reality of an afterlife, a world of the spirit where their sufferings would be at an end, replaced by ultimate peace and love. For many people with an interest in esotericism, it became evident that the war was very much a war between Good and Evil in the cosmic sense: a battle between the powers of Light and Darkness. The Nazis were using (or perhaps being used by) monstrous occult powers, and the only way to have even a chance of stopping them was to employ the opposing magical powers of goodness and love. This the Spiritualist community did, paying special attention to British pilots fighting in the Battle of Britain. It is a little-known fact that there was an additional battle being waged at the time, by Spiritualists giving psychic aid to the brave pilots defending the nation's skies. This came to be known as the Magical Battle of Britain.

The Spiritualists were in turn aided in their efforts by the white witches who feared that a Nazi invasion of Britain would see their extermination. By raising their own occult forces, they hoped to stave off the invasion in the summer of 1940. Travelling to the Kent coast, the witches threw a substance known as 'go-away powder' into the sea. Made according to an ancient recipe, this substance, combined with certain potent magical spells, had the effect (so the witches believed) of raising an impassable psychic barrier around the shores of Britain. Another coven travelled to the Hampshire coast with the intention of raising a magical cone of power that would turn back the advancing forces of Darkness. Indeed, magical operations were carried out by covens all over the country, concentrating on the idea of confusing the minds of Hitler's High Command and making them think that to invade Britain would be too difficult. (In the autumn of 1940, the invasion of Britain was postponed indefinitely.)

At this point, I should pause to note that at various points in this book I shall be using two phrases that at first sight might appear to be synonymous but which actually have very different meanings. The first is 'Nazi occultism', by which I mean the Nazi *belief* in the occult and supernatural; the second is 'Nazi occult power', by which I mean the belief of occultists and crypto-historians that the Nazis wielded *genuine supernatural powers*, achieved through their alleged contact with transhuman intelligences. It will become clear in the course of the book, I hope, that the latter concept, while far less verifiable in historical terms, is nevertheless of considerable importance in the mythology of the twentieth century and the manner in which we view reality today.

That said, let us now turn to a brief overview of the subjects that we shall be examining in the following pages. This survey can in many ways be categorised as conspiracy literature. As such, it presents certain problems both for the writer who explores it and the reader who agrees to accompany him or her. With regard to *Invisible Eagle*, it will become clear that the early sections refer to data that have been verified and are accepted by professional historians. However, as the reader proceeds through the book, it will also become clear that ideas about the involvement of leading Nazis with occultism and black magic grow more outlandish and less believable, particularly when presented by writers who have little or no official training in the history of fascism and the Second World War.

It might therefore appear to the reader that this book itself is only half legitimate, based as it is partly on verifiable historical data and partly on bizarre and spurious notions that have few claims to historical accuracy. Such a conclusion would, however, be a mistake: the various claims made regarding Nazi involvement with the occult have come to occupy a central place in the mythologising of the Third Reich that has developed in the years since the end of the Second World War. Just as the Nazis mythologised the history of their so-called 'Aryan' ancestors in order to legitimise (in their own minds, at least) their claims to racial superiority, so they themselves have, to a great extent, been mythologised by writers in the fields of occultism and conspiracy theory.

The result is that a body of wild historical speculation now exists alongside what we know for certain about Nazi Germany, and it is an unpalatable but undeniable fact that this speculation forms a significant element in the public attitude to Hitler and the Nazis. However spurious the ideas that we shall examine in the later stages of this book, it is essential that we do discuss them in order to gain some understanding of the awful fascination the Third Reich still holds for us.

Thus, in Chapter One, we will examine the origins of occultist belief in Nazi Germany in movements such as *völkisch* nationalism and Pan-Germanism, the adoption of Theosophical concepts, the development of the occult-racist doctrine known as Ariosophy, and the occult societies that were used as conduits for the propagation of racist esotericism and the doctrine of Aryan supremacy. In Chapter Two, we will concentrate on the bizarre mythology adopted by the Nazis, which centred on the idea of a lost Aryan homeland in the far North, and will examine the occult origin of the swastika.

The first two chapters contain information that is historically verifiable and accepted by serious historians. With Chapter Three, we find ourselves departing from this path of respectability and entering what the French writers Louis Pauwels and Jacques Bergier call the Absolute Elsewhere: an intellectual realm of extreme notions that is the equivalent of Godwin's 'twilight zone between fact and fiction'. Much of the remainder of this book will deal with these notions, not through any misguided belief in their veracity but rather in an attempt to establish the reasons for their inclusion in the mythology that has been imposed upon the history of the Third Reich in the last five decades. Chapter Three, therefore, will introduce us to the mysterious Vril Society and its use of a vast and hidden power known as 'vril' and said to be wielded by a race of subterranean superhumans. In Chapter Four we will travel to Tibet to examine the curious notion that the Nazis were in contact with certain high lamas, through whom they intended to ally themselves with the powerful race living beneath the Himalayas. Chapter Five will be devoted to an examination of one of the most enduring myths regarding Nazi occult power: that of Hitler's quest for the so-called Spear of Destiny, the Holy Lance said to have pierced the side of Christ during the crucifixion and whose possession would enable those who understood its mysteries to control the world. In Chapter Six we will chart the origins and ritual practices of the SS and attempt to establish how much of what has been written regarding its use of black magic is true. Chapter Seven will see us plunging ever deeper into the Absolute Elsewhere, where we will encounter the fantastic principles of Nazi cosmology, including the theory that the Earth is hollow (a theory that has enjoyed more or less constant currency in certain UFO circles – the fringe of the fringe, one might say).

Although at first sight it might appear out of place in a book dealing with the subject of Nazi occultism, I have devoted Chapter Eight to an examination of the radical and highly advanced aircraft designs on which the Nazis were working towards the end of the war, and which were captured, along with many of the scientists and engineers who were attempting to put them into practice, by the Allies in 1945. I have included this subject because it provides a connection between the alleged occult philosophy of the Third Reich and the sinister but increasingly popular concept of Nazi survival to the present day. It has been suggested by a number of researchers and commentators that modern sightings of UFOs (unidentified flying objects) may be due to the development by America and Russia of captured Nazi secret weapon designs. It is certainly beyond dispute that both Allied and German air crews encountered highly unusual aerial phenomena over Europe in the form of small (three- to four-foot diameter) illuminated spheres, which appeared to follow their fighters and bombers and interfered with the electrical systems of the aircraft. These glowing balls of light were known as 'foo fighters'. Others (including certain neo-Nazi groups) have suggested in all seriousness that some UFOs are actually operated by Nazis and are powered by vril energy, and that the Third Reich survives today in the icy fastnesses of the North and South polar regions, in particular the region of Antarctica known as Queen Maud Land (so named by Norwegian explorers) which the Nazis claimed for Germany in 1939 and renamed *Neu Schwabenland*.

In Chapter Nine we will examine the notion of Nazi survival in various secret locations, which has it that the Third Reich (or, perhaps more accurately, the Fourth Reich) is alive and well and continuing its quest for world domination. Finally, in the Conclusion we will attempt a summing up of the material we have covered.

By the end of the book, I hope to make it clear that the history of Nazi occultist beliefs, in combination with the attempt to enlist the Nazis' quest for genuine supernatural power to explain the motivations of Hitler and the Third Reich, has resulted in an elaborate mythological system that has had a definite influence upon our attitude to the practice of official secrecy and the putative abuses of political and economic power in the post-war world. The structure of belief we will be discussing is thus twofold: on the one hand, we can identify the pernicious esotericism of the Nazis themselves and the revolting cruelties it engendered; and on the other, the modern mythological system that has developed in the years since the end of the Second World War, and which has Nazi occultist beliefs as its starting point. Readers will find themselves embarking on a journey into realms both *outré* and unsettling; we will of necessity be exploring concepts from which most academics would turn away with the utmost disdain. We will look at claims and beliefs that most rational people would find it hard to accept anyone could seriously entertain – were it not for the atrocities committed in their name that have irreparably demeaned our species. And we will see how the frightful and irrational concepts of Nazi mysticism and pseudo-science have survived to the present day to cast a fearsome shadow over the future.

1 Ancestry, blood and nature

The Mystical Origins of National Socialism

Historical Perspective

W E MUST BEGIN OUR JOURNEY in the convulsed but well-mapped territory of nineteenth-century Europe, in which arcane and esoteric concepts might be expected to be far removed from the complex political processes, intellectual rationalism and rapid industrialisation occurring at the time. Nevertheless, the origins of the Nazi fascination with occult and esoteric belief systems can be traced to the political, cultural and economic conditions prevalent in Prussia and Austria in the second half of the century. As noted by the British authority on the history of the Third Reich, Nicholas Goodrick-Clarke, Austria in the late 1800s was the product of three major political changes: 'These changes consisted in the exclusion of Austria from the German Confederation, the administrative separation of Hungary from Austria, and the establishment of a constitutional monarchy in the "Austrian" or western half of the empire.'' The German Confederation had been created by the Congress of Vienna to replace the Holy Roman Empire, and lasted from 1815 to 1866; it consisted of a union of 39 German states, with 35 monarchies and four free cities. Its main organ was a central Diet under the presidency of Austria. However, the establishment of the confederation failed to meet the aspirations of German nationalists, who had hoped for a consolidation of these small monarchies into a politically unified Greater Germany.

As a step towards the ascendancy of Prussia over Austria and the unification of Germany under Prussian dominance, Otto von Bismarck provoked the Austro-Prussian War in June 1866, using the dispute over the administration of Schleswig-Holstein as a pretext. In this conflict, also known as the Seven Weeks' War, Prussia was allied with Italy, and Austria with a number of German states, including Bavaria, Württemberg, Saxony and Hanover. Prussia easily overcame Austria and her allies. Austria was excluded from German affairs in the Treaty of Prague (23 August 1866). The war notwithstanding, Bismarck considered Austria a potential future ally and so avoided unnecessarily weakening the state, settling for the annexation of Hanover, Hesse, Nassau, Frankfurt and Schleswig-Holstein. (These moderate peace terms were to facilitate the Austro-German alliance of 1879.) The war resulted in the destruction of the German Confederation, and its replacement with the North German Confederation under the sole leadership of Prussia. The defeat of Austria was an additional blow to German nationalism: Austrian Germans found themselves isolated within the Habsburg Empire, with its multitude of national and ethnic groups. A look at the political divisions within the empire will give some idea of the extent of its multiculturalism. They included:

Austria;
the kingdoms of Bohemia, Dalmatia and Galicia-
   Lodomeria;
the archduchies of Lower Austria and Upper Austria;
the duchies of Bukovina, Carinthia, Carniola Salzburg
   and Styria;
the margraviates of Istria and Moravia;
the counties of Gorizia-Gradisca, Tyrol and Vorarlberg;
the crownland of Austrian-Silesia;
Bosnia-Hercegovina;

Lombardy (transferred to Italy in 1859), Modena
(transferred to Italy in 1860), Tuscany (transferred to
Italy in 1860) and Venetia (transferred to Italy in
1866);
and the town of Trieste.[2]

As Goodrick-Clarke states, fears that the supremacy of the
German language and culture within the empire would be
challenged by the non-German nationalities resulted in a
conflict of loyalties between German nationality and Austrian
citizenship. This in turn resulted in the emergence of two
principal nationalist movements: *völkisch* nationalism and the
Pan-German movement, which we will discuss a little later.

The second major change was the *Ausgleich* ('Compro-
mise') of 1867, whereby the Habsburgs set up the Dual
Monarchy of Austria-Hungary. The intention was to curb the
nationalist aspirations of Slavs in both states, inspired by
Slavs in the Ottoman Empire (including Serbs, Montenegrins
and Albanians) who had taken advantage of the Turkish
decline to establish their own states. As noted by the
American historian Steven W. Sowards, 'The former
revolutionaries [of 1848] – German and Magyar – became de
facto "peoples of state", each ruling half of a twin country
united only at the top through the King-Emperor and the
common Ministries of Foreign Affairs and of War'.[3]

However, according to Norman Davies, the *Ausgleich* only
served to make matters worse:

> There was no chance that the German-speaking élite
> could impose its culture throughout Austria, let alone
> extend it to the whole of the Dual Monarchy. After all,
> 'Austria was a Slav house with a German façade'. In
> practice the three 'master races' – the Germans, the
> Magyars, and the Galician Poles – were encouraged to
> lord it over the others. The administrative structures
> were so tailored that the German minority in Bohemia
> could hold down the Czechs, the Magyars in Hungary
> could hold down the Slovaks, Romanians, and Croats,
> and the Poles in Galicia could hold down the Ruthenians

(Ukrainians). So pressures mounted as each of the excluded nationalities fell prey to the charms of nationalism.[4]

The *Ausgleich* resulted in aspirations towards autonomy among a number of groups within the Austro-Hungarian Empire; the empire as a whole was home to eleven major nationalities: Magyars, Germans, Czechs, Poles, Ruthenians, Slovaks, Serbs, Romanians, Croats, Slovenes and Italians. The largest and most restless minority consisted of about 6.5 million Czechs living in Bohemia, Moravia and Austrian Silesia. However, their desires for autonomy were constantly frustrated by the Hungarian determination to preserve the political structure established by the *Ausgleich*.

German nationalism had been frustrated on two main occasions in the first half of the nineteenth century: at the Congress of Vienna in 1815, and after the revolutions of 1848. According to Goodrick-Clarke:

> As a result of this slow progress towards political unification, Germans increasingly came to conceive of national unity in cultural terms. This tendency had begun in the late eighteenth century, when writers of the pre-Romantic *Sturm und Drang* movement had expressed the common identity of all Germans in folk-songs, customs, and literature. An idealized image of medieval Germany was invoked to prove her claim to spiritual unity, even if there had never been political unity. This emphasis on the past and traditions conferred a strongly mythological character upon the cause of unification.[5]

He goes on:

> The exclusion of Austria from the new Prussian-dominated Reich had left disappointed nationalists in both countries. Hopes for a Greater Germany had been dashed in 1866, when Bismarck consolidated the ascendancy of Prussia through the military defeat of

Austria, forcing her withdrawal from German affairs. The position of German nationalists in Austria-Hungary was henceforth problematic. In 1867 the Hungarians were granted political independence within a dual state. The growth of the Pan-German movement in Austria in the following decades reflected the dilemma of Austrian Germans within a state of mixed German and Slav nationalities. Their programme proposed the secession of the German-settled provinces of Austria from the polyglot Habsburg empire and their incorporation in the new Second Reich across the border. Such an arrangement was ultimately realized by the *Anschluss* of Austria into the Third Reich in 1938.[6]

The idealised, romantic image of a rural, quasi-medieval Germany suffered under the programme of rapid modernisation and industrialisation undertaken by the Second Reich. For many, who saw their traditional communities destroyed by the spread of towns and industries, the foundations of their mystical unity had become threatened. In addition, these anti-modernist sentiments resulted in the rejection of both liberalism and rationalism, while paradoxically hijacking the scientific concepts of anthropology, linguistics and Darwinist evolution to 'prove' the superiority of the German race.

A set of inner moral qualities was related to the external characteristics of racial types: while the Aryans (and thus the Germans) were blue-eyed, blond-haired, tall and well-proportioned, they were also noble, honest, and courageous. The Darwinist idea of evolution through struggle was also taken up in order to prove that the superior pure races would prevail over the mixed inferior ones. Racial thinking facilitated the rise of political anti-Semitism, itself so closely linked to the strains of modernization. Feelings of conservative anger at the disruptive consequences of economic change could find release in the vilification of the Jews, who were blamed for the collapse of traditional values and institutions. Racism indicated that the Jews were not just a religious community but biologically different from other races.[7]

The Völkisch Movement and Pan-Germanism

As mentioned earlier, the fears and aspirations of German nationalists led to the formation of two highly influential movements, *völkisch* nationalism and Pan-Germanism. The intention of the *völkisch* movement was to raise the cultural consciousness of Germans living in Austria, particularly by playing on their fears for their identity within the provinces of mixed nationality in the Austro-Hungarian Empire. The word *völkisch* is not easy to translate into English, containing as it does elements of both nationalism and a profound sense of the importance of folklore. The main principles of *völkisch* thought were the importance of living naturally (including a vegetarian diet); an awareness of the wisdom of one's ancestors, expressed through the appreciation of prehistoric monuments; and an understanding of astrology and cosmic cycles. (As more than one commentator has noted, there is a distinct and rather sinister similarity between these principles and those of the modern New Age movement.)

The ideas of the *völkisch* movement were propagated through educational and defence leagues called *Vereine*. In 1886, Anton Langgassner founded the *Germanenbund*, a federation of *Vereine*, at Salzburg under the banner of Germanic *Volkstum* (nationhood). The *Vereine* were particularly popular amongst young people and intellectuals; such was their popularity, in fact, that an unsettled Austrian government dissolved the *Germanenbund* in 1889, although it re-emerged in 1894 as the *Bund der Germanen*. Goodrick-Clarke estimates that by 1900, as many as 150,000 people were influenced by *völkisch* propaganda.

According to the historian of Nazism, Eugene Davidson, the followers of the *völkisch* movement

believed the troubles of the industrial order – the harshness, the impersonality, the sharp dealing, the ruthless speculators – would only be exorcised by a return to Ur-Germanism, to the German community, the ancient Teutonic gods, and a Germanic society unsullied by inferior, foreign intrusions. Nations might endure such foreign elements, but a *Volk* was an organic unity with a common biological inheritance. *The culture-bearing Volk of the world, incomparably superior among the races, was the German;* therefore, the only proper function of a German state was to administer on behalf of the *Volk*; everything international was inferior and to be rejected. A sound economy would be based on agriculture rather than on industry with its international, especially Jewish influences; and in religion, a German God would have to replace the Jewish God.[8] [Original emphasis.]

Völkisch ideology was propagated through a number of racist publications, one of the most virulent of which was the satirical illustrated monthly *Der Scherer*, published in Innsbruck by Georg von Schönerer (1842–1921), a leader in the movement, whom Davidson describes as 'anti-Catholic, anti-Semitic, and often ludicrous'.[9] The anti-Catholic and anti-Semitic articles in *Der Scherer* were accompanied by drawings of fat priests and big-nosed Jews, the latter a prototype of the Jewish stereotype that would be later used in National Socialist propaganda. In one picture, a Jew and a priest are sitting on a mound of writhing people, who represent the *Volk*, while another shows the Devil in Hell, with a sign saying: 'Spa for Jews and Jesuits.'[10]

Jews were consistently attacked from two directions: *völkisch* anticlerical groups linked them with the reactionary Church, while clerical anti-Semites linked them with *völkisch* heathenism. Jews were therefore seen as 'either godless socialists or capitalist exploiters ... and the hidden, international rulers of financial and intellectual life'.[11] As we shall see later, these views would survive Nazism, and have extended their pernicious influence through various right-wing groups active today. One Catholic paper, *Die Tiroler Post*, wrote in 1906 that the goal of the Jew was world domination, while another, the *Linzer Post*, defended anti-Semitism as no more than healthy self-preservation. In the same year, the *völkisch Deutsche Tiroler Stimmen* called for the extermination of the Jewish race.[12]

If the *völkisch* movement attempted to raise German national and cultural consciousness, Pan-Germanism operated in a more political context, beginning with the refusal of Austrian Germans to accept their exclusion from German affairs after the Austro-Prussian War of 1866. The movement originated among student groups in Vienna, Graz and Prague, which were inspired by earlier German student clubs (*Burschenschaften*) following the teachings of Friedrich Ludwig Jahn (1778–1850). Jahn, a purveyor of *völkisch* ideology, advocated German national unity, identity and romantic ritual. These groups advocated *kleindeutsch* (or 'little German') nationalism, which called for the incorporation of German Austria into the Bismarckian Reich. As Goodrick-Clarke notes, 'This cult of Prussophilia led to a worship of force and a contempt for humanitarian law and justice.'[13]

Georg von Schönerer's involvement with Pan-Germanism transformed it from a nebulous 'cult of Prussophilia' into a genuine revolutionary movement. Following his election to the *Reichsrat* in 1873, Schönerer followed a progressive Left agenda for about five years, before making demands for a German Austria without the Habsburgs and politically united with the German Reich. Schönerer's Pan-Germanism was not characterised merely by national unity, political democracy and social reform: its essential characteristic was racism, 'that is, the idea that blood was the sole criterion of all civil rights'.[14]

The Pan-German movement experienced something of a setback in 1888, when Schönerer was convicted of assault after barging into the offices of *Das Neue Wiener Tageblatt* and attacking the editor for prematurely reporting the death of the German emperor, Wilhelm I. He was sentenced to four months' imprisonment, lost his title of nobility[15] and was deprived of his political rights for five years.

When the Austrian government decided in 1895 that Slovene should be taught in the German school at Celje in

Carniola, and two years later the Austrian premier, Count Casimir Badeni, ruled that all officials in Bohemia and Moravia should speak both Czech and German (thus placing Germans at a distinct disadvantage), the flames of nationalism were once again fanned throughout the empire. The result was that the Pan-Germans, together with the democratic German parties, followed a strategy of blocking all parliamentary business, which in turn led to violent public disorder in the summer of 1897.

By this time, Schönerer had identified an additional enemy in the Catholic Church, which he regarded as inimical to the interests of Austrian Germans. 'The episcopate advised the emperor, the parish priests formed a network of effective propagandists in the country, and the Christian Social party had deprived him of his earlier strongholds among the rural and semi-urban populations of Lower Austria and Vienna.'[16] The association of Catholicism with Slavdom and the Austrian state could further be emphasised, Schönerer believed, by a movement for Protestant conversion; this was the origin of the slogan 'Los von Rom' ('Away from Rome'). The movement claimed approximately 30,000 Protestant conversions in Bohemia, Styria, Carinthia and Vienna between 1899 and 1910,[17] although it was not at all popular among either the völkisch leagues or the Pan-Germans, who saw it as 'a variation of old-time clericalism'.[18] For that matter, the Protestant Church itself was rather dissatisfied with Los von Rom, and felt that its profound connection of religion with politics would make religious people uneasy. By the same token, those who were politically motivated felt religion itself to be irrelevant.

By the turn of the century, Pan-Germanism could be divided into two groups: those who, like Schönerer, wanted political and economic union with the Reich, and those who merely wanted to defend German cultural and political interests within the Habsburg empire. These interests were perceived as being radically undermined, not only by the Badeni language decrees, but also by the introduction in 1907 of universal male suffrage. This could only exacerbate the growing German-Slav conflict within the empire, and was one of the main factors in the emergence of the racist doctrine of Ariosophy, which we will discuss later. In 1853–55, Arthur de Gobineau had written an essay on the inequality of races, in which he had made claims for the superiority of the Nordic-Aryan race, and warned of its eventual submergence by non-Aryans. This notion, along with the ideas about biological struggle of Social Darwinism, was taken up at the turn of the twentieth century by German propagandists who claimed that Germans could defend their race and culture only by remaining racially pure.[19]

The *völkisch* nationalists and Pan-Germans found further inspiration in the work of the zoologist Ernst Haeckel who, in 1906, founded the Monist League to spread his racist interpretation of Social Darwinism. Seven years earlier, Haeckel's colleague, Wilhelm Bölsche, had written a book entitled *Vom Bazillus zum Affenmenschen* (*From the Bacillus to the Apeman*), in which he had described the 'naked struggle for dominance between the zoological species "Man"' and 'the lowest form of organic life [microscopic organisms]'.[20] This 'struggle for dominance' was to have a profound effect upon the development of German anti-Semitism in the early years of the twentieth century. Hitler would later express his own anti-Semitism in these biological terms, in order to deprive Jews of all human attributes. On one occasion in 1942, for instance, Hitler said:

> The discovery of the Jewish virus is one of the greatest revolutions the world has seen. The struggle in which we are now engaged is similar to the one waged by Pasteur and Koch in the last century. How many diseases must owe their origin to the Jewish virus! Only when we have eliminated the Jews will we regain our health.[21]

German Theosophy

The revival of Germanic mythology and folklore in Austria in the last two decades of the nineteenth century was of enormous importance to the development of Nazi esotericism and cosmology, yet it must be viewed in the context of a much wider occult revival that had been taking place in Europe for about one hundred years. The central concepts of what would become Western occultism, such as Gnosticism, Hermeticism and the Cabala, which originated in the eastern Mediterranean more than 1,500 years ago, had been largely banished from Western thought by the scientific revolution of the seventeenth century.

At this point, it is worth pausing to consider the meanings of these concepts. Gnosticism (*gnosis* simply means direct knowledge), as practised by early Christian heretics, contains two basic tenets. The first is dualism, which can, according to Michael Baigent and Richard Leigh, be defined thus:

> Dualism, as the word itself suggests, presupposes an opposition, often a conflict, between two antithetical principles, two antithetical hierarchies of value, two antithetical realities. In dualism, certain aspects or orders of reality are extolled over others. Certain aspects of reality are repudiated as unreal, or inferior, or evil. In its distinction between soul and body, between spirit and 'unregenerate nature', Christianity is, in effect, dualist.[22]

The second tenet concerns the evil of matter:

> Matter was rejected as intrinsically evil. Material creation, the phenomenal world, was deemed to be the handiwork of a lesser and malevolent god. In consequence, matter and material creation had to be transcended in order to attain union with a greater and truer god, whose domain was pure spirit; and it was this union that the term 'gnosis' signified ... [Gnostic] thinking had probably originated in the similar dualism of Persian Zoroastrianism. It was subsequently to surface again in Persia, under a teacher known as Mani, and to be called Manicheism.[23]

Hermeticism derives from Hermes Trismegistus ('the thrice-greatest Hermes'), the name given by the Greeks to the Egyptian god Thoth, the god of wisdom and of literature. To the Greeks, this 'scribe of the gods' was author of all sacred books, which they called 'Hermetic'. The ancient wisdom of Hermes is said to reside in 42 books, the surviving fragments of which are known as the Hermetica. The books of Hermes were written on papyrus and kept in the great library of Alexandria. When the library was destroyed by fire, most of this wisdom was forever lost; however, some fragments were saved and, according to legend, buried in a secret desert location by initiates.

Hermetic works such as *The Divine Pymander* and *The Vision* describe the means by which divine wisdom was revealed to Hermes Trismegistus, and also contain discourses on the evolution of the human soul. The *Tabula smaragdina* or *Emerald Tablet* is said to contain the most comprehensive summation of Egyptian philosophy, and was of central importance to the alchemists, who believed that it was encoded with the mystical secrets of the Universe. Hermes Trismegistus is said to have been the greatest philosopher, king and priest, and was also a somewhat prolific writer, being credited with 36,525 books on the principles of nature. A composite of the Egyptian god Thoth and the Greek god Hermes, both of whom were associated with the spirits of the dead, Hermes Trismegistus was the personification of universal wisdom. However, it is likely that the writings attributed to him were actually the anonymous works of early Christians.

The third element in the threefold foundation of Western occultism was the Cabala, the mystical system of classical Judaism. Translated from the Hebrew as 'that which is received', the Cabala is founded on the Torah (Jewish scriptures) and is a kind of map, given to Adam by angels and handed down through the ages, by which our fallen species may find its way back to God. The primary document of Cabalism is the *Sefer Yetzirah* (*Book of Creation*), which was possibly written in the third century by Rabbi Akiba, who was martyred by the Romans. According to the *Sefer Yetzirah*, God created the world by means of 32 secret paths: the ten *sephirot* (or emanations by which reality is structured) and the 22 letters of the Hebrew alphabet.

Between 1280 and 1286, the Spanish Cabalist Moses de León wrote the *Sefer ha-Zohar* (*Book of Splendour*), the primary document of classical Cabalism. It is centred upon the *Zohar*, a body of teachings developed by the second-century sage Rabbi Simeon bar Yohai during his meditation in a cave near Lod, Israel. In the *Zohar*, God is referred to as *Ein-Sof* (without end), and as such cannot be represented or known by fallen humanity. The human goal is to realise a union with God and, since all of reality is connected, thereby to elevate all other souls in the Universe.

In the West, Cabalism came to form a principal foundation of occultism, with its magical amulets and incantations, seals and demonology, and its concentration on the power inherent in the letters of the Hebrew alphabet. Christian occultists focused on the Tetragrammaton YHVH, the unspeakable name of God, through which it was possible to gain power over the entire Universe.[24]

The occult revival in Europe came about primarily as a reaction to the rationalist Enlightenment and materialism of the eighteenth and early nineteenth centuries. This lamentably but necessarily brief look at its esoteric origins brings us to the emergence of Theosophy in the 1880s. The prime mover behind Theosophy was Helena Petrovna Blavatsky (1831–1891). Her parents, Baron von Hahn, a soldier and member of the lesser Russian-German nobility, and Madame von Hahn, a romantic novelist and descendant of the noble house of Dolgorouky, led a somewhat unsettled life: the baron's regiment was constantly on the move. Madame von Hahn died in 1842, when Helena was eleven, an event which seems to have contributed to her waywardness and powerful sense of individuality.

At seventeen she married Nikifor Blavatsky, Vice-Governor of Yerevan in the Caucasus, and 23 years her senior in July 1848. The marriage failed after only a few weeks and Helena left her husband with the initial intention of returning to her father. However, she suddenly decided instead to leave her family and country behind, boarded a steamer on the

Black Sea and headed for Constantinople.[25] For the next 25 years, she wandered through Europe, Asia and the Americas. Although she may have had an allowance from her father, she also supported herself in a variety of ways, including as a bareback rider in a circus, a piano teacher in London and Paris, and also as an assistant to the famous medium Daniel Dunglas Home. This is pretty much all that is known with any certainty about this period in her life: the rest is a confusing jumble of rumour, contradiction and legend, much of which originated with Blavatsky herself.

During a trip to the United States in 1873, Blavatsky observed the enormous popularity of Spiritualism. She had arrived with no money and had to live in a hostel for working women, doing menial jobs such as sewing purses. At about this time, she met Henry Olcott (1832–1907), whose New Jersey family claimed descent from the pilgrims. Apparent financial difficulties forced Olcott to take up farming in Ohio, at which he seems to have excelled, gaining a position as Agricultural Editor of the *New York Tribune*, until the outbreak of the Civil War, in which he fought as a signals officer in the Union Army. When the war ended, Olcott headed to New York to study for the Bar, and established a law practice there in the late 1860s.[26] In spite of a fair degree of success in his profession, Olcott seems to have been rather dissatisfied with his lot: his marriage was not happy, and eventually he divorced his wife. In search of some form of intellectual diversion, he became interested in Spiritualism.

As his interest in the subject grew, Olcott began to investigate individual cases of alleged psychic manifestations, including those occurring on the Eddy farm at Chittenden, Vermont. His investigation of the events at Chittenden (which included spirit materialisations) were written up as articles for a New York paper, the *Daily Graphic*. On 14 October 1874, Olcott met Blavatsky at the Eddy farmhouse during one of his many visits there. Blavatsky had been intrigued by the articles she had read in the *Daily Graphic*, and had decided to cultivate Olcott's friendship.

Greatly impressed with her apparent mediumistic skills, Olcott became Blavatsky's devotee and publicist. From then until 1875, when she founded the Theosophical Society, Blavatsky earned a comfortable living as a medium, only falling on hard times when the nationwide interest in Spiritualism began to wane. In 1877, Blavatsky published *Isis Unveiled*, an exposition of Egyptian occultism that, she claimed, had been dictated to her by spirits *via* a form of automatic writing, and which argues, essentially, for the acceptance of occultism (hidden laws of nature) to be accepted by orthodox science. Its effect – the book sold widely – was to soothe the minds of those whose religious faith had been undermined by scientific rationalism, in particular the theories on evolution and natural selection of Charles Darwin. Perhaps unsurprisingly, the book was fiercely attacked in scholarly circles both for intellectual incompetence and out-and-out plagiarism, with one critic identifying more than 2,000 unacknowledged quotations.[27]

Central to the mythos Blavatsky constructed for herself was her experience of living and travelling for seven years in Tibet. (The number seven is of considerable magical significance, and is the number of years required for initiates into occult mysteries to complete their apprenticeship.[28]) She made the rather astonishing claim that she had studied with a group of Hidden Masters in the Himalayas, under whose guidance she had reached the highest level of initiation into the mysteries of the Universe. It is, however, extremely unlikely that a single white woman with a considerable weight problem and no mountaineering experience could have made the arduous trip up the Himalayas, succeeded in finding these 'Hidden Masters', and done so without being spotted by the numerous Chinese, Russian and British patrols that were in the area at that time.[29]

One of the Tibetan adepts with whom Blavatsky studied was named Master Morya. She actually met him at the Great Exhibition in London in July 1851 (although she claimed to have met him in visions on numerous occasions previously). Master Morya was a member of the Great White Brotherhood of Masters, immortal, incorporeal beings who had achieved ultimate enlightenment, but had elected to remain on Earth to guide humanity towards the same goal. We shall have a good deal more to say on the Great White Brotherhood in Chapter Five, but for now let us return to Madame Blavatsky.

In 1879, with the Theosophical Society not doing particularly well at recruiting converts, Blavatsky decided to go to India, a logical choice in view of the emphasis placed on eastern philosophy in *Isis Unveiled*. She and Olcott enjoyed a warm reception from various members of Indian society, including the journalist A. P. Sinnett and the statesman Allen O. Hume. In 1882, they moved the society's headquarters to Adyar, near Madras. The new headquarters included a shrine room in which the Hidden Masters would manifest in physical form. However, while Blavatsky and Olcott were away touring Europe, Emma Coulomb and her husband, who had managed the household but been dismissed after repeatedly attempting to secure financial loans from the society's wealthy members, decided to take their revenge by publishing letters said by them to have been written by Blavatsky and which contained instructions on how to operate the secret panels in the shrine room, through which the 'Masters' appeared.

Unfortunately for Blavatsky, it was at this time that the Society for Psychical Research (SPR) decided to investigate the mediumistic claims of Theosophy. Needless to say, when the Coulombs' revelations of trickery came to light, the SPR issued a scathing report on Blavatsky and her claims.

Injured by the scandal and with her health failing (she would later die of Bright's Disease), Blavatsky left India and settled in London, where she began work on her second and (it is generally acknowledged) greater book, *The Secret Doctrine* (published in 1888). Comprising two main sections, 'Cosmogenesis' and 'Anthropogenesis', the book is nothing less than a history of the Universe and intelligent life. *The Secret Doctrine* is allegedly a vast commentary on a fantastically old (several million years) manuscript called *The Stanzas of Dzyan*, written in the Atlantean language Senzar, and seen by Blavatsky in a monastery hidden far beneath the Himalayas. The *Stanzas* tell how the Earth was colonised by spiritual beings from the Moon. Humanity as we know it is descended from these remote ancestors via a series of so-called 'root races'.

Lack of space prevents us from going too deeply into the contents of *The Secret Doctrine*. Suffice to say that at the beginning of the Universe, the divine being differentiated itself into the multitude of life forms that now inhabit the cosmos. The subsequent history of the Universe passed through seven 'rounds' or cycles of being. The Universe experienced a fall from divine grace through the first four rounds, and will rise again through the last three, until it is redeemed in ultimate, divine unity, before the process begins again. (We would perhaps be well advised to resist the temptation to compare this scheme with the similar-sounding Big Bang/Big Crunch theory of universal evolution proposed by modern physicists: there is little else in the *Stanzas* that orthodox science would find palatable.)

Each of these cosmic rounds saw the rise and fall of seven root races, whose destiny mirrored exactly that of cosmic evolution, with the first four descending from the spiritual into the material and the last three ascending once again. According to Blavatsky, humanity in its present form is the fifth root race of Earth, which is itself passing through the fourth cosmic round. (The reader may thus find it a considerable relief that we have a long period of spiritual improvement ahead of us.) The first root race were completely noncorporeal Astral beings who lived in an invisible land; the second race were the Hyperboreans, who lived on a lost polar continent (we will examine the important concept of Hyperborea in detail in the next chapter); the third root race were the Lemurians, fifteen-foot-tall brown-skinned hermaphrodites with four arms, who had the misfortune to occupy the lowest point in the seven-stage cycle of humanity. For this reason, the Lemurians, who lived on a now-sunken continent in the Indian Ocean, suffered a Fall from divine grace: after dividing into two distinct sexes, they began to breed with beautiful but inferior races, this miscegenation resulting in the birth of soulless monsters. The fourth root race were the Atlanteans, who possessed highly advanced psychic powers and mediumistic skills. Gigantic like the Lemurians and physically powerful, the Atlanteans built huge cities on their mid-Atlantic continent. Their technology was also highly advanced, and was based on the application of a universal electro-spiritual force known as Fohat – similar, it seems, to the vril force (see Chapter Four). Unfortunately for the Atlanteans, although they were intelligent and powerful, they were also possessed of a childlike innocence that made them vulnerable to the attentions of an evil entity that corrupted them and caused them to turn to the use of black magic. This was to result in a catastrophic war that led to the destruction of Atlantis.[30] The fifth root race, from which we today are descended, was the Aryan race.

Theosophy placed a heavy emphasis on the importance of reincarnation and the concept of hierarchy. Through reincarnation, the movement's followers could imagine themselves to have participated in the fabulous prehistory of humanity in a variety of magical, exotic and long-lost locations, while feeling assured that their souls were on a definite upward trajectory, heading for spiritual salvation and ultimate unity with God. Of equal importance to the cosmic scheme were hierarchy and élitism. As mentioned earlier, the Hidden Masters or Mahatmas of Tibet, such as Master Morya and Koot Hoomi, were enlightened beings who had decided to remain on Earth to guide the rest of humanity towards spiritual wisdom. This concept, along with Blavatsky's own claim to hidden occult knowledge, is clearly based on the value of authority and hierarchy. Indeed, this value is illustrated by the fate of the Lemurians, whose miscegenation caused their Fall from divine grace. The only section of that society to remain pure was the élite priesthood, which eventually retired to the wondrous city of Shambhala in what is now the Gobi Desert (more of which in Chapter Four) and which is linked with the Hidden Masters of Tibet.[31]

As we have already noted, the central tenets of Theosophy offered a way for people in the late nineteenth century to maintain their religious faith (or, at least, their faith in the existence of some form of spirituality in the cosmos) while simultaneously accepting the validity of new theories, such as evolution, that threatened to undermine their previously held world view. However, for many people in Europe and America, scientific rationalism, rapid industrialisation and urbanisation presented another threat to their long-established way of life. As an antidote to the fears and uncertainties of modern life, Theosophy was particularly readily accepted in Germany and Austria. As Goodrick-Clarke notes, it was well suited to the German protest movement known as *Lebensreform* (life reform). 'This movement represented a middle-class attempt to palliate the ills of modern life, deriving from the growth of the cities and industry. A variety of alternative life-styles – including herbal and natural medicine, vegetarianism, nudism and self-sufficient rural communes – were embraced by small groups of individuals who hoped to restore themselves to a natural existence ... Theosophy was appropriate to the mood of *Lebensreform* and provided a philosophical rationale for some of its groups.'[32]

Interest in Theosophy increased in Germany with the founding of the German Theosophical Society on 22 July 1884 at Elberfeld. Blavatsky and Olcott were staying there at the home of Marie Gebhard (1832–1892), a devotee of occultism who had corresponded frequently with the famous French occultist and magician Eliphas Lévi (Alphonse Louis Constant) (c. 1810–1875). Its first president was Wilhelm Hübbe-Schleiden, then a senior civil servant at the Colonial Office in Hamburg. Hübbe-Schleiden, who had travelled extensively throughout the world and was a keen advocate of German colonial expansion abroad, was instrumental in gathering the isolated Theosophists scattered throughout Germany into a consolidated German branch of the society.

Hübbe-Schleiden also did much to increase occult interest in Germany through the founding in 1886 of his periodical *Die Sphinx*, a scholarly blend of psychical research, the paranormal, archaeology and Christian mysticism from a scientific viewpoint. As such it was firmly Theosophical in tone, and included contributions from scientists, historians and philosophers.[33]

Another great populariser of scientific occultism in Germany was Franz Hartmann (1838–1912), who had also led a highly eventful life in Europe and the Americas, following a number of careers such as soldier, doctor, coroner and mining speculator. Already interested in Spiritualism, Hartmann was converted to Theosophy after reading *Isis Unveiled* and decided to travel to Adyar to meet Blavatsky and Olcott in 1883. So impressed was Blavatsky with him that she appointed him acting president of the Theosophical Society while she and Olcott travelled to Germany to start the branch there. Hartmann remained there until 1885, when the Theosophists left India following the Coulomb scandal.

Hartmann went on to found the occult periodical *Lotusblüthen* (*Lotus Blossoms*), which ran from 1892 to 1900 and was the first German publication to feature the swastika on its cover.[34] (In eastern mysticism, the swastika is a symbol with many positive connotations; we will examine it in detail in the next chapter.) The increased public interest generated by this periodical prompted a number of German publishers to issue long book series dealing with a wide range of occult and esoteric subjects, including the work of Annie Besant and Charles Leadbeater who took over the Theosophical Society on Blavatsky's death in 1891.

The German branch of the society had been dissolved in 1885 when the Theosophists left India, but was replaced by a new society founded in Berlin in August 1896 as a branch of the International Theosophical Brotherhood in America, with Hartmann as president. Also on the executive committee was one Paul Zillmann, who founded the monthly *Metaphysische Rundschau* (*Metaphysical Review*) and who would later publish the works of the Ariosophists (whom we shall meet shortly). By 1902, German Theosophy, which had hitherto suffered from internecine rivalry, became far better coordinated under the two main centres at Berlin and Leipzig.

In 1906, a Theosophical Publishing House was founded at Leipzig by Hugo Vollrath, a disciple of Hartmann's, possibly to counter the new influence in occult circles of Theosophist Rudolf Steiner, whose mystical Christian stance did not endear him to Annie Besant whose own outlook was firmly Hindu. (Steiner would later leave and form his own Anthroposophical Society in 1912.) The Theosophical Publishing House produced a large number of occult magazines and book series, in competition with other publishers such as Karl Rohm, Johannes Baum and Max Altmann who had turned their attention to this potentially lucrative field.

The public interest in occultism quickly grew in Vienna, which already had its own tradition of esotericism and interest in paranormal phenomena. New occult groups were founded, including the Association for Occultism, which had its own lending library, the Sphinx Reading Club and the First Viennese Astrological Society.[35] In fact, it was in Vienna that the seeds of Germanic occult racism were most liberally sown. The public disquiet at economic change, scientific rationalism and rapid industrialisation and the threat they appeared to pose to traditional 'natural' ways of life was palliated not only by occultist notions of the centrality and importance of humanity within the wider cosmos (of the essential *meaningfulness* of existence), but also by the *völkisch* ideology that assured Germans of the value and importance of their cultural identity. This combination of culture and spirituality was expressed most forcefully through the doctrine of Ariosophy, which originated in Vienna.

Ariosophy

The bizarre theories of Ariosophy constituted a mixture of racist *völkisch* ideology and the Theosophical concepts of Madame Blavatsky. (As with the philosophy of Nietzsche, Blavatsky's ideas were hijacked and warped by German occultists and it should be remembered that neither of these two would have advocated the violence and suffering that would later be perpetrated by the Nazis: indeed, Nietzsche disavowed anti-Semitism and called German nationalism an 'abyss of stupidity'.)

The two principal personalities behind Ariosophy were Guido von List (1848–1919) and Jörg Lanz von Liebenfels (1874–1954), both of whom added the undeserved particle 'von' (denoting nobility) to their names. Born in Vienna to a prosperous middle-class family, List dreamed of the reunification of Austria with Germany, and hated both Jews and Christians for the attacks he perceived them to have made upon German culture, spirituality and territorial rights. A journalist by trade, List also wrote novels about the ancient Teutons and the cult of Wotan, whose hierarchy he came to call the *Armanenschaft*, a name derived from his spurious interpretation of a Teutonic myth. According to the Roman author Tacitus in his *Germania*, the Teutons believed that their people were descended from the god Tuisco and his son, Mannus. Mannus had three sons, after whom the ancient German tribes were named: Ingaevones, Hermiones and Istaevones. With no scholarly evidence to back him up, List decided that these names referred to the agricultural, intellectual and military estates within the Germanic nation. The word *Armanenschaft* derived from List's Germanisation of Hermiones, the intellectual or priestly estate, to 'Armanen'. List claimed that the profoundly wise *Armanenschaft* was the governing body of the ancient society.[36]

List's codification of his beliefs regarding the ancient and racially pure Teutons led to a profound interest in the symbolism of heraldry and the secrets allegedly contained in the runic alphabet, an interest that included the mystical significance of the swastika which he identified (at least in terms of its power and significance) with the Christian Cross and the Jewish Star of David. (As indicated earlier, we shall examine the origin and meaning of the swastika in the next chapter.) By 1902, as a result of a period of enforced inactivity following a cataract operation that left him blind for eleven months, List had devoted much thought to the nature of the proto-Aryan language he believed was encoded in the ancient runes.

His occult-racist-mystical theories, including an exposition on the Aryan proto-language, did not find particular favour with the Imperial Academy of Sciences in Vienna, which returned without comment a thesis he had sent. Nevertheless, the anti-Semitic elements in German and Austrian society began to take note, and in 1907 a List Society was formed to provide financial aid in his researches. List's spurious historiography and archaeology provided a pseudo-scientific basis for both racism and extreme nationalism, and enabled the German *Volk* to trace their ancestry back to the splendour and racial purity of the ancient Teutons and their cult of Wotanism.

The cult of Wotan arose primarily from List's beliefs regarding the religious practices of the ancient Teutons, whom he considered to have been persecuted by Christians in early medieval Germany. In List's view, the Old Norse poems of Iceland, Norway, Denmark and Sweden, the *Eddas*, were actually chronicles of the myths of the ancient Germans. The *Eddas* were composed of songs, manuals of poetry and works of history telling the story of the ancient Teutonic pantheon of gods and the numerous secondary divinities who were their cohorts. In fact, we have almost no record of the myths and beliefs of the ancestors of the Germans and Anglo-Saxons. According to conventional studies of mythology:

> For the Germanic tribes of the West, the ancestors of the Germans and Anglo-Saxons, documentary sources of information are sparse. Latin historians like Caesar and Tacitus had at their disposal only second-hand information and they attempted to explain Teutonic religion in terms of Roman religion. For instance, Donar, the thunder-god, became for them *Jupiter tonans*. Woden received the name Mercury and Tiw [the sky-god] was called Mars. The missionaries, monks and clerks who, from the eighth century, pursued their work of conversion and were at the same time the first to write the German language could, had they wished to, have given us a complete picture of German mythology in the early centuries. But their chief concern was to save souls. Hence they scarcely alluded to pagan myths except to condemn them. We should know practically nothing of the old German beliefs if 'popular' tales and epics had not preserved much that pertains to secondary divinities, demons, giants and spirits of all sorts.[37] [Original emphasis.]

In the *Eddas*, Wotan (whose name derives from the word in all Germanic languages meaning fury, and which in modern German is *wüten*, to rage) was the god of war, whom dead heroes met in Valhalla. It was Wotan who gained an understanding of the runes after being wounded by a spear and hanging from a tree for nine nights, and who related the eighteen runic spells that held the secrets of immortality, invincibility in battle, healing abilities and control of the elements. In Norse legend, the runes are not only a system of writing but also possess an inherent magical power. Goodrick-Clarke describes List as 'the pioneer of *völkisch* rune occultism',[38] since he was the first to link the runes of a certain written series with Wotan's runic spells. 'List attributed a specific individual rune to each of Wotan's verses, adding occult meanings and a summary motto of the spell. These occult meanings and mottoes were supposed to represent the doctrine and maxims of the rediscovered religion of Wotanism. Typical mottoes were: "Know yourself, then you know everything!" . . . and "Man is one with God!" '[39]

The central tenet of Wotanism was the cyclical nature of the Universe, which proceeded through a series of transformations: 'birth', 'being', 'death' and 'rebirth'. This cyclical cosmology was a primal law and represented the presence of God in Nature. Since Man was part of the cosmos, he was bound by its laws and thus required to live in harmony with the natural world. 'A close identity with one's folk and race was reckoned a logical consequence of this closeness to Nature.'[40]

List also utilised Theosophical concepts in his development of Wotanism, in particular those of Max Ferdinand Sebaldt von Werth who wrote extensively on Aryan sexuality and racial purity. Sebaldt believed that the Universe was whisked into being by the god Mundelföri, and that its fundamental nature was one of the interaction of opposites, such as matter and spirit, and male and female. Aryan superiority could therefore only be achieved through a union of racially 'pure opposites'. In September 1903, List published an article in the Viennese occult periodical *Die Gnosis* that drew heavily on this idea, referring to ancient Aryan cosmology and sexuality. The phases of this cosmology were illustrated with variations on the swastika, the Hindu symbol of the Sun, that List appropriated and corrupted to denote the unconquerable and racially pure Germanic hero.[41]

List was also heavily influenced by legends of lost civilisations and sunken continents, such as the fabled lands of Atlantis and Lemuria, and by the theosophical writings of Madame Blavatsky. He went so far as to compare the Wotanist priesthood with the hierophants of Blavatsky's *The Secret Doctrine*. Theosophical concepts also formed the basis of his *Die Religion der Ario-Germanen* (1910), in which he devoted considerable space to the Hindu cosmic cycles which had inspired Blavatsky's concept of 'rounds' or cosmological cycles. List identified the four rounds of fire, air, water and earth with 'the mythological Teutonic realms of Muspilheim, Asgard, Wanenheim and Midgard, which were tenanted respectively by fire-dragons, air-gods, water-giants and mankind'.[42] These realms lie at the centre of the Nordic creation myth. At the dawn of time, there was nothing but a vast, yawning abyss. Niflheim, a realm of clouds and shadows, formed to the north of the abyss, while to the south formed the land of fire called Muspilheim. When Ymir, the first living being and the father of all the giants, was slain in battle, his body was raised from the sea and formed the earth, Midgard.[43] According to List, the Ario-Germans were the fifth race in the present round, the preceding four corresponding to the mythical Teutonic giants.

Wotanist doctrine held that the natural evolutionary cycle of the Universe was from unity to multiplicity and back to unity. The first stage of this evolution (unity to multiplicity) was represented symbolically by anticlockwise triskelions and swastikas and inverted triangles. The second stage (multiplicity back to the unity of the godhead) was represented by clockwise and upright symbols. In this scheme, the Ario-German was seen as the highest possible form of life, since he occupied the 'zenith of multiplicity at the outermost limit of the cycle'.[44]

List was a fervent believer in the lost civilisations of Atlantis and Lemuria, and claimed that the prehistoric megaliths of Lower Austria were actually Atlantean artefacts.

In his *Die Ursprache der Ario-Germanen* (*The Proto-Language of the Ario-Germans*) (1914), he included a chart comparing the geological periods of Earth with a Hindu *kalpa* (4,320,000,000 years), which also corresponded to a single theosophical round. We will have much more to say on the Ariosophist belief in lost civilisations later in this chapter, and in the next.

For now, let us turn our attention to the other principal personality in Ariosophy, List's young follower Jörg Lanz von Liebenfels, who founded the notorious anti-Semitic hate sheet *Ostara* and created the Order of the New Templars in 1907. Like his mentor List, Liebenfels had a middle-class Viennese upbringing, which he would later deny in favour of an imagined aristocratic background.

Liebenfels chose as a headquarters for the Order of the New Templars a ruined castle, Burg Werfenstein, perched on a cliff on the shores of the River Danube between Linz and Vienna. He was obsessed with the idea of a Manichaean struggle between the 'blond' race (characterised by creativity and heroism) and the dark 'beast-men', who were consumed with lust for 'blonde' women and who were bent on the corruption of human culture. Two years earlier, Liebenfels had established the racist periodical *Ostara* (named after the pagan goddess of spring) that called repeatedly for the restoration of the 'blond race' as the dominant force in the world. This could only be achieved through racial purity, the forced sterilisation or extermination of inferior races, and the destruction of socialism, democracy and feminism.[45]

These racist concerns led Liebenfels to conceive the bizarre notion of founding a chivalrous order based on the monastic and military orders of the Crusades. As Goodrick-Clarke notes, Liebenfels had been drawn since childhood to 'the Middle Ages and its pageant of knights, noblemen, and monks. His decision to enter the Cistercian noviciate owed much to these sentiments, and it is likely that his adult desire to identify with the aristocracy derived from similar fantasies.'[46] Liebenfels's fantasies also included holy orders, which perhaps naturally resulted in an intense interest in the Order of the Knights Templar. This interest was fuelled by the medieval Grail Romances, which were at the time enjoying a widespread popularity due to their treatment by Richard Wagner in his operas. To Liebenfels and many of his contemporaries, such romances were significant in their painting of the Grail Knights as searchers after sublime and eternal values: this view provided a powerful antidote to the hated modern world with its rampant industrialisation and materialism.

The most renowned and applauded Order in Christendom at the time of the Crusades was undoubtedly the Knights Templar, and Liebenfels developed a fantasy in which these knights became champions of a racist struggle for a Germanic order that would enjoy a hegemony over the Mediterranean and the Middle East. According to Goodrick-Clarke:

> In 1913 he published a short study, in which the grail was interpreted as an electrical symbol pertaining to the 'panpsychic' powers of the pure-blooded Aryan race. The quest of the 'Templeisen' for the Grail was a metaphor for the strict eugenic practices of the Templar knights designed to breed god-men. The Templars had become the key historical agent of [Liebenfels's] sexo-racist gnosis before 1914.[47]

At this point, it is worth looking very briefly at the history of the Knights Templar and how their rise and fall influenced Liebenfels's *Weltanschauung* (world view). The Order of the Knights Templar became one of the most powerful monastic societies in twelfth-century Europe, and came to symbolise the Christian struggle against the infidel. In AD 1118, a knight from Champagne named Hugh of Payens persuaded King Baldwin I of Boulogne (whose elder brother, Godfrey, had captured Jerusalem nineteen years before) to install Payens and eight other French noblemen in a wing of the royal palace, the former mosque al-Aqsa, near the site where King Solomon's Temple had allegedly once stood in the Holy Land. The Order later comprised three classes: the knights, all of noble birth; the sergeants, drawn from the bourgeoisie, who were grooms and stewards; and the clerics, who were chaplains and performed non-military tasks.[48] Choosing the name Militia Templi (Soldiers of the Temple),[49] they vowed to defend the mysteries of the Christian faith and Christians travelling to the holy places. The Order initially derived its power from St Bernard of Clairvaux, head of the Cistercian Order, and from Pope Honorius II, who officially recognised the Templars as a separate Order in 1128.[50] It is believed that the Templars took their inspiration from the Hospitallers, who protected Catholic pilgrims in Palestine and pledged themselves to a life of chastity and poverty.

The Seal of the Templars showed two knights riding on a single horse – a sign of their poverty (at least in their early days); the design was retained for decades after the Order had become one of the richest of the time.[51] The vast wealth that the Templars were to acquire was partly the result of the Order's exemption from local taxes, coupled with their ability to levy their own taxes on the community. The Templars honoured their vow of poverty for the first nine years of their existence, relying on donations from the pious even for their clothes. Their battle standard was a red eight-pointed cross on a black-and-white background; their battle cry was 'Vive Dieu, Saint Amour' ('God Lives, Saint Love'), and their motto was 'Non nobis, Domine, non nobis, sed Nomini Tuo da gloriam' ('Not for us, Lord, not for us, but to Thy Name give glory').[52]

Over the next century and a half, the Templars amassed a truly staggering amount of wealth, property (with over seven thousand estates in Europe) and power, and had branches throughout Europe and the Middle East, all run from their headquarters in Paris. This led to jealous rivalries, and during the Crusades rumours began to circulate that the Templars were not the pious Christian knights many believed them to be. Attention was focused on their secret rituals, which their enemies claimed were centred upon their worship of Allah; others suspected them of actually worshipping the demon Baphomet, practising horrendous black magic rites involving sodomy, bestiality and human sacrifice, of despising the Pope and the Catholic Church, and various other crimes.

In 1307, King Philip IV of France, heavily in debt to the Templars, decided to use these rumours in an attempt to engineer their downfall. On 13 October, he seized their

Temple in Paris and arrested the Grand Master, Jacques de Molay, and 140 Templars, whom he subjected to horrible tortures in order to secure confessions. Philip persuaded Pope Clement V to authorise the seizure of all Templar properties. Pope Clement abolished the Order in 1312 at the Council of Vienne, and transferred its properties to the Hospitallers, in return for the money Philip claimed was owed by the Templars.[53]

Jacques de Molay was promised life in prison if he made a public confession of the Order's crimes. Instead, he made a public proclamation of the Order's innocence of all crimes with which it had been charged, and for this he was burned at the stake. However, this was apparently not the end of the Knights Templar: there have been persistent rumours that those Templars who managed to evade capture fled to Scotland disguised as stonemasons and created the society of Freemasons. It has also been suggested that a Templar named Geoffroy de Gonneville received a message from de Molay shortly before his death and took it to a group of Templars meeting in Dalmatia. The message stated that the Order would be revived in 600 years' time. Before disbanding, the Templars at this meeting allegedly created the Order of the Rose-Croix, or Rosicrucians.[54]

To Lanz von Liebenfels, the brutal suppression of the Knights Templar and the appropriation of their wealth and property represented the victory of racial inferiors over a society of heroic men. The result was racial chaos, the corruption of 'ario-Christian' civilisation and the disorder of the modern world.[55] For this reason, Liebenfels decided to resurrect the Order in the form of his Ordo Novi Templi (ONT). He described the Order as an 'Aryan mutual-aid association founded to foster racial consciousness through genealogical and heraldic research, beauty-contests, and the foundation of racist utopias in the underdeveloped parts of the world'.[56]

The early activities of the ONT revolved around festivals and concerts, with hundreds of guests being shipped in by steamer from Vienna. They were routinely reported in the press, thus ensuring a wider audience for Liebenfels and the racist ideas presented in Ostara. Membership of the ONT was naturally restricted to those who could prove that they were of pure Aryan blood and who would vow to protect the interests of their (racial) brothers.

Two years before he founded the ONT, Liebenfels had published a book with the incredibly odd title *Theozoologie oder die Kunder von den Sodoms-Äfflingen und dem Götter-Elektron* (*Theo-zoology or the Lore of the Sodom-Apelings and the Electron of the Gods*). The word 'theo-zoology' was arrived at through the amalgamation of Judaeo-Christian doctrine and the principles of the then-burgeoning field of life-sciences. Using the Old and New Testaments as departure points, Liebenfels divided his book into two sections, the first dealing with the origin of humanity in a race of beast-men (*Anthropozoa*) spawned by Adam. In his warped and bizarre view of antiquity, Liebenfels utilised new scientific discoveries such as radiation and radio communication, which at that time had a powerful hold on the public imagination.

Liebenfels applied these discoveries in his description of the gods, which held that they were not really gods at all, but higher forms of life (*Theozoa*) who possessed fantastic mental faculties including telepathy (which was actually the transmission of electrical signals between the brains of the *Theozoa*). Through the millennia, these god-men gradually lost these faculties through miscegenation with the beast-men of Adam, until their telepathic sense organs became atrophied as the pineal and pituitary glands of modern humanity. As Goodrick-Clarke notes,[57] Liebenfels based this declaration in part on the work of the zoologist Wilhelm Bölsche (1861–1939), who in turn seems to have been inspired by Theosophy. At any rate, Liebenfels believed that the only way for Germans to reclaim their ancient godhood was through the enforced sterilisation and castration of 'inferior races', to prevent the pollution of pure Aryan blood.[58]

The second section of Liebenfels's book concerned the life of Christ (whose powers were once again electrical in nature) and the redemption of the Aryan people, who had been corrupted by the promiscuous activities of the other races of Earth. This idea of the Aryan struggle against the pernicious vices of other races in effect replaced the traditional

Judaeo-Christian concept of the struggle between good and evil. Liebenfels argued for the most extreme measures in the pursuit of Aryan re-deification: since the poor and underprivileged in society were identified with the progeny of the inferior races, they would have to be either exterminated (by incineration as a sacrifice to God), deported or used as slave labour. This constituted the inversion of traditional Judaeo-Christian compassion for the poor, weak and handicapped in the new form of Social Darwinism, with its central tenet of survival of the fittest at the expense of the weakest. These horrific methods of ensuring the survival of pure-blooded Aryans proposed by Liebenfels would, of course, become hideous reality in the Third Reich.

Although List's and Liebenfels's ideas were inherently hateful and violent, they remained just that: ideas. Many of their followers became more and more restless and dissatisfied with their lack of action against the perceived threat to the Aryan race from the various inferior beings with whom they were forced to share their nation, in particular the Jews, who were blamed for the perceived evils of urbanisation, industrialisation and the threat to the traditional rural way of life of the Aryan peasant-hero. Many came to believe that the time for scholarly theorising was past, that the time for direct action had come.

The Germanenorden

In May 1912, a meeting was held at the Leipzig home of Theodor Fritsch. At this meeting were approximately twenty prominent Pan-Germans and anti-Semites. Their purpose was to found two groups to alert Germans to the dangers to small businesses they perceived as arising from the influence of Jewish business and finance. These groups were known as the *Reichshammerbund* and the *Germanenorden* (Order of Germans). Born on 28 October 1852, Fritsch, the son of Saxon peasants, had trained as a milling engineer, and had edited the *Kleine Mühlen-Journal* (*Small-Mills Journal*). In common with other activists of the time, his anti-Semitism arose principally from a fear of rapid industrialisation, technology and mass production, driven by international Jewish influence, and the threat it posed to small tradesmen and craftsmen.

In spite of his political leanings, Fritsch decided against becoming a candidate for either of the two German anti-Semitic parties, the *Deutsch-Soziale Partei* and the *Antisemitische Volkspartei*, which had been established at Bochum in 1889, since he did not believe that anti-Semitism would prove successful in parliament. As Goodrick-Clarke notes, Fritsch's 'conviction in the ineffectiveness of parliamentary anti-Semitism proved to be correct. When more than one party existed after the Bochum conference, their competition led to a reduction in the number of successful anti-Semitic candidates at the Reichstag elections.'[59] In addition, the merging of the two parties in 1894 as the *Deutsch-Soziale Reformpartei* resulted in a significant reduction in anti-Semitism in favour of 'an appeal to more conservative and middle-class economic interests'.[60]

At this time, in the mid-1860s, racist writers such as the French aristocrat Comte Vacher de Lapouge and the Germanised Englishman Houston Stewart Chamberlain were influenced by biology and zoology, and were concentrating more on 'scientific' studies of race (although they were, of course, nothing of the kind). It was these writers who identified the Jews as the greatest threat to the supremacy of the Aryan race, and attempted to back up their ideas with reference to physical characteristics such as hair and eye colouring, and the shape of the skull.[61] For de Lapouge, Jews were more pernicious than any other race because they had insinuated themselves so completely into European society,[62] while Chamberlain in particular did much to popularise mystical racism in Germany. According to Stanley G. Payne:

Beyond the Aryan racial stereotype (tall, blond, blue-eyed) [Chamberlain] affirmed the existence of a special 'race soul' that created a more imaginative and profound spirit in Aryans and produced a 'German religion', though the latter was still (in part) vaguely related to Christianity. The ultimate anti-Aryan and most bitter racial foe was the Jew. Chamberlain combined Social Darwinism with racism and thus emphasized an endless racial struggle on behalf of the purity of Aryanism and against Jews and lesser peoples [including Slavs and Latins], virtually creating a scenario for race war.[63]

In order to fulfil his ambition to create a powerful anti-Semitic movement outside the ineffectual parliament, Fritsch founded a periodical called the *Hammer* in January 1902. By 1905, its readership had reached 3,000. These readers formed themselves into *Hammer-Gemeinden* (Hammer-Groups), changing their name in 1908 to *Deutsche Erneuerungs-Gemeinde* (German Renewal Groups). '[T]heir membership was interested in anti-capitalist forms of land reform designed to invigorate the peasantry, the garden city movement, and *Lebensreform*.'[64]

The Reichstag elections of January 1912 saw a humiliating defeat for Conservatives and anti-Semites, who lost 41 of their 109 seats, while the Social Democratic Party increased their seats from 43 to 110.[65] In the *Hammer*, Fritsch favourably reviewed a violently anti-Semitic book entitled *Wenn ich der Kaiser wär!* (*If I were Kaiser!*) by the chairman of the Pan-German League, Heinrich Class, and decided that the time was right to act in the formation of an anti-Semitic organisation that would not be subject to the control or influence of any party.

As already stated, at the meeting in Fritsch's Leipzig home on 24 May 1912 two groups were established: the *Reichshammerbund*, which combined all existing Hammer-Groups, and the *Germanenorden*, whose secret nature reflected the conviction of anti-Semites that Jewish influence in public life could only be the result of a secret international conspiracy and as such could only be combated by a quasi-Masonic lodge whose members' names would be withheld to prevent enemy infiltration.[66]

Germanenorden lodges were established throughout Northern and Eastern Germany that year, and called for the rebirth of a racially pure Germany from which the 'parasitic' Jews would be deported. By July, lodges had been established at Breslau, Dresden, Königsberg, Berlin and Hamburg. By the end of 1912, the *Germanenorden* claimed 316 brothers.[67] The main purpose of these lodges was to monitor Jewish activities; in addition, lodge members aided each other in business dealings and other matters.

The *Germanenorden* was heavily influenced by the doctrines of Ariosophy. Any German wishing to join the order was required to supply details of hair, eye and skin colour, and also had to prove beyond any doubt that they were of pure Aryan descent. Anyone suffering from a physical handicap – and for that matter, anyone who looked 'unpleasant' – was barred from membership. Ariosophy also inspired the emblems used by the Order. According to Goodrick-Clarke: 'From the middle of 1916 the official Order newsletter, the *Allgemeine Ordens-Nachrichten*, began to display on its front cover a curved-armed swastika superimposed upon a cross . . . Although the swastika was current among several contemporary *völkisch* associations in Germany, it was through the *Germanenorden* and the Thule Society, its successor organization in post-war Munich, that this device came to be adopted by the National Socialists.'[68]

The initiation rituals of the *Germanenorden* were somewhat bizarre, to say the least. Initiation would take place in the ceremonial room of the lodge, where the blindfolded novice would encounter the Master, two Knights in white robes and horned helmets, the Treasurer and Secretary with white Masonic sashes, and the Herald, who stood at the centre of the room. 'At the back of the room in the grove of the Grail stood the Bard in a white gown, before him the Master of Ceremonies in a blue gown, while the other lodge brothers stood in a semicircle around him as far as the tables of the Treasurer and Secretary. Behind the grove of the Grail was a music room where a harmonium and piano were accompanied by a small choir of "forest elves".'[69]

Upon commencement of the ceremony, the brothers sang the Pilgrims' Chorus from Wagner's *Tannhäuser*, while the brothers made the sign of the swastika. The novice was then informed of the Order's world-view, and the Bard lit the sacred flame in the grove of the Grail. 'At this point the Master seized Wotan's spear and held it before him, while the two Knights crossed their swords upon it. A series of calls and responses, accompanied by music from *Lohengrin*, completed the oath of the novices.'[70]

With the outbreak of the First World War in 1914, the *Germanenorden* began to suffer problems, both with membership and finance. Many members of the Order were killed in action, and the Order's chief, Hermann Pohl, feared that the war would ultimately result in its destruction. At that time, Pohl's leadership abilities were coming under attack from several high-ranking members who were becoming tired of the emphasis he placed on ritual and ceremony of the type indicated above. On 8 October 1916, representatives of the Berlin lodge suggested that Pohl should be relieved of his position, to which Pohl responded by declaring the formation of a breakaway order, the *Germanenorden Walvater* of the Holy Grail. The original Order was then headed by General-major Erwin von Heimerdinger.[71]

Following the schism of 1916, the *Germanenorden* became seriously weakened, with many members confused as to its status (many assumed that it had been disbanded). However, the end of the war in November 1918 saw attempts to revive its fortunes and influence. Grand Master Eberhard von Brockhusen believed that the Order would benefit from a constitution, which he succeeded in establishing in 1921, 'which provided for an extraordinarily complex organization of grades, rings, and provincial "citadels" (*Burgen*) supposed to generate secrecy for a nationwide system of local groups having many links with militant *völkisch* associations . . .'[72]

In the post-war period, the *Germanenorden*'s verbal violence was transformed into murderous activities against public figures. The new Republic was, of course, despised as a symbol of defeat, and it was the *Germanenorden* that ordered the assassination of Matthias Erzberger, the former Reich Finance Minister and head of the German delegation to Compiègne (one of the so-called 'November criminals'[73]) who had signed the armistice. His killers, Heinrich Schulz and Heinrich Tillessen, had settled in Regensburg in 1920, where they met Lorenz Mesch, the local leader of the *Germanenorden*. Since they had become interested in *völkisch* ideology after the end of the war, and were heavily influenced by its propaganda, the Order chose them to assassinate Erzberger, which they did in August 1921.

From 1921, the *Germanenorden* became the focus for right-wing and anti-Semitic sentiments in the hated Weimar Republic. When Rudolf von Sebottendorff joined Hermann Pohl's breakaway *Germanenorden Walvater* in 1917, the seed of the legendary Thule Society was sown.

The Thule Society

The mythology surrounding the Arctic realm of Thule has its origins in another myth, that of Atlantis. Although the 'lost continent' of Atlantis was held for centuries to have existed in the Atlantic Ocean 'beyond the Pillars of Hercules' (according to Plato in two of his dialogues, the *Timaeus* and *Critias*), this view was challenged in the late seventeenth century by the Swedish writer Olaus Rudbeck (1630–1702) who claimed that the lost civilisation, which had conquered North Africa and much of Europe 9,000 years before, had actually been centred in Sweden.

This curious notion was taken up in the mid-eighteenth century by a French astronomer and mystic named Jean-Sylvain Bailly (1736–1793) who came to the conclusion that the great achievements of civilisations such as Egypt and China were the result of knowledge inherited from a vastly superior antediluvian culture that had resided in the far North. According to Bailly, when the Earth was younger, its interior heat was much greater, and consequently the North Polar regions must have enjoyed a temperate climate in remote antiquity. Combining this idea with his belief that such climates are the most conducive to science and civilisation, Bailly identified Rudbeck's Atlanteans with the Hyperboreans of classical legend. The placing of this high civilisation in the far north resulted in the Nordic physique (tall, blond-haired and blue-eyed) being seen as the ultimate human ideal.

The origin of the Nazi concept of Thule and the Thule Society can be traced to Guido von List, Jörg Lanz von Liebenfels and Rudolf von Sebottendorff (1875–1945). As we have already noted (see page 38), all three added the particle 'von', suggesting noble descent, to their otherwise undistinguished names. As Joscelyn Godwin observes in his study of Polar mythology, *Arktos* (1993), 'One of the hallmarks of master-race philosophy is that no one is known to have embraced it who does not consider himself a member of that race. And what is more tempting, having once adopted the belief that one's own race is chosen by Nature or God for pre-eminence, than to put oneself at its aristocratic summit?'[74]

As we have seen, in 1907, Liebenfels founded the ritualistic and virulently racist Order of the New Templars, which had the dubious distinction of serving as the prototype for Heinrich Himmler's SS (*Schützstaffel*). Liebenfels was an avid student of Madame Blavatsky, who developed the notion that humanity was descended from a series of 'Root Races' that had degenerated throughout the millennia from a pure spiritual nature to the crude and barbarous beings of the present. According to Blavatsky, the origin of the anthropoid apes could be explained as the result of bestiality committed by the Third Root Race of humanity with monsters. Liebenfels in effect hijacked this concept and twisted it in the most appalling way, claiming that the non-Aryan races were the result of bestiality committed by the original Aryans after their departure from the paradise of their northern homeland, a lost continent he called Arktogäa (from the Greek, meaning 'northern earth').

These ideas found favour with Guido von List, like Liebenfels a native of Vienna, who was instrumental in the development of the *völkisch* movement. As we saw earlier, this movement was characterised by a love of unspoiled Nature, vegetarianism, ancient wisdom, astrology and earth energies. List had already played a crucial role in the founding of the secret, quasi-Masonic *Germanenorden*, whose aim was to counter what its members saw as the corruption by Jewry of German public life that was clearly the result of a secret international conspiracy. The *Germanenorden* was still active during the First World War, publishing a newsletter and placing advertisements in newspapers inviting men and women 'of pure Aryan descent' to join its ranks. It was in response to one of these advertisements that Rudolph von Sebottendorff met the leader of the *Germanenorden*, Hermann Pohl.

Sebottendorff had originally intended to be an engineer; however, having failed to complete his studies at the Berlin-Charlottenburg Polytechnic, and thus having little chance of qualified employment in Germany, he decided to go to sea. In 1900, after service on a number of steamships, and an abortive career as a gold prospector in Western Australia, Sebottendorff made his way first to Egypt and then to Turkey, where he immersed himself in a study of the Turkish people and cultivated an intense interest in occult science and ancient theocracies.

By 1916, Sebottendorff, now married, had settled in Bad Aibling, a fashionable Bavarian spa. At their meeting in Berlin in September of that year, Sebottendorff learned of Pohl's conviction that contamination by other races (particularly Jews) had robbed the Aryan race of its knowledge of magical power, and that this knowledge could only be regained through racial purity. On his return to Bad Aibling, Sebottendorff immediately set about organising a recruitment campaign for the *Germanenorden* in Bavaria.

In 1918, Sebottendorff met an art student named Walter Nauhaus who had been badly wounded on the Western Front in 1914 and had been invalided out of the war. Nauhaus shared Sebottendorff's intense interest in the occult, and soon became an invaluable colleague in the Bavarian recruitment campaign for the *Germanenorden*. It was Nauhaus who suggested that the name of the order be changed from *Germanenorden* to *Thule Gesellschaft* (Thule Society), in order, according to Goodrick-Clarke, to 'spare it the unwelcome attentions of socialist and pro-Republican elements'.[75] The ceremonial foundation of the Thule Society took place on 17 August 1918. The society met at the fashionable Hotel Vierjahreszeiten in Munich, in rooms decorated with the

Thule emblem: a long dagger, its blade surrounded by oak leaves, superimposed on a shining, curved-armed swastika.

On the eve of the Armistice that signalled German defeat in the First World War, the Thule Society, appalled at the prospect of the Kaiser abdicating, not to mention the revolution in Bavaria which had seen the seizure of authority by the Soviet Workers' and Soldiers' Councils, held a meeting on 9 November 1918, at which Sebottendorff made an impassioned exhortation to his fellow Thuleans:

> Yesterday we experienced the collapse of everything which was familiar, dear and valuable to us. In the place of our princes of Germanic blood rules our deadly enemy: Judah. What will come of this chaos, we do not know yet. But we can guess. A time will come of struggle, the most bitter need, a time of danger [. . .] I am determined to pledge the Thule Society to this struggle. Our Order is a Germanic Order, loyalty is also Germanic. [. . .] And the eagle is the symbol of the Aryans. In order to depict the eagle's capacity for self-immolation by fire, it is coloured red. From today on our symbol is the red eagle, which warns us that we must die in order to live.[76]

The Thule Society continued to meet at the Hotel Vierjahreszeiten, while Sebottendorff extended its influence from the upper and middle classes to the working classes via the use of popular journalism. He achieved this by purchasing for 5,000 marks a minor weekly newspaper, published in Munich and called the *Beobachter*, in 1918. Renaming the paper the *Münchener Beobachter und Sportblatt*, Sebottendorff added sports features to attract a more youthful, working-class readership for the anti-Semitic editorials that had been carried over from the paper's previous proprietor, Franz Eher. (In 1920, the *Münchener Beobachter und Sportblatt* became the *Völkischer Beobachter*, which would later be the official newspaper of the Nazi Party.)

On 26 April 1919, seven members of the Thule Society were captured by Communists and taken to the Luitpold

Gymnasium, which had served as a Red Army post for the previous two weeks. The hostages included Walter Nauhaus, Countess Hella von Westarp (secretary of the society) and Prince Gustav von Thurn und Taxis (who had many relatives in the royal families of Europe). Four days later, on 30 April, the hostages were shot in the cellar of the Gymnasium as a reprisal for the killing of Red prisoners at Starnberg. The killing of the Thule Society members had the effect of catalysing a violent popular uprising in Munich that, with the aid of White troops entering the city on 1 May, ensured the demise of the Communist Republic.

In 1918, Sebottendorff had succeeded in extending the journalistic influence of the Thule Society to the working classes by asking a sports reporter on a Munich evening paper, Karl Harrer, who had an intense interest in *völkisch* ideology, to form a workers' ring. This small group met every week throughout the winter of 1918, and discussed such topics as the defeat of Germany and the Jewish enemy. At the instigation of Anton Drexler, the workers' ring became the *Deutsche Arbeiterpartei* (German Workers' Party) (DAP) on 5 January 1919. In February 1920, the DAP was transformed into the National Socialist German Workers' Party (NSDAP). By that time, the party had already been infiltrated by an army spy whose orders had been to monitor its activities. Instead, he supported it, drafted new regulations for the committee, and soon became its President. His name was Adolf Hitler.

The Edda Society

As we saw earlier in this chapter, Guido von List and his followers believed that the Icelandic *Eddas* were chronicles of the ancient Aryans. List's occult-historical system was elaborated upon by Rudolf John Gorsleben (1883–1930), a playwright-turned-journalist who was born in Metz and grew up in Alsace-Lorraine (annexed by the German Reich in 1871). In this environment, in which people's loyalties were divided between France and Germany, Gorsleben was exposed to Pan-German nationalism and succeeded in tracing his ancestry back to a fourteenth-century noble family in Thuringia.[77]

At the outbreak of the First World War, Gorsleben fought first in a Bavarian regiment and then in a unit attached to the Turkish army in Arabia. When the war ended he went to Munich, where he became involved with the Thule Society and right-wing politics. During an eventful three years, Gorsleben became Gauleiter of the South Bavarian section of the *Deutschvölkischer Schutz- und Trutzbund*, an anti-Semitic group that was competing with the early Nazi Party. He formed associations with right-wing figures such as Julius Streicher, who would later edit the Nazi organ *Der Stürmer*, and Lorenz Mesch, the *Germanenorden* chief who had been instrumental in the assassination of Erzberger.

Through his periodical *Deutsche Freiheit (German Freedom)* – later renamed *Arische Freiheit (Aryan Freedom)* – Gorsleben disseminated his occult racist ideas, which centred upon the concept of racial purity and the reactivation of the occult powers that every Aryan possessed but which had become atrophied. With these magical powers once more at their fullest, the Aryan would hold complete sway over the processes of nature, and would thus be in a position to dominate and rule the world. He reiterated the *völkisch* notion that racial mixing was not only detrimental to the superior partner but also that a female could be tainted merely by intercourse with a racial inferior, and that all subsequent offspring, even if conceived with a racial equal, would likewise be tainted.[78]

With regard to the *Eddas*, Gorsleben believed that the Scandinavian runes contained an inherent magical power that provided those who understood their significance with a spiritual conduit through which could flow the force that drives the Universe itself. By far the most powerful was the asterisk-like hagall rune, since within it could be found hidden all the other runes. In addition, Gorsleben was perhaps the first occultist to promote the magical significance of crystals, which he considered to be three-dimensional projections of the runes. According to this theory, the spirit of every human individual can be correlated to a specific type of crystal that can be apprehended through the faculty of mediumship.

In November 1925, Gorsleben founded the Edda Society in the medieval town of Dinkelsbühl in Franconia. The treasurer of the society was Friedrich Schaefer, an associate of Karl Maria Wiligut, who would come to exert a great influence upon Heinrich Himmler. When Gorsleben died from heart disease in August 1930, the Edda Society was taken over by Werner von Bülow (1870–1947), who had designed a 'world-rune-clock' which illustrated the correspondences between the runes, the zodiac, numbers and gods.[79] Bülow also took over the running of Gorsleben's periodical, and changed its name from *Arische Freiheit* to *Hag All All Hag*, and then *Hagal*.

Although the primary intention of the Edda Society was to conduct research into the ancient Aryan religion through the interpretation, via the runes, of Norse mythology, the history of the lost Atlantean civilisation and the numerous prehistoric monuments of Europe, it nevertheless declared its allegiance to National Socialism in 1933, stating in an article in *Hagal* that the rise of Nazism was occurring in accordance with universal laws. *Hagal* also included material on the ancestral clairvoyant memories of Wiligut, which were felt to be of extreme significance to an understanding of the ancient occult heritage of the Germanic people.

Interestingly, not all rune scholars subscribed wholeheartedly to the racist, anti-Semitic interpretation of the *Eddas*. For example, one rune occultist, Friedrich Bernhard Marby (1882–1966), synthesised rune scholarship with astrology after encountering the writings of Guido von List. In his paper *Der eigene Weg* (established 1924) and his book series *Marby-Runen-Bücherei* (begun in 1931), Marby emphasised the health benefits gained from meditation on the runes. He was denounced as an anti-Nazi by the Third Reich in 1936, and sent first to Welzheim concentration camp, and then to Flossenbürg and Dachau, and was only freed when the camps were liberated by the Allies in April 1945.[80]

Although he lacked the virulently racist outlook of the other *völkisch* occultists of the period, Marby subscribed to a similar theory to that espoused by Liebenfels: namely, the essentially electrical nature of the cosmos, inspired (as noted earlier) by the recent discovery of radiation and the new uses to which electricity was being put. In Marby's opinion, the Universe was awash with cosmic rays, which could be both received and transmitted by human beings. In addition, the beneficial influences of these rays could be increased by adopting certain physical postures in imitation of rune-forms (a practice with an obvious similarity to yoga).

In 1927, Siegfried Adolf Kummer (b. 1899) founded a rune school called 'Runa' at Dresden. Runa concentrated on the practice of ritual magic, including the drawing of magic circles containing the names of the Germanic gods and the use of traditional magical tools such as candelabra and censers. During these rituals, the names of runes were called out and rune shapes were traced in the air as an aid to the magical process. Like Marby, Kummer was denounced by Wiligut, who considered their methods disreputable.[81]

Other occultists were more concerned with astrology and more overtly paranormal (in today's parlance) subjects than rune occultism. Georg Lomer (1877–1957) trained as a physician, but after encountering Theosophy turned his attention to alternative methods of medicine, particularly the use of dream symbolism and palmistry in the diagnosis of illness. By 1925, Lomer had added astrology to his occult interests, resulting in a synthesis of pagan Germanic mysticism with astrology. As Goodrick-Clarke observes: 'In common with the other post-war Aryan occultists, Lomer essentially used occult materials to illuminate the forgotten Aryan heritage.'[82]

The defining element in the occultism practised in Germany and Austria in the late nineteenth and early twentieth centuries was the perceived evil and corruption of the modern world, particularly that of the despised Weimar Republic with its stench of defeat, weakness and decadence. For people like List, Liebenfels, Sebottendorff and their followers, the future of humanity lay not in industrialisation, urbanisation and international finance (which they saw as causing the destruction of traditional, rural ways of life and the brutalisation of their ancestral homelands) but in the resurgence of ancient Aryan culture and the maintenance of racial purity. For the Aryans were heirs to a fabulous mystical legacy stretching far into prehistory, all the way back to the lost realms of Atlantis, Lemuria, Hyperborea and Ultima Thule. From out of the mists of time shone this lost Golden Age of giants and god-men endowed with fantastic, super-human abilities but who had been subsumed through miscegenation with inferior races – and were now gone. The *völkisch* occultists hoped, through their activities, to forge a magical and cultural link with these lost times, and through racial segregation and later genocide re-establish the global hegemony of the Aryan Superman.

Having completed our survey of Germanic occultism as developed and practised around the turn of the twentieth century, we must now leap back several thousand years into the past and turn our attention to that lost Golden Age itself. We are about to enter the strange realm of crypto-history, which will require us to travel far from Germany in the inter-war years – indeed, far from the orthodox view of humanity's entire history. In this way, we shall be able to identify the mythological origins of *völkisch* occultism in the legends of the lost Aryan homeland. In the following chapter, we will find ourselves traversing the icy fastness of the far North, as well as an ancient sea in what is now the Gobi Desert. We shall also reacquaint ourselves with Madame Blavatsky and her theories of the Root Races of humanity; and, by the end of the chapter, we will have examined the origins, mystical significance and ultimate corruption of the swastika, at which point we will have prepared ourselves for the harrowing journey into the nightmarish world of Nazi occultism itself.

2 Fantastic prehistory

The Lost Aryan Homeland

A S WE HAVE SEEN, the idea of a fabulous and mysterious homeland of the Aryan people, lying hidden somewhere in the far northern latitudes, was not an invention of the Nazis but had a rich provenance not only in the tradition of Western occultism but also in the burgeoning science of anthropology. (Indeed, the very concept of an 'Aryan Race' owed its existence as much to philology as any other branch of enquiry.[1])

Until the Enlightenment, of course, biblical tradition had been assumed to be the ultimate authority on the origin and history of humanity, that origin being Mount Ararat on which Noah's Ark made landfall after the Deluge. This idea made sense even to those scientists of the Enlightenment who rejected biblical authority, since mountainous regions would have provided the only possible protection against natural disasters such as the putative prehistoric flood.

The German Romantics were greatly attracted to Oriental philosophy and mysticism, in particular the *Zend-Avesta*, the sacred text of the ancient Persians. Thinkers of the calibre of Goethe, Nietzsche, Arthur Schopenhauer and Richard Wagner found in the Orient a system of philosophy and historiography that allowed them to abandon the unsatisfactory world view of Judeo-Christianity.[2] As Joscelyn Godwin notes, allied with this admiration for the Orient was a rediscovery of the German *Volk*, the pre-Christian Teutonic tribes whose descendants, the Goths, had brought about the final destruction of the decadent Roman Empire. The problem faced by the German Romantics was how to forge a historical connection between themselves and the Orient, which they considered to be the cradle of humanity and the origin of the highest human ideals.

Godwin asks, concerning the early Teutons:

> But where had those noble and gifted tribes come from? Were they, too, sons of Noah, or dared one sunder them from the biblical genealogy? The time was ripe to do so. The French Encyclopedists had set the precedent of contempt for the Hebrew scriptures as a source of accurate information. The British School of Calcutta, with their *Asiatic Researches*, had revealed another world, surely more learned, and to many minds philosophically and morally superior to that of Moses. If the Germans could link their origins to India, then they would be forever free from their Semitic and Mediterranean bondage.[3]

Of course, in order to establish and strengthen the link between the Germans and the Orient, Hebrew had to be abandoned as the original language of humanity, to be replaced by Sanskrit, the language of classical Hinduism. Instrumental in the forging of this link was the classical scholar Friedrich von Schlegel (1772–1829), who attempted to establish a historical and cultural contact between the Indians and the Scandinavians through which the Scandinavian languages could have been influenced by the Indian. Schlegel solved this problem by supposing that the ancient Indians had travelled to the far north as a result of their veneration for the sacred mountain, Meru, which they believed to constitute the spiritual centre of the world.

It was actually Schlegel who coined the term 'Aryan' in 1819 to denote a racial group (as opposed to a group of people speaking the Proto-Indo-European language, which is the proper definition of the term). Schlegel took the word 'Aryan', which had already been borrowed from Herodotus (who had used the word *Arioi* to describe the people of Media, an ancient western Asian country in what is now northern Iran) and applied to the ancient Persians, and connected it spuriously with the German word *Ehre*, meaning honour. At that point, the word 'Aryan' came to denote the highest, purest and most honourable racial group.⁴ This historical scheme was added to by other thinkers such as the anti-Semitic Christian Lassen, who claimed that the Indo-Germans were inherently biologically superior to the Semites.

The philologist Max Müller would later urge the adoption of the term 'Aryan' instead of 'Indo-Germanic', since the latter term did not include other European peoples who could, like the Indians and Germans, trace the origin of their languages to Sanskrit. According to the historian Léon Poliakov, by 1860 cultivated Europeans had come to accept that there was a fundamental division between Aryans and Semites. Godwin expresses this dogma in straightforward terms: '(1) Europeans were of the Aryan Race; (2) This race had come from the high plateaus of Asia. There had dwelt together the ancestors of the Indians, Persians, Greeks, Italians, Slavonians, Germans, and Celts, before setting off to populate Europe and Asia.'⁵

As we noted in Chapter One, the ideas of Charles Darwin were hijacked at this time by the proponents of Aryan racial superiority, and the concept of the survival of the fittest was readily applied to the interaction between racial groups (however spurious and misguided this system of grouping might have been). Darwin's assumption that evolution through natural selection would necessarily result in gradual improvements to each species was inverted by Aryan racism, which maintained that the White Race had long ago reached perfection and was being corrupted and undermined through miscegenation with inferior races.

As Godwin informs us, plans were being laid in some quarters for the biological 'improvement' of the human race back in the late nineteenth century. The French writer Ernest Renan believed that selective breeding in the future would result in the production of 'gods' and 'devas':

A factory of Ases [Scandinavian heroes], an *Asgaard*, might be reconstituted in the center of Asia. If one dislikes such myths, one should consider how bees and ants breed individuals for certain functions, or how botanists make hybrids. One could concentrate all the nervous energy in the brain ... It seems that if such a solution should be at all realizable on the planet Earth, it is through Germany that it will come.[6]

The Polar Paradise

In their desire to rediscover the ultimate mythical and cultural roots of their self-designated master race, the proponents of Aryanism turned away from the heat of the biblical Mesopotamian Eden and looked instead to the cool and pristine fastness of the Far North. The eighteenth-century polymath Jean-Sylvain Bailly (1736–1793) had already done much of the groundwork for a radical re-interpretation of humanity's origin with his highly original combination of Eastern mysticism and astronomy. According to Bailly, the ancient cultures of Egypt, Chaldea, China and India were actually the heirs of a far older body of knowledge, possessed in the distant past by a long-lost superior culture living in the antediluvian North.[7]

Bailly believed that it was this ancient culture that invented the zodiac in around 4600 BC. After the Flood, members of this civilisation moved from northern Asia to India. For Bailly, this assertion was supported by the similarity of certain legends in later cultures living far from each other: for example, the legend of the Phoenix, which is found both in Egypt and in the Scandinavian *Eddas* (discussed in Chapter One). Bailly equated the details of the Phoenix's death and rebirth with the annual disappearance of the Sun for 65 days at 71° North latitude. He went on to compare the Phoenix with the Roman god Janus, the god of time, who is represented with the number 300 in his right hand, and the number 65 in his left (corresponding, of course, with the 300 days of daylight and 65 days of darkness each year in the far northern latitudes). Bailly thus concluded that Janus was actually a northern god who had moved south with his original worshippers in the distant past. In support of his theory, Bailly also cited the legend of Adonis, who was required by Jupiter to spend one third of each year on Mount Olympus, one third with Venus and one third in Hades with Persephone. Bailly connected this legend with conditions in the geographical area at 79° North latitude, where the Sun disappears for four months (one third) of the year.[8]

To Bailly, this strongly suggested the preservation of the ancient knowledge of a hitherto unknown Nordic civilisation, which had been encoded in numerous legends passed down to subsequent cultures. These ideas corresponded somewhat with the work of one Comte de Buffon, who had concluded in 1749 that the Earth had formed much earlier than the Christian date of 4004 BC (although Buffon's date of 73,083 BC is still quite far from the Earth's actual age of approximately 4,000 million years). Buffon made the logical suggestion (within his scheme of creation) that the polar regions would have been the first to cool sufficiently to allow the development of life, and therefore placed the first human civilisation in the far northern latitudes. For Bailly, this was ample justification for his own ideas concerning the Arctic region as the cradle of humanity. The reason for the southerly migration of this first civilisation became obvious: since temperate climates are the most conducive to social, intellectual and scientific advancement, it clearly became necessary to move away gradually from the polar regions as they became too cold and the temperatures in the southern latitudes cooled from arid to temperate. The migration was finally complete when Chaldea, India and China were reached.[9]

The idea of a polar homeland for humanity was also elaborately developed by the Indian Bâl Gangâdhar Tilak (1856–1920) who wrote an epic work, *The Arctic Home in the Vedas*, while in prison in 1897 for publishing anti-British material in his newspaper, *The Kesari*. Published in 1903, Tilak's book concentrates on the age and original location of the Indian Vedic civilisation, from its origin in the Arctic around 10,000 BC, through its destruction in the last Ice Age; the migration to northern Europe and Asia in 8000–5000 BC and the composition of the Vedic hymns; the loss of the Arctic traditions around 3000–1400 BC; to the Pre-Buddhistic period in 1400–500 BC.[10]

Tilak's reading of the ancient Vedic texts supported his assertion of a prehistoric homeland in the far north, describing as they did a realm inhabited by the gods where the sun rose and fell once a year. Godwin has this to say regarding Tilak's interpretation of the Vedic hymns:

> The hymns are full of images that make nonsense in the context of a daily sunrise, such as the 'Thirty Dawn-Sisters circling like a wheel,' and the 'Dawn of Many Days' preceding the rising of the sun. If, however, they are applied to the Pole, they fall perfectly into place. The light of the sun circling beneath the horizon would be visible for at least thirty days before its annual rising. One can imagine the sense of anticipation felt by the inhabitants, as the wheeling light became ever brighter and the long winter's night came to an end.[11]

Tilak's ideas on the origin of humanity were further developed by the Zoroastrian scholar H. S. Spencer in his book *The Aryan Ecliptic Cycle* (1965), in which he examines the Zoroastrian scriptures in much the same way that Tilak examined the Vedic texts. Spencer compared events in the scriptures with the various positions of the sun during the precession of the equinoxes. (At this point, we should pause briefly to examine this phenomenon. The rotational axis of the Earth is not perpendicular to the plane occupied by the Solar System: instead, it is tilted at an angle of 23½°. Due to gravitational forces from the Sun and the Moon, the axis of the Earth's rotation 'wobbles' very slightly; or, to be more precise, it describes a circle. As the planet rotates, its axis also rotates, describing a complete circle once every 26,000 years.) In this way, Spencer was able to date with considerable accuracy the events described in the Zoroastrian scriptures. Spencer set the date for the first appearance of the

Aryans in the polar regions at 25,628 BC, during the Interglacial Age. The Aryans were forced to leave their homeland as the environment grew steadily colder and more hostile, and enormous reptiles began to appear. (How the reptiles themselves could have withstood the cold is another matter.) According to Spencer, the advent of the Ice Age that scattered the Aryans from their pleasant homeland was just one of a number of global catastrophes that proved the downfall of at least three other ancient civilisations: Atlantis, Lemuria and the culture occupying what is now the Gobi Desert.[12] According to Spencer, the Aryan tradition influenced the great civilisations of Egypt, Sumer and Babylon.

From Hyperborea to Atlantis

The great Russian occultist Helena Blavatsky, whom we met in Chapter One, had considerable information to divulge on the nature of the lost civilisations whose philosophy and knowledge were passed down, in frequently garbled form, to the great civilisations of the Middle and Far East. According to Blavatsky, who claimed to have consulted a fantastically old document entitled the *Stanzas of Dzyan* while in Tibet, our remote ancestors occupied a number of lost continents, the first of which she describes as 'The Imperishable Sacred Land', an eternal place unencumbered by the sometimes violent fates reserved for other continents, that was the home of the first human and also of 'the last divine mortal'.

The Second Continent was Hyperborea, 'the land which stretched out its promontories southward and westward from the North Pole to receive the Second Race, and comprised the whole of what is now known as Northern Asia'. The 'Second Race' refers to one of the Root Races (see page 34). Blavatsky continues:

The land of the Hyperboreans, the country that extended beyond Boreas, the frozen-hearted god of snows and hurricanes, who loved to slumber heavily on the chain of Mount Riphaeus, was neither an ideal country, as surmised by the mythologists, nor yet a land in the neighbourhood of Scythia and the Danube. It was a real continent, a *bonâ-fide* land which knew no winter in those early days, nor have its sorry remains more than one night and day during the year, even now. The nocturnal shadows never fall upon it, said the Greeks; for it is the *land of the Gods*, the favourite abode of Apollo, the god of light, and its inhabitants are his beloved priests and servants. This may be regarded as poetised *fiction* now; but it was poetised *truth* then.[13] [Original emphasis.]

The Third Continent was Lemuria (so called by the zoologist P. L. Sclater in reference to a hypothetical sunken continent extending from Madagascar to Sri Lanka and Sumatra). Blavatsky claimed that the gigantic continent of Lemuria actually existed, its highest points now forming islands in the Pacific Ocean.

The Fourth Continent was Atlantis. 'It would be the first historical land, were the traditions of the ancients to receive more attention than they have hitherto. The famous island of Plato of that name was but a fragment of this great Continent.'[14]

In her description of the Fifth Continent, Blavatsky evokes images of cataclysmic seismic shifts in the land mass of the Earth:

The Fifth Continent was America; but, as it is situated at the Antipodes, it is Europe and Asia Minor, almost coeval with it, which are generally referred to by the Indo-Aryan Occultists as the fifth. If their teaching followed the appearance of the Continents in their geological and geographical order, then this classifica-tion would have to be altered. But as the sequence of the Continents is made to follow the order of evolution of the Races, from the first to the fifth, our Aryan Root-race, Europe must be called the fifth great Continent. The Secret Doctrine takes no account of islands and peninsulas, nor does it follow the modern geographical distribution of land and sea. Since the day of its earliest teachings and the destruction of the great Atlantis, the face of the earth has changed more than once. There was a time when the delta of Egypt and Northern Africa belonged to Europe, before the formation of the Straits of Gibraltar, and a further upheaval of the continent, changed entirely the face of the map of Europe. The last serious change occurred some 12,000 years ago, and was followed by the submersion of Plato's little Atlantic island, which he calls Atlantis after its parent continent.[15]

Blavatsky claimed to have read in the *Stanzas of Dzyan* that the Earth contained seven great continents, 'four of which have already lived their day, the fifth still exists, and two are to appear in the future'. In *The Secret Doctrine*, she calls them Jambu, Plaksha, Salmali, Kusa, Krauncha, Sâka and Pushkara. She continues:

> We believe that each of these is not strictly a continent in the modern sense of the word, but that each name, from Jambu down to Pushkara, refers to the geographical names given (i) to the dry lands covering the face of the whole earth during the period of a Root-Race, in general; and (ii) to what remained of these after a geological [cataclysm]: and (iii) to those localities which will enter, after the future cataclysms, into the formation of new *universal* 'continents,' [or] peninsulas . . . each continent being, in one sense, a greater or smaller region of dry land surrounded with water. [Original emphasis.][16]

Aside from the *Stanzas of Dzyan*, Blavatsky drew on a huge number of religious texts, including the Hindu Puranas, which speak of a land called *Svita-Dvîpa* (Hyperborea), or the White Island, at the centre of which is Mount Meru, the spiritual centre of the world. (We will have more to say of Mount Meru in Chapter Four.) If we accept the attributes given to Mount Meru in the sacred texts of the Hindus –

including its height of 672,000 miles – then it must be conceded that the mountain does not exist anywhere on the physical Earth. This has led Orientalists to speculate that the White Island and Mount Meru are situated in what might best be described as another dimension occupying that same space as Earth and which is visible (and reachable) to beings possessing a sufficiently advanced spirituality.[17]

The legendary realm of Hyperborea also formed a centrepiece in the writings of the French occultist René Guénon (1886–1951) who, like Blavatsky (whom he nevertheless considered a charlatan), claimed to have received his information from hidden Oriental sources. Guénon's Hyperborea is very similar to Blavatsky's, although its origin is placed much more recently. According to Guénon, the present cycle of humanity began a mere 64,800 years ago in the Hyperborean land of Tula (Thule). Along with the later Atlantean civilisation, which lasted for 12,960 years (or half of one precessional cycle), Hyperborea was the origin of all religious and spiritual tradition in our own modern world. Guénon also wrote of Mount Meru, although in symbolic terms: 'It seems from his essays on symbology that Guénon did not regard Meru as an actual mountain situated at the North Pole, but rather as a symbol of the earth's axis that passes through the pole and points to the *Arktoi*, the constellations of the Great and Little Bears. (Guénon also claimed that the inclination of the Earth's axis at 23 ½° was a result of the Fall of humanity.)'[18]

At this point, we should pause to consider a question that may have occurred to the reader: assuming the existence of the prehistoric Root Races of humanity, why have none of their remains ever been discovered and excavated by archaeologists and palaeontologists? Apart from the obvious but not particularly satisfactory answer that the vast majority of the Earth's fossil record has yet to be discovered, it should be remembered that, according to Guénon, Blavatsky and the other Theosophists, the early Earth and its fabulous primordial inhabitants were not solid, corporeal entities, but were composed of a rarefied spiritual substance that only later descended into the material state. It is for this reason that their remains have never been discovered.[19]

For a basic chronology of the Earth according to this system, we can look to Godwin, who summarises the development of Guénon's work by Jean Phaure. Between 62,000 and 36,880 BC was the Golden Age (*Krita Yuga*), which lasted for one full precessional cycle (25,920 years) beginning with the Age of Leo. This was the period before the descent into matter, when Paradise existed. Then came the period from 36,880 to 17,440 BC, the Silver Age (*Treta Yuga*), lasting 19,440 years. This age lasted from Leo to Sagittarius, and included the descent into matter. It also saw the rise of Hyperborea and the other continents of Lemuria and Mu. This was followed by the period from 17,440 to 4,480 BC, the Bronze Age (*Dvapara Yuga*), which lasted for half of one precessional cycle, and from Scorpio to Gemini. This age saw the fall of Atlantis around 10,800 BC, the colonisation of other parts of the world by Atlantean refugees, the biblical Flood and the invention of writing. The period between 4,480 BC and AD 2000 is the Iron Age (*Kali Yuga*), which lasts for 6,480 years, from Taurus, through Aries to Pisces. This period includes our own history. The cycle ends with the Millennium and the beginning of the Age of Aquarius. Phaure has no problem with an incarnated humanity living in the Arctic, and suggests that they were able to do so with the aid of a spiritual energy source unknown to our own narrow, materialistic science. In support of this, he cites the case of certain Tibetan adepts who are able to live quite happily in the frigid Himalayan regions with little clothing.[20]

It is easy to see how the central tenets of Theosophy – the ancient and fantastic civilisations, the origins of the Aryan race and that race's position of high nobility – were attractive to the German occultists and nationalists who so hated the modern world of the late nineteenth and early twentieth centuries. As the researcher Peter Levenda observes: 'Modernism in general was seen as being largely an urban, sophisticated, intellectual (hence "Jewish") phenomenon, and this included science, technology, the Industrial Revolution, and capitalism.'[21] The doctrines of the Theosophists successfully fused science and mysticism, taking Darwin's theories regarding natural selection and the survival of the fittest and applying them to the concept of a spiritual struggle between the races of Earth (resulting in the Aryan race), which was a necessary component in the evolution of the spirit.[22]

Levenda continues:

It should be remembered that Blavatsky's works ... appear to be the result of prodigious scholarship and were extremely convincing in their day. The rationale behind many later Nazi projects can be traced back – through the writings of von List, von Sebottendorff, and von Liebenfels – to ideas first popularized by Blavatsky. A caste system of races, the importance of ancient alphabets (notably the runes), the superiority of the Aryans (a white race with its origins in the Himalayas), an 'initiated' version of astrology and astronomy, the cosmic truths coded within pagan myths ... all of these and more can be found both in Blavatsky and in the Nazi Party itself, specifically in the ideology of its Dark Creature, the SS. It was, after all, Blavatsky who pointed out the supreme occult significance of the swastika. And it was a follower of Blavatsky who was instrumental in introducing the *Protocols of the Elders of Zion* to a Western European community eager for a scapegoat.[23]

It will be remembered that the notorious document known as the *Protocols of the Elders of Zion* was an anti-Semitic forgery created by the *Okhrana* (the Czarist secret police) and occultists in St Petersburg and Paris to discredit the enemies of Rachkhovsky, the head of the *Okhrana* in Paris.[24] Produced in St Petersburg in 1902 and translated into German in 1919, the document purported to be the minutes of a meeting of the putative secret Jewish world conspiracy,[25] a conspiracy that, it appeared, was approaching the fulfilment of its goals. The *Protocols* indicated that Democracy, Communism and international commerce had been successfully infiltrated and taken over by the Jews, who 'had "infected" all governments, all commerce, all of the arts and media'.[26] Information regarding the *Protocols* was initially provided to the press by a Madame

Yuliana Glinka, a believer in Spiritualism who would do much to promote the anti-Semitic falsehoods contained within the document.

As is well known, Hitler himself came to believe wholeheartedly in the veracity of the *Protocols*, which formed a principal basis for his own anti-Semitism:

> To what an extent the whole existence of this people is based on a continuous lie is shown incomparably by the *Protocols of the Wise Men [Elders] of Zion*, so infinitely hated by the Jews. They are based on a forgery, the *Frankfurter Zeitung* moans and screams once every week: the best proof that they are authentic. What many Jews may do unconsciously is here consciously exposed. And that is what matters. It is completely indifferent from what Jewish brain these disclosures originate; the important thing is that with positively terrifying certainty they reveal the nature and activity of the Jewish people and expose their inner contexts as well as their ultimate final aims. The best criticism applied to them, however, is reality. Anyone who examines the historical development of the last hundred years from the standpoint of this book will at once understand the screaming of the Jewish press. For once this book has become the common property of a people, the Jewish menace may be considered as broken.[27]

Hitler's reference to the *Frankfurter Zeitung* is especially interesting and ironic, in view of the startling and intriguing suggestion made by that paper's Munich correspondent, the anti-Nazi Konrad Heiden. Heiden began reporting on Hitler's activities in 1921; when Hitler took power in 1933, Heiden was forced to flee to France. In his biography of Hitler, *Der Fuehrer*, written in exile and published in 1944, Heiden suggests a profound connection between Hitler and the *Protocols*, a connection which is summarised by Rosenbaum:

> Heiden's stunning conjecture, which deserves attention because of his intimate acquaintance with the Hitler

Party from the very beginning of the Führer's rise, was that the secret of that rise lay in Hitler's adapting the modernized Machiavellian tactics attributed to his archenemy, the Elders of Zion, and *putting them to his own use* in manipulating the media, subverting the institutions of the state, and crafting his own successful conspiracy to rule the world. Heiden argues that Hitler did not merely adopt the counterfeit Jewish conspiracy as his vision of the world, he adopted the *tactics* falsely attributed to Jews by czarist forgers as his own – and used them with remarkable success. A success that made Hitler himself a kind of creation of a counterfeit. [Original emphasis.][28]

I hope the reader will forgive this seeming digression from the subject we were discussing: while the apparent influence of the *Protocols* on Hitler may seem a long way from the lost Aryan homeland of the prehistoric north, it is worth introducing the idea at this point, not only because it was a supporter of Blavatsky who promoted the *Protocols* in western Europe but also because it is of profound importance to the rest of our study. If Heiden was correct in his conjecture, and Adolf Hitler, and hence Nazi Germany, were the creation of a counterfeit, this demonstrates quite convincingly the power and influence that bizarre falsehoods can have over the collective psyche of a people. This will have special significance in the last three chapters of this book, which will deal with Nazi cosmology and the belief in a hollow Earth, the theory that German scientists were responsible for the wave of UFO sightings in the late 1940s (and perhaps still are responsible for such sightings today), and the persistent rumours regarding the survival of key Nazis in a hidden Antarctic colony.

Before moving on, however, we must return briefly to Blavatsky and Theosophy in order to address the implication that the movement possessed fascist elements. In spite of its proclamation of the supremacy of thc Aryan race (not to mention Madame Glinka's unfortunate promotion of the *Protocols*), Theosophy was not inherently fascist, and

Blavatsky herself did not become overtly involved in politics.[29] (Indeed, although it had inspired a large number of German occultists and nationalists at the turn of the century, Theosophy would later be attacked and suppressed by the Nazis, along with all other organisations showing any resistance whatsoever to Hitler.[30]) Nevertheless, some of Blavatsky's followers, most notably Annie Besant (1847–1933), became active in politics. In Besant's case, it was Indian politics, and it was under her presidency after Henry Olcott's death in 1907 that the Theosophical Society became an important element in the Indian Nationalist Movement. As Levenda notes, the Nazis would later attempt to exploit Indian nationalism and the desire for home rule by claiming a similarity of ideals and objectives between Indian nationalism and National Socialism.[31]

Iceland and Antarctica

It is a matter of historical record that the Nazis mounted expeditions to Iceland, Antarctica and Tibet (the Tibetan expeditions will be examined more closely in the next chapter). The true reasons for these expeditions, however, have been the subject of considerable debate throughout the decades since the end of the war. As we have already noted, the Nazi concept of Thule can be traced to Guido von List, Jörg Lanz von Liebenfels and Rudolf von Sebottendorff, who conceived of it as the ancient homeland of the Aryan race. (At some time between the third and fourth centuries BC, Pytheas of Massilia undertook a voyage to the north. He reached Scotland, and sailed on for six more days, probably reaching the North Shetland Islands. He then claimed to have reached the land of Thule, which may have been Iceland, or perhaps Norway, before encountering a frozen sea.[32])

The *völkisch* fascination with the Scandinavian *Eddas* led von Sebottendorff to conclude that the supposedly long-vanished land of Thule was actually Iceland. This link with the lost Aryan homeland prompted an intense interest in the possibility of discovering further clues to their remote history, indeed, to their very origin, among the caves and prehistoric monuments of the island.[33]

According to Peter Levenda, an organisation called the Nordic Society was established at Lübeck by Alfred Rosenberg (1893–1945), the Nazi mystic, philosopher, editor of the *Völkischer Beobachter* and later Reich Minister for the occupied eastern territories. The society counted among its members representatives from Norway, Sweden, Finland, Denmark and Iceland, who were drawn together in order to defend the Nordic nations against the Soviet, Jewish and Masonic threat. On 22 August 1938, the *Völkischer Beobachter* carried an article on one of the Nordic Society's meetings, at which Rosenberg was quoted thus:

'We all stand under the same European destiny, and must feel obliged to this common destiny, because finally the existence of the white man depends altogether upon the unity of the European continent! Unanimous must we oppose that terrible attempt by Moscow to destroy the world, the sea of blood into which already many people have dived!'[34]

Rosenberg explained his Thulean mythology in his book *Der Mythus des 20. Jahrhunderts* (*The Myth of the Twentieth Century*), published in 1930, which was a massive best-seller in Germany, despite the fact that it was widely considered to be appallingly-written nonsense. (Hitler himself, who, once in power, had little time for paganism, Thulean or otherwise, described it as 'stuff nobody can understand'.[35]) In the first chapter of the book, Rosenberg explains the basis of his belief in an ancient Aryan homeland in the north:

The geologists show us a continent between North America and Europe, whose remains we can see today in Greenland and Iceland. They tell us that islands on the other side of the Far North (Novaia Zemlya) display former tide marks over 100 metres higher than today's; they make it probable that the North Pole has wandered, and that a much milder climate once reigned in the present Arctic. All this allows the ancient legend of Atlantis to appear in a new light. It seems not impossible that where the waves of the Atlantic Ocean now crash and pull off giant icebergs, once a blooming continent rose out of the water, on which a creative race raised a mighty, wide-ranging culture, and sent its children out into the world as seafarers and warriors. But even if this Atlantean hypothesis is not thought tenable, one has to assume that there was a prehistoric northern center of culture.[36]

Despite these assertions concerning the great secrets of a long-vanished Aryan civilisation that might be found in Iceland, Rosenberg, who was looked upon with a mixture of amusement and contempt by most of the leading Nazis, was not involved with the actual expeditions sent there. They were authorised by Heinrich Himmler under the auspices of the *Ahnenerbe* – the SS Association for Research and Teaching on Heredity. Levenda has retrieved numerous documents regarding these missions, some of which he includes in his fascinating study *Unholy Alliance* (1995). One of these documents, addressed to the *Ahnenerbe* from a Dr Bruno Schweizer, contains a proposal for a research journey to Iceland, and is dated 10 March 1938:

From year to year it becomes more difficult to meet living witnesses of Germanic cultural feelings and Germanic soul attitudes on the classical Icelandic soil uninfluenced by the overpowerful grasp of western civilization. In only a few years has the natural look of the country, which since the Ur-time has remained mostly untouched in stone and meadow, in desert and untamed mountain torrents, revealed its open countenance to man and has fundamentally changed from mountainsides and rock slabs to manicured lawns, nurseries and pasture grounds, almost as far from Reykjavik as the barren coast section, a feat accomplished by the hand of man; the city itself expands with almost American speed as roadways and bridges, power stations and factories emerge and the density of the traffic in Reykjavik corresponds with that of a European city.

Dr Schweizer goes on to bemoan the loss of ancient agricultural techniques such as forging, wood-carving, spinning, weaving and dyeing; along with the forgetting of myths and legends and the lack of belief in a 'transcendent nature'. After describing the lamentable rise of materialism that drew people from rural areas to the city (and gave an unfavourable impression to good German visitors!), the doctor continues:

> Every year that we wait quietly means damage to a number of objects, and other objects become ruined for camera and film due to newfangled public buildings in the modern style. For the work in question only the summer is appropriate, that is, the months of June through August. Furthermore, one must reckon that occasionally several rainy days can occur, delaying thereby certain photographic work. The ship connections are such that it is perhaps only possible to go to and from the Continent once a week.
>
> All this means a minimum period of from 5–6 weeks for the framework of the trip.
>
> The possible tasks of an Iceland research trip with a cultural knowledge mission are greatly variegated. Therefore it remains for us to select only the most immediate and most realizable. A variety of other tasks . . . should be considered as additional assignments.
>
> Thus the recording of human images (race-measurements) and the investigation of museum treasures are considered to be additional assignments.[37]

As Levenda wryly observes, it is not clear how the people of Iceland would have reacted to the taking of 'race measurements' or, for that matter, the 'investigation of museum treasures', which almost certainly would not have remained in the museums for very long!

German interest in Antarctic exploration goes back to 1873, when Eduard Dallman mounted an expedition in his steamship *Grönland* on behalf of the newly founded German Society of Polar Research. Less than 60 years later, the Swiss explorer Wilhelm Filchner, who had already led an expedition to Tibet in 1903–05, planned to lead two expeditions to Antarctica with the intention of determining if the continent was a single piece of land. Filchner's plans called for two ships, one to enter the Weddell Sea and one to enter the Ross Sea. Two groups would then embark on a land journey and attempt to meet at the centre of the continent. This plan, however, proved too expensive, and so a single ship, the *Deutschland*, was used. The *Deutschland* was a Norwegian ship specifically designed for work in polar regions, and was acquired with the help of Ernest Shackleton, Otto Nordenskjöld and Fridtjof Nansen. The expedition reached the Weddell Sea in December 1911. Another expedition was mounted in 1925 with the polar expedition ship *Meteor* under the command of Dr Albert Merz.

In the years running up to the Second World War, Germany wanted a foothold in Antarctica, both for the propaganda value of demonstrating the power of the Third Reich and also because of the territory's strategic significance in the South Atlantic. On 17 December 1938, an expedition was despatched under the command of Captain Alfred Ritscher to the South Atlantic coast of Antarctica and arrived there on 19 January 1939. The expedition's ship was the *Schwabenland*, an aircraft carrier that had been used since 1934 for transatlantic mail delivery. The *Schwabenland*, which had been prepared for the expedition in the Hamburg shipyards at a cost of one million Reichsmarks, was equipped with two Dornier seaplanes, the *Passat* and the *Boreas*, which were launched from its flight deck by steam catapults and which made fifteen flights over the territory which Norwegian explorers had named Queen Maud Land. The aircraft covered approximately 600,000 square kilometres, took more than 11,000 photographs of the Princess Astrid and Princess Martha coasts of western Queen Maud Land, and dropped several thousand drop-flags (metal poles with swastikas). The area was claimed for the Third Reich, and was renamed *Neu Schwabenland*.

Perhaps the most surprising discovery made by this expedition was a number of large, ice-free areas, containing lakes and sparse vegetation. The expedition geologists suggested that this might have been due to underground heat sources.

In mid-February 1939, the *Schwabenland* left Antarctica and returned to Hamburg. Ritscher was surprised at the findings of the expedition, particularly the ice-free areas, and immediately began to plan another journey upon his arrival home. These plans, however, were apparently abandoned with the outbreak of war.

At this point, orthodox history gives way to strange rumours and speculations regarding the true reason for the Third Reich's interest in Antarctica. It has been suggested, for instance, that the 1938-39 expedition had been to look for a suitable ice-free region on the continent that could be used for a secret Nazi base after the war. According to the novelist and UFO researcher W. A. Harbinson: 'Throughout the war, the Germans sent ships and aircraft to *Neu Schwabenland* with enough equipment and manpower (much of it slave labour from the concentration camps) to build massive complexes under the ice or in well-hidden ice-free areas. At the close of the war selected Nazi scientists and SS troops fled to Antarctica . . .'[38]

Such speculations properly belong to the field known as 'Nazi survival', which we will discuss in depth in the final chapter of this book. Therefore, let us place them aside and turn our attention to another important element in the concept of a lost Aryan homeland: a symbol that once signified good fortune but was irreparably corrupted by the Nazis, and which now signifies nothing but terror and death.

The Swastika

In antiquity, the swastika was a universal symbol, being used from the Bronze Age onwards on objects of every kind. The word 'swastika' comes from the Sanskrit: *su* (Greek *eu*, meaning 'good'), *asti* (Greek *estô*, meaning 'to be') and the suffix *ka*.[39] The symbol means 'good luck' (the Sanskrit-Tibetan word *Swasti* means 'may it be auspicious'). According to Joscelyn Godwin, the shape of the swastika derives from the constellation Arktos, also known as the Great Bear, the Plough and the Big Dipper. To the observer in the Northern Hemisphere, this constellation appears to rotate around Polaris, the Pole Star (an effect caused by the rotation of the Earth). If the positions of Arktos in relation to Polaris are represented in pictorial form (corresponding to the four seasons), the result is highly suggestive of a swastika; in 4000 BC, they were identical to the symbol. It is for this reason that the swastika (aside from denoting good fortune) has been used to represent the Pole.[40]

The swastika gained in importance in European culture in the nineteenth century, primarily in the fields of comparative ethnology and Oriental studies. The absence of the symbol from Egypt, Chaldea, Assyria and Phoenicia led the ethnologists to believe that the swastika was an Aryan sun-symbol.[41] Madame Blavatsky saw the significance of the symbol, and incorporated it into the seal of the Theosophical Society to signify the harmony of universal movement. According to Godwin: 'So innocent were the "good luck" associations of the swastika that during World War I, it was used as the emblem of the British War Savings Scheme, appearing on coupons and stamps.'[42]

The swastika appears in two forms: left-handed and right-handed. However, confusion quickly arises when one is faced with the question of how to define 'left' and 'right' with regard to this symbol. Some occultists and historians favour a definition based on the direction taken by the arms as they extend outward from the centre; while others prefer to define 'left' and 'right' in terms of the apparent direction of rotation. The confusion arises from the fact that a swastika whose arms proceed to the *left* appears to be rotating to the *right*, and vice versa.

Each swastika variant has been taken to mean different things by writers on the occult, such as the Frenchman André

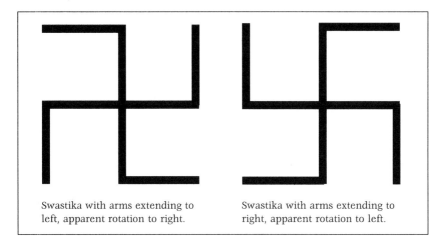

Swastika with arms extending to left, apparent rotation to right.

Swastika with arms extending to right, apparent rotation to left.

Brissaud who says that the counter-clockwise-spinning swastika represents the rotation of the Earth on its axis and is the 'Wheel of the Golden Sun', symbolising creation, evolution and fertility. The clockwise-spinning swastika is, according to Brissaud, the 'Wheel of the Black Sun', representing man's quest for power in opposition to Heaven.[43] The Chilean diplomat, esotericist and Hitler apologist Miguel Serrano (b. 1917), whom we shall meet again in the final chapter, has another explanation of the left- and right-handed swastikas: the left-handed (clockwise-turning) symbol represents the migration of the ancient Aryan Race from its homeland at the North Pole, while the right-handed (counter-clockwise-turning) symbol – the one used by the Nazis – represents the destiny of the Aryans to return to their spiritual centre at the South Pole.[44]

After informing us of the complexities attached to the interpretation of left- and right-handed swastikas, Godwin continues:

Whatever the validity of these theories, the ancient decorative swastikas show no preference whatsoever for one type over the other. The place where the left-right distinction is supposed to be most significant is Tibet, where both Nicholas Roerich and Anagarika Govinda observed that the swastika of the ancient Bön-Po religion points to the left, the Buddhist one to the right. Now it is true that the Bön-Pos perform ritual circumabulations counter-clockwise, the Buddhists clockwise, but almost all the Buddhist iconography collected by Thomas Wilson shows left-handed swastikas, just like the ones on the Bön-Pos' ritual scepter, their equivalent of the Buddhist *vajra*. One can only say that the swastika should perhaps be left-handed if (as in Bön-Po) it denotes polar revolution, and right-handed if (as in Buddhism) it symbolizes the course of the sun. But the root of the problem is probably the inherent ambiguity of the symbol itself, which makes the left-handed swastika appear to be rotating to the right, and vice versa.[45]

As we saw in the first chapter, the swastika gained popularity among German anti-Semitic groups through the writings of Guido von List and Lanz von Liebenfels, who took the symbol of good fortune and universal harmony and used it to denote the unconquerable Germanic hero. As might be expected, the counter-clockwise orientation of the swastika used as a banner by the National Socialist German Workers' Party (NSDAP) has also aroused considerable controversy in occult and esoteric circles.

According to the occult historian Francis King, when Hitler called for suggestions for a banner, all of the submissions included a swastika. The one Hitler finally chose had been designed by Dr Friedrich Krohn, a dentist from Sternberg. However, the design incorporated a clockwise-turning swastika, symbolising good fortune, harmony and spirituality. Hitler decided to reverse the design, making the swastika counter-clockwise, symbolising evil and black magic.[46] Here again, we encounter the problem of defining what is a right- and left-handed swastika. Was the Nazi symbol right-handed (traditionally denoting good) or left-handed (denoting evil)? In one sense, the Nazi swastika could be said to be right-handed because the hooked arms extend to the right; conversely, it could be said to be left-handed, since the apparent rotation is counter-clockwise. As the journalist Ken Anderson notes: 'What we are dealing with is subjective definition ... We can speculate that Hitler had chosen to reverse the cross *because* of the connotations of black magic and evil in Krohn's cross and *for* the purpose of evoking the positive images of good luck, spiritual evolution, etc., for his fledgling party!'[47] (Original emphasis.) Anderson gives the impression of having his tongue slightly in his cheek, but his interpretation is almost certainly correct, for two reasons. Firstly, we must remember that Hitler himself had very little time for occult mumbo-jumbo, and was certainly not the practising black magician many occultists claim him to have been (more on this in Chapter Five); and secondly, the idea that Hitler considered himself 'evil' (as he would have had to have done in order to take the step of reversing a positive symbol to a negative one), or that evil was an attractive concept for him is ridiculous. As we noted in the Introduction (page 78), one of the most terrifying and baffling aspects of Adolf Hitler is that he did not consider himself 'evil': as Trevor-Roper states, Hitler was convinced of his own rectitude, that he was acting correctly in exterminating the Jews and the other groups targeted for destruction by the Nazis.

In addition, Hitler himself makes no mention of such an alteration in his repulsive *Mein Kampf*. In view of the fact that he took most of the credit for the design himself, neglecting even to mention Krohn's name, he would surely have explained the reasons for his making such a fundamental alteration to the design of the NSDAP banner:

> ... I was obliged to reject without exception the numerous designs which poured in from the circles of the young movement ... I myself – as Leader – did not want to come out publicly at once with my own design, since after all it was possible that another should produce one just as good or perhaps even better. Actually, a dentist from Starnberg [sic] did deliver a design that was not bad at all, and, incidentally, was quite close to my own, having only the one fault that a swastika with curved legs was composed into a white disk

I myself, meanwhile, after innumerable attempts, had laid down a final form; a flag with a red background, a white disk, and a black swastika in the middle. After long trials I also found a definite proportion between the size of the flag and the size of the white disk, as well as the shape and thickness of the swastika.[48]

The reader will notice that Hitler says the submission he received that was quite close to his own had only one fault: the swastika had curved legs. Anderson is undoubtedly correct when he states that 'the major importance of the decision [was] – for a man who prided himself on being a thwarted artist of great merit – not some unidentified occultic myth, but rather balance and aesthetic value'.[49]

3 A hideous strength

The Vril Society

W E HAVE NOW REACHED THE POINT in our survey of Nazi involvement with the occult where we must depart from what is historically verifiable and enter an altogether more obscure and murky realm, a place that Pauwels and Bergier call the 'Absolute Elsewhere'.[1] Serious historians (at least, those who deign to comment on the subject at all) regard the material we shall be examining for the rest of this book with contempt – and, it must be said, not without good reason. Much of what follows may well strike the reader as bizarre and absurd in equal measure; and yet, as we shall see, amongst the notions we are about to address (products, apparently, of fevered imaginations) will be found unsettling hints of a thread running through the collective mind of humanity in the late twentieth century – ominous, dangerous and, by the majority, unseen.

As we shall see, the 'twilight zone between fact and fiction' can produce significant shifts in our collective awareness of the world, our place in it and the unstated intentions of those who rule us. The world view of those who subscribe to the idea of genuine Nazi occult power includes a number of outrageous conspiracy theories that revolve around the claim that many leading Nazis (including, according to some, Hitler himself) escaped from the ruins of Berlin and continue with their plans for world domination from some hidden headquarters. At first sight, these theories can surely have little to do with known reality. And yet, the idea that the American Central Intelligence Agency (CIA) could have smuggled many personnel from Nazi intelligence and the German secret weapons programme into the United States in the post-war years might likewise seem outlandish – until we remember that this, too, is a documented historical fact. Project PAPERCLIP proves that some senior elements of the Third Reich did indeed survive in this way, their lives bought with scientific and military knowledge that the American government desperately wanted.

So, for the rest of this book, we shall concentrate on the elements of Nazi occultism that find no home in orthodox history but that nevertheless stretch their pernicious tentacles through modern popular and fringe culture and refuse to vanish in the glare of the light of reason. The Vril Society, our departure point into the Absolute Elsewhere, might seem to have been better placed in the first chapter, were it not that there is so little evidence for its influence over the activities of the Third Reich. In spite of this, it has come to occupy a central position in the dubious study of Nazi occult power and so demands a chapter of its own. But what was the strangely named Vril Society?

The first hint of the Vril Society's existence was discovered in a scene that would not have been out of place in one of Dennis Wheatley's occult thrillers. On 25 April 1945, so the story goes, a group of battle-weary Russian soldiers were making their cautious way through the shattered remnants of Berlin, mopping up the isolated pockets of German resistance that remained in the heart of the Third Reich. The soldiers moved carefully from one wrecked building to another, in a state of constant readiness against the threat of ambush.

In a ground-floor room of one blasted building, the soldiers made a surprising discovery. Lying in a circle on the floor were the bodies of six men, with a seventh corpse in the centre. All were dressed in German military uniforms, and the dead man in the centre of the group was wearing a pair of bright green gloves. The Russians' assumption that the bodies were those of soldiers was quickly dispelled when they realised that the dead men were all Orientals. One of the

Russians, who was from Mongolia, identified the men as Tibetans. It was also evident to the Russian soldiers that the men had not died in battle but seemed to have committed suicide. Over the following week, hundreds more Tibetans were discovered in Berlin: some of them had clearly died in battle, while others had committed ritual suicide, like the ones discovered by the Russian unit.[2]

What were Tibetans doing in Nazi Germany towards the end of the Second World War? The answer to this question may be found in a curious novel entitled *The Coming Race* by Edward Bulwer-Lytton (1803–1873), first Baron Lytton. A prolific and very successful writer (his output included novels, plays, essays and poetry) Bulwer-Lytton was considered in his lifetime to be one of the greatest writers in the English language. Unfortunately, his reputation for vanity, ostentation and eccentricity attracted a good deal of hostility from the press and this has damaged his subsequent literary reputation to a disproportionate extent, with the result that today his books are extremely hard to find and his work is seldom – if at all – taught in universities in the English-speaking world.[3]

Throughout his career, Bulwer-Lytton wrote on many themes, including romance, politics, history, social satire, melodrama and the occult. It is perhaps unsurprising, therefore, that he should have turned to the subject of utopian science fiction with *The Coming Race*, published in 1871. In this novel, the narrator, a traveller and adventurer of independent means, explores a mine in an unnamed location and discovers a vast subterranean world, inhabited by a superior race of humans called the Vril-ya. Once tenants of the Earth's outer surface, the Vril-ya were forced to retreat underground by a natural catastrophe similar to the biblical Flood many thousands of years ago. Their technology is far in advance of anything to be found in the world of ordinary humanity, and is based on the application of a force known as 'vril'. Befriended by a young female Vril-ya named Zee, the narrator asks about the nature of the vril force.

Therewith Zee began to enter into an explanation of which I understood very little, for there is no word in any language I know which is an exact synonym for vril. I should call it electricity, except that it comprehends in its manifold branches other forces of nature, to which, in our scientific nomenclature, differing names are assigned, such as magnetism, galvanism, &c. These people consider that in vril they have arrived at the unity in natural energetic agencies, which has been conjectured by many philosophers above ground, and which Faraday thus intimates under the more cautious term of correlation:

'I have long held an opinion,' says that illustrious experimentalist, 'almost amounting to a conviction, in common, I believe, with many other lovers of natural knowledge, that the various forms under which the forces of matter are made manifest have one common origin; or, in other words, are so directly related and mutually dependent, that they are convertible, as it were, into one another, and possess equivalents of power in their action.'[4]

According to Zee, all Vril-ya are trained in the application of vril, which can be used to control the physical world, including the minds and bodies of others, as well as to enhance the telepathic and telekinetic potentials of the human mind. The vril force is most often applied through the use of a device known as the Vril Staff which, like the vril force itself, requires many years to master. (The narrator is not allowed to hold one, 'for fear of some terrible accident occasioned by my ignorance of its use'.) The Vril Staff 'is hollow, and has in the handle several stops, keys, or springs by which its force can be altered, modified, or directed – so that by one process it destroys, by another it heals – by one it can rend the rock, by another disperse the vapour – by one it affects bodies, by another it can exercise a certain influence over minds'.[5]

During his protracted stay in the subterranean realm, the narrator learns of the system of government by which the Vril-ya live. They are ruled by a single supreme magistrate who abdicates the position at the first sign of advancing age.

Although their society is entirely free of crime or strife of any kind, they consider strength and force to be among the finest virtues, and the triumph of the strong over the weak to be in perfect accordance with Nature. Democracy and free institutions are, to them, merely the crude experiments of an immature culture.

> The government of the tribe of Vril-ya ... was apparently very complicated, really very simple. It was based upon a principle recognised in theory, though little carried out in practice, above ground – viz., that the object of all systems of philosophical thought tends to the attainment of unity, or the ascent through all intervening labyrinths to the simplicity of a single first cause or principle. Thus in politics, even republican writers have agreed that a benevolent autocracy would insure the best administration, if there were any guarantees for its continuance, or against its gradual abuse of the powers accorded to it. There was ... in this society nothing to induce any of its members to covet the cares of office. No honours, no insignia of higher rank were assigned to it. The supreme magistrate was not distinguished from the rest by superior habitation or revenue. On the other hand, the duties awarded to him were marvellously light and easy, requiring no preponderant degree of energy or intelligence.[6]

After a number of adventures in the subterranean world – and a great many conversations with its denizens – the narrator comes to the following conclusion regarding the ultimate origins of the fantastic Vril-ya race:

> [T]his people – though originally not only of our human race, but, as seems to me clear by the roots of their language, descended from the same ancestors as the great Aryan family, from which in varied streams has flowed the dominant civilisation of the world; and having, according to their myths and their history, passed through phases of society familiar to ourselves,

– had yet now developed into a distinct species with which it was impossible that any community in the upper world could amalgamate: And that if they ever emerged from these nether recesses into the light of day, they would, according to their own traditional persuasions of their ultimate destiny, destroy and replace our existent varieties of man.[7]

Although greatly impressed with the knowledge and accomplishments of the Vril-ya, the narrator is nevertheless terrified by their power and the ease with which they wield it, implying at one point that, should he have angered them at any time, they would have had no compunction in turning their Vril Staffs on him and reducing him to cinders. This uneasiness, coupled with his natural desire to return to the upper world and the life with which he is familiar, prompts the narrator to begin seeking a means of escape from the subterranean world of the Vril-ya. Aid comes in the unlikely form of Zee, who has fallen in love with him and has attempted to persuade him to stay, but who nevertheless understands that an unrequited love cannot result in happiness for either of them. It is she who leads him back to the mine shaft through which he first entered the realm of the Vril-ya.

Upon his return home, the narrator begins to ponder the wonders he has beheld far below the surface of the Earth, and once again hints at the possible dreadful fate awaiting a blissfully unaware humanity at the hands of the 'Coming Race'. In the final chapter, we read:

[T]he more I think of a people calmly developing, in regions excluded from our sight and deemed uninhabit-able by our sages, powers surpassing our most disciplined modes of force, and virtues to which our life, social and political, becomes antagonistic in proportion as our civilisation advances, – the more devoutly I pray that ages may yet elapse before there emerge into sunlight our inevitable destroyers.[8]

It is an assumption of many occultists that *The Coming Race* is fact disguised as fiction: that Bulwer-Lytton based his engaging novel on a genuine body of esoteric knowledge. He was greatly interested in the Rosicrucians, the powerful occult society which arose in the sixteenth century and which claimed to possess ancient wisdom, discovered in a secret underground chamber, regarding the ultimate secrets of the Universe. There is some evidence that Bulwer-Lytton believed in the possibility of a subterranean world, for he wrote to his friend Hargrave Jennings in 1854: 'So Rosenkreuz [the founder of the Rosicrucians] found his wisdom in a secret chamber. So will we all. There is much to be learned from the substrata of our planet.'[9]

Some writers, including Alec Maclellan, author of the fascinating book *The Lost World of Agharti* (1996), have suggested that *The Coming Race* revealed too much of the subterranean world, and was as a result suppressed in the years following Bulwer-Lytton's death in 1873. Indeed, he describes the book as 'one of the hardest to find of all books of mysticism',[10] and informs us of his own search for a copy, which for some years met with no success. While doubtless an intriguing piece of stage-setting on Maclellan's part, the rarity of the book can surely be accounted for by the unjust waning of Bulwer-Lytton's posthumous literary reputation (mentioned earlier). The present author searched for some months for a copy of *The Coming Race*, before finding an extremely affordable paperback edition in a high-street bookshop.

What is the connection between Bulwer-Lytton's strange novel and Nazi Germany? If there really was a large colony of Tibetan monks in Berlin in the 1940s, what were they doing there? It seems that the connection was none other than the Bavarian Karl Haushofer (1869–1946) whose theories of Geopolitics gave rise to the concept of *Lebensraum* (living space), which Hitler maintained would be necessary to the continued dominance of the superior Aryan race and which he intended to take, primarily, from the Soviet Union. Haushofer, along with Dietrich Eckart (1868–1923) – an anti-Semitic journalist and playwright who influenced Hitler's racial attitudes and introduced him to influential social circles after the First World War – is frequently described by believers in genuine Nazi occult power as a practising black magician, and the 'Master Magician of the Nazi Party'.[11]

Haushofer excelled at Munich University, where he began to develop his lifelong interest in the Far East. After leaving university, he entered the German army, where his great intelligence ensured a rapid rise through the ranks. His knowledge of the Far East earned him a posting as military attaché in Japan. The idea that Haushofer was an occult adept, with secret knowledge of powerful trans-human entities, was first suggested by Louis Pauwels and Jacques Bergier in their fascinating but historically unreliable book *The Morning of the Magicians* (which served as the model for a number of subsequent treatments of Nazi occultism in the 1960s and early 1970s).

According to Pauwels and Bergier:

[Haushofer] believed that the German people originated in Central Asia, and that it was the Indo-Germanic race which guaranteed the permanence, nobility and greatness of the world. While in Japan, Haushofer is said to have been initiated into one of the most important secret Buddhist societies and to have sworn, if he failed in his 'mission', to commit suicide in accordance with the time-honoured ceremonial.[12]

Haushofer was also apparently a firm believer in the legend of Thule, the lost Aryan homeland in the far north, which had once been the centre of an advanced civilisation possessed of magical powers. Connecting this legend with the Thule Society, Pauwels and Bergier have this to say:

Beings intermediate between Man and other intelligent beings from Beyond would place at the disposal of the [Thule Society] Initiates a reservoir of forces which could be drawn on to enable Germany to dominate the world again and be the cradle of the coming race of Supermen which would result from the mutations of the human species. One day her legions would set out to annihilate everything that had stood in the way of the spiritual destiny of the Earth, and their leaders would be men who knew everything, deriving their strength from the very fountain-head of energy and guided by the Great Ones of the Ancient World . . . It would seem that it was under the influence of Karl Haushofer that [the Thule Society] took on its true character of a society of Initiates in communion with the Invisible, and became the magic centre of the Nazi movement.[13]

Serious historians such as Nicholas Goodrick-Clarke take issue with the claims of Pauwels and Bergier and the later writers who reiterated them. Goodrick-Clarke, who has perhaps conducted more research into primary German sources than any other writer in this curious field, states that the claims regarding the secret guiding power of the Thule Society are 'entirely fallacious. The Thule Society was dissolved in 1925 when support had dwindled.' He goes on to assure us that 'there is no evidence at all to link Haushofer to the group'.[14] Nevertheless, Haushofer's alleged skill in the Black Arts has become an important link in the Nazi occult chain as described by writers on such fringe subjects.

After the end of the First World War, Haushofer returned to Munich, where he gained a doctorate from the university. He divided his time between teaching and writing and founded the *Geopolitical Review* in which he published his ideas on *Lebensraum*, which could 'both justify territorial conquest by evoking the colonizing of Slav lands by Teutonic knights in the Middle Ages and, emotively, conjure up notions of uniting in the Reich what came to be described as *Volksdeutsche* (ethnic Germans) scattered throughout eastern Europe'.[15]

While incarcerated in the fortress of Landsberg am Lech following the failure of the Munich *Putsch* in 1924, Adolf Hitler read and was influenced by Haushofer's books on geopolitics (he had already been introduced to Haushofer by the professor's student assistant, Rudolf Hess). There is no doubt that Hitler occupied his time in Landsberg judiciously, reading widely in several fields, though not for the sake of education so much as to confirm and clarify his own preconceptions. (He later said that Landsberg was his 'university paid for by the state'.[16])

According to Pauwels and Bergier and other fringe writers, Haushofer visited Hitler every day in Landsberg, where he explained his geopolitical theories and described his travels through India in the early years of the century. While in India, he had heard stories of a powerful civilisation living beneath the Himalayas:

> Thirty or forty centuries ago in the region of Gobi there was a highly developed civilization. As the result of a catastrophe, possibly of an atomic nature, Gobi was transformed into a desert, and the survivors emigrated, some going to the extreme North of Europe, and others towards the Caucasus. The Scandinavian god Thor is supposed to have been one of the heroes of this migration.
>
> . . . Haushofer proclaimed the necessity of 'a return to the sources' of the human race – in other words, that it was necessary to conquer the whole of Eastern Europe, Turkestan, Pamir, Gobi and Thibet. These countries constituted, in his opinion, the central core, and whoever had control of them controlled the whole world.[17]

After the cataclysm that destroyed the Gobi civilisation, the survivors migrated to a vast cavern system beneath the Himalayas where they split into two groups, one of which followed the path of spirituality, enlightenment and meditation while the other followed the path of violence and materialistic power. The first of these centres was called Agartha, the other Shambhala. (These names have many different spellings: for Agartha, I use the simplest; for Shambhala, the spelling favoured by Orientalists.) We shall return for a closer look to the realms of Agartha and Shambhala in the next chapter.

According to Alec Maclellan, among the many books Hitler read while languishing in Landsberg was Bulwer-Lytton's *The Coming Race*, which, Haushofer informed him, was an essentially correct description of the race of Supermen living far beneath the surface of the Earth and corroborated much of what the professor had himself learned while travelling in Asia. Bulwer-Lytton's novel apparently galvanised Hitler's imagination, and he 'began to yearn for the day when he might establish for himself the actuality of the secret civilization beneath the snows of Tibet . . .'[18]

In the following year, 1925, the Vril Society (also known as the Luminous Lodge) was formed by a group of Berlin Rosicrucians including Karl Haushofer. As Joscelyn Godwin informs us, there is only one primary source of information on the Vril Society: Willy Ley, a German rocket engineer who fled to the United States in 1933 and followed a successful career writing popular science books. In 1947, Ley published an article entitled 'Pseudoscience in Naziland'. Following a description of Ariosophy, Ley writes:

The next group was literally founded upon a novel. That group which I think called itself *Wahrheitsgesellschaft* – Society for Truth – and which was more or less localized in Berlin, devoted its spare time looking for *Vril*. Yes, their convictions were founded upon Bulwer-Lytton's 'The Coming Race'. They knew that the book was fiction, Bulwer-Lytton had used that device in order to be able to tell the truth about this 'power'. The subterranean humanity was nonsense, *Vril* was not. Possibly it had enabled the British, who kept it as a State secret, to amass their colonial empire. Surely the Romans had had it, inclosed [sic] in small metal balls, which guarded their homes and were referred to as *lares*. For reasons which I failed to penetrate, the secret of *Vril* could be found by contemplating the structure of an apple, sliced in halves.

No, I am not joking, that is what I was told with great solemnity and secrecy. Such a group actually existed, they even got out the first issue of a magazine which was to proclaim their credo.[19]

Although they apparently interviewed Ley, Pauwels and Bergier could learn nothing more from him about this mysterious society; however, they later discovered that the group actually called itself the Vril Society, and that Karl Haushofer was intimately connected with it. (Joscelyn Godwin kindly reminds us of the unreliability of the splendid Pauwels and Bergier: although they cite Jack Fishman's *The Seven Men of Spandau* with regard to Haushofer's connection to the Vril Society, Fishman actually makes no such reference.)[20]

Pauwels and Bergier go on to inform us that, having failed in his mission, Haushofer committed suicide on 14 March 1946, in accordance with his pledge to his masters in the secret Japanese society into which he had been initiated. Once again, the truth is somewhat different: Haushofer did not commit *hara kiri* but died from arsenic poisoning on 10 March. In addition, Ley's reference to 'contemplating the structure of an apple, sliced in halves' (thus revealing the five-pointed star at its centre) echoes Rudolf Steiner's suggestion in *Knowledge of Higher Worlds and Its Attainment*. Indeed, as Godwin reminds us,[21] the Theosophists were themselves interested in the concept of the vril force, which bears some resemblance to Reichenbach's Odic force, and to the Astral Light, also known as the Akashic Records: a subtle form of energy said to surround the Earth, in which is preserved a record of every thought and action that has ever occurred.

In spite of the sober research of writers like Goodrick-Clarke and Godwin, the idea of an immensely sinister and powerful Vril Society secretly controlling the Third Reich has lost nothing of its ability to fascinate. Many still maintain that Haushofer introduced Hitler to the leader of the group of Tibetan high lamas living in Berlin, a man known only as 'The Man with the Green Gloves', and that this man knew the locations of the hidden entrances to the subterranean realms of Agartha and Shambhala.[22]

These rumours doubtless gave rise to the famous legends about Hitler's obsessive search for the entrances to the inner world. According to Maclellan: 'The first expeditions were dispatched purely under the auspices of the Luminous Lodge, beginning in 1926, but later, after coming to power, Hitler took a more direct interest, overseeing the organization of the searches himself.'[23] Maclellan also states that Hitler believed unequivocally that 'certain representatives of the under-ground super-race were already abroad in the world',[24] citing Hermann Rauschning's famous book *Hitler Speaks: A Series of Political Conversations with Adolf Hitler on his Real Aims* (1939). The conversations recorded by Rauschning have served as source material for many writers on the Third Reich, including serious ones. Proponents of genuine Nazi occult power have repeatedly pointed to the mystical elements in Hitler's conversations as relayed by Rauschning, who says that he repeatedly had the feeling that Hitler was a medium, possessed of supernatural powers. It seems that on one occasion, Hitler actually met one of the subterranean Supermen. Rauschning claims that Hitler confided to him: 'The new man is among us. He is here! Now are you satisfied? I will tell you a secret. I have seen the vision of the new man – fearless and formidable. I shrank from him.'[25]

To his credit, Maclellan states that this was more than likely a deranged fantasy on Hitler's part. However, Rausch-ning's very description should be treated with extreme caution: it should be noted that, in spite of the widespread interest it stimulated, *Hitler Speaks* has not stood the test of time as an accurate historical document. In fact, Ian Kershaw, one of the foremost authorities on Hitler and the author of *Hitler 1889–1936: Hubris* (1998), does not cite Rauschning's book anywhere in his monumental study, and states that it is 'a work now regarded to have so little authenticity that it is best to disregard it altogether'.[26]

As the story goes, Hitler ordered a number of expeditions into German, Swiss and Italian mines to search for the entrances to the cavern cities of the Supermen. He is even said to have ordered research to be conducted into the life of Bulwer-Lytton, in an effort to determine whether the author himself had visited the realm of the Vril-ya. While serious writers ignore these rumours, there is an interesting event on record that Maclellan quotes in his *The Lost World of Agharti* and that illustrates the frustrating nature of the 'twilight zone between fact and fiction' in which we find ourselves when discussing Nazi occultism.

Maclellan cites the testimony of one Antonin Horak, an expert speleologist and member of the Slovak Uprising, who accidentally discovered a strange tunnel in Czechoslovakia in October 1944. Dr Horak kept quiet about the discovery until 1965, when he published an account in the *National Speleological Society News*. In his article, Dr Horak stated that he and two other Resistance fighters found the tunnel near the villages of Plavince and Lubocna (he is quite specific about the location: 49.2 degrees north, 20.7 degrees east). Having just survived a skirmish with the Germans, the three men (one of whom was badly injured) asked a local peasant for help. He led them to an underground grotto where they could hide and rest. The peasant told the Resistance men that the cave contained pits, pockets of poison gas, and was also haunted, and warned them against venturing too far inside. This they had no intention of doing, such was their weariness. They attended to the wounds of their comrade and fell asleep.

The following day, Horak's curiosity got the better of him and, while he waited for the injured man to recover enough strength to travel again, he decided to do a little exploring inside the cave. Presently, he came to a section that was completely different from the rest of the cave. 'Lighting some torches, I saw that I was in a spacious, curved, black shaft formed by cliff-like walls. The floor in the incline was a solid lime pavement.'[27] The tunnel stretched interminably into the distance. Dr Horak decided to take a sample of the wall, but was unable to make any impression with his pickaxe. He took his pistol and fired at the wall (surely an unwise thing to do, given the risk of a ricochet and with German soldiers possibly still in the vicinity).

'The bullet slammed into the substance of the walls with a deafening, fiery impact,' he wrote. 'Sparks flashed, there was a roaring sound, but not so much as a splinter fell from the substance. Only a small welt appeared, about the length of half my finger, which gave off a pungent smell.'

Dr Horak then returned to his comrades and told them about the apparently man-made tunnel. 'I sat there by the fire speculating. How far did it reach into the rocks? I wondered.

Who, or what, put it into the mountain? Was it man-made? And was it at last proof of the truth in legends – like Plato's – of long-lost civilisations with magic technologies which our rationale cannot grasp or believe?'[28] No one else, apparently, has explored this tunnel since Dr Horak in 1944. The peasants who lived in the region obviously knew of its existence, but kept well away.

In addition to the stories of Nazi mine expeditions in Central and Eastern Europe during the Second World War, occult writers have frequently made reference to the Nazi Tibet Expeditions, allegedly an attempt to locate and make contact with a group of high lamas with access to fantastic power. Once again, Pauwels and Bergier have plenty to say on this subject, which is in itself enough to give pause to the cautious.

The American researcher Peter Levenda experienced a similar scepticism with regard to the supposed Nazi-Tibet connection, until he began to search for references in the microfilmed records in the Captured German Documents Section of the National Archives in Washington, DC. He discovered a wealth of material, running to many hundreds of pages, dealing with the work of Dr Ernst Schäfer of the *Ahnenerbe*. These documents included Dr Schäfer's personal notebooks, his correspondence, clippings from several German newspapers, and his SS file, which describes an expedition to East and Central Tibet from 1934–1936, and the official SS-Tibet Expedition of 1938–1939 under his leadership.[29]

As Levenda demonstrates, the expedition was not so much concerned with contacting Tibetan representatives of the subterranean super-race as with cataloguing the flora and fauna of the region (an activity of little military value to the Third Reich, which accounts for the difficulty Schäfer occasionally had in securing funding for his trips).

Born in Cologne on 14 March 1910 into a wealthy industrialist family, Ernst Schäfer attended school in Heidelberg and Göttingen, and embarked on his first expedition to Tibet in 1930 under the auspices of the Academy of Natural Sciences in Philadelphia when he was only twenty years old. The following year, he joined the American Brooke Dolan expedition to Siberia, China and Tibet. He became a member of the SS in mid-1933, finally reaching the rank of Sturmbannführer in 1942. In addition to being an SS officer, Schäfer was also a respected scientist who published papers in various journals, such as the *Proceedings of the Academy of Natural Sciences, Philadelphia*. As Levenda wryly notes, Schäfer was 'a man of many parts: one part SS officer and one part scholar, one part explorer and one part scientist: a Nazi Indiana Jones'.[30] Schäfer was also deeply interested in the religious and cultural practices of the Tibetans, including their sexuality. (Indeed, the members of the 1938–1939 expedition displayed a somewhat prurient fascination with intimate practices: the film-maker Ernst Krause, for instance, took great care to record his observation of a fifteen-year-old Lanchung girl masturbating on a bridge beam.[31])

When not cataloguing flora and fauna (and spying on teenage girls), the members of the expedition managed to conduct other research, which included an exhaustive study of the physical attributes of the Tibetan people. Schäfer noted height and weight, the shape of hands and feet, the colour and shape of eyes, and even took plaster casts of Tibetans' faces. On 21 July 1939, *Der Neue Tag* published the following article:

SACRED TIBETAN SCRIPTURE
ACQUIRED BY THE DR SCHÄFER-EXPEDITION ON NINE ANIMAL LOADS ACROSS THE HIGH-COUNTRY

(SPECIAL) FRANKFURT – 20 JULY The Tibet Expedition of Dr Ernst Schäfer, which during its expedition through Tibet stayed a long time in Lhasa and in the capital of the Panchen Lama, Shigatse, is presently on its return trip to Germany. Since the monsoons began unusually early, the return march of the expedition was hastened in order to secure the shipment of the precious collections. The expedition has singularly valuable scientific research results to inventory. In addition to outstanding accomplishments in the areas of geophysical and earth-magnetic research they succeeded in obtaining an extra-rich ethnological collection including, along with cult objects, many articles and tools of daily life.

With the help of the regent of Lhasa it was Dr Schäfer who also succeeded in obtaining the *Kangschur*, the extensive, 108-volume sacred script of the Tibetans, which required nine animal loads to transport. Also especially extensive are the zoological and botanical collections that the expedition has already shipped, in part, to Germany, the remainder of which they will bring themselves. The zoological collection includes the total bird-fauna of the research area. Dr Schäfer was also able, for the first time, to bag a Schapi, a hitherto unknown wild goat. About 50 live animals are on the way to Germany, while numerous other live animals are still with the expedition. An extensive herbarium of all existing plants is also on its way. Furthermore, valuable geographical and earth-historical accomplishments were made. Difficulties encountered due to political tensions with the English authorities were eliminated due to personal contact between Dr Schäfer and members of the British authorities in Shangtse, so that the unimpeded return of the expedition out of Tibet with its valuable collections was guaranteed.[32]

Levenda informs us that he was unable to discover the fate of the *Kangschur*, the 'core document' of Tibetan Buddhism, although he suspects that it was taken to Vienna. With regard to the expedition itself, while it must be conceded that it had very little to do with the occult or magical ambitions of the Third Reich, it is possible that the 'earth-magnetic' and 'geophysical' experiments had a firm foundation in a very shaky theory. Levenda suggests that the Tibet Expedition of 1938–1939 attempted to prove the pseudo-scientific World Ice Theory of Hans Hörbiger. This bizarre theory will be discussed in detail in Chapter Seven. But for now, let us return to the concept embodied in the rumours about the Vril

Society, with its alleged attempts to contact (and enlist the aid of) a mysterious group of vastly powerful Eastern adepts. To examine the origins of this idea, we must ourselves embark on a journey to Tibet, known in some quarters as 'the Phantom Kingdom'.

4 The phantom kingdom

The Nazi-Tibet Connection

A T FIRST SIGHT, IT MIGHT SEEM STRANGE in the extreme that the architects of the Third Reich would be interested in a region that many consider to be the spiritual centre of the world; until, that is, we remember that, according to Thulean mythology, this centre was once the Aryan homeland in the Arctic, and was displaced with the fall of Atlantis around 10,800 BC (see Chapter Two). Since then, the spiritual centre, while remaining hidden from the vast majority of humanity who are unworthy of its secrets, has nevertheless been the primary force controlling the destiny of the planet.[1] The two hidden realms of Agartha and Shambhala constitute the double source of supernatural power emanating from Tibet, and have come to occupy an important place in twentieth-century occultism and fringe science.

Before we address the Third Reich's alleged interest in Agartha and Shambhala, it is essential that we pause for a (necessarily brief) examination of the rôle of Shambhala in Tibetan mysticism. In this way, we may chart the course of its warping and degradation as it was fitted into the Nazi scheme of crypto-history.

The Land of the Immortals

The writer Andrew Tomas spent many years studying the myths and legends of the Far East, and his book *Shambhala:*

Oasis of Light is an eloquent argument in favour of the realm's actual existence. In the book, Tomas cites the ancient writings of China, which refer to Nu and Kua, the 'Asiatic prototypes of Adam and Eve' and their birthplace in the Kun Lun Mountains of Central Asia. It is something of a mystery why such a desolate, forbidding place should serve as the Chinese Garden of Eden rather than more hospitable regions such as the Yangtse Valley or the province of Shantung, and Tomas speculates that the Gobi Desert may at one time have been an inland sea with accompanying fertile land.[2] As we shall see later in this chapter, the Gobi is a prime candidate as a site for one of the ancient and unknown civilising cultures whose wisdom has been passed down through the ages.

The Kun Lun Mountains hold a very important place in Chinese mythology, since it is in this range that the Immortals are believed to live, ruled by Hsi Wang Mu, the Queen Mother of the West. Hsi Wang Mu, who is also called Kuan Yin, the goddess of mercy, is said to live in a nine-storeyed palace of jade. Surrounding this palace is a vast garden in which grows the Peach Tree of Immortality. Only the most wise and virtuous of human beings are permitted to visit the garden and eat the fruit, which appears only once every 6,000 years.[3]

The Immortals who aid Hsi Wang Mu in her attempts to guide humanity towards wisdom and compassion possess perfect, ageless bodies, and are said to be able to travel anywhere in the Universe, and to live on the planets of other star systems. As Tomas notes, whether the ancient Chinese believed that the Immortals could travel in space in their physical bodies or by projecting their minds, this is still a remarkable concept to entertain, since it is based on an acceptance of the plurality of inhabited worlds in the Cosmos.

Ancient Chinese texts are replete with legends regarding the attempts of many people to cross the Gobi Desert to the Kun Lun Mountains. The most famous of these searchers is surely the great philosopher Lao Tzu (c. 6th century BC), author of the book of Taoist teaching *Tao Te Ching*, who is said to have made the journey across the Gobi towards the end of his life. The Vatican archives also contain many reports made by Catholic missionaries concerning deputations from the emperors of China to the spiritual beings living in the mountains. These beings possess bodies that are visible, but which are not made of flesh and blood: they are the 'mind-born' gods whose bodies are composed of elementary atomic matter, which allow them to live anywhere in the Universe, even at the centres of stars.

The people of India also believe in a place of wisdom and spiritual perfection; they call it Kalapa or Katapa, and it is said to lie in a region north of the Himalayas, in Tibet. According to Indian tradition, the Gobi Desert is the floor of what was once a great sea, which contained an island called Sweta-Dvipa (White Island). The great Yogis who once lived there are believed to live still in the high mountains and deep valleys that once formed the island of Sweta-Dvipa. This island has been identified by Orientalists with the Isle of Shambhala of Puranic literature, which is said to stand at the centre of a lake of nectar.

In the seventeenth century, two Jesuit missionaries, Stephen Cacella and John Cabral, recorded the existence of Chang Shambhala, as described to them by the lamas of Shigatse, where Cacella lived for 23 years until his death in 1650. (Chang Shambhala means Northern Shambhala, which differentiates the abode of the spiritual adepts from the town called Shamballa, north of Benares, India.[4]) Nearly 200 years later, a Hungarian philologist named Csoma de Körös, who lived for four years from 1827–30 in a Buddhist monastery in Tibet, claimed that Chang Shambhala lay between 45° and 50° north latitude, beyond the river Syr Daria.[5]

Legends of a hidden spiritual centre, a sacred zone whose inhabitants secretly guide the evolution of life on Earth, are widespread in the ancient cultures of the East. The writer Victoria Le Page describes this wondrous realm thus:

> . . . [S]omewhere beyond Tibet, among the icy peaks and secluded valleys of Central Asia, there lies an inaccessible paradise, a place of universal wisdom and ineffable peace called Shambhala . . . It is inhabited by

adepts from every race and culture who form an inner circle of humanity secretly guiding its evolution. In that place, so the legends say, sages have existed since the beginning of human history in a valley of supreme beatitude that is sheltered from the icy arctic winds and where the climate is always warm and temperate, the sun always shines, the gentle airs are always beneficient and nature flowers luxuriantly.[6]

Only the purest of heart are allowed to find this place (others, less idealistically motivated, who search for it risk an icy grave) where want, evil, violence and injustice do not exist. The inhabitants possess both supernatural powers and a highly advanced technology; their bodies are perfect, and they devote their time to the study of the arts and sciences. The concept of the hidden spiritual centre of the world is to be found in Hinduism, Buddhism, Taoism, shamanism and other ancient traditions. In the Bön religion of pre-Buddhist Tibet, Shambhala is also called 'Olmolungring' and 'Dejong'. In Tibetan Buddhism, the Shambhalic tradition is enshrined within the Kalachakra texts, which are said to have been taught to the King of Shambhala by the Buddha before being returned to India.[7]

As might be expected with such a marvellous, legend-haunted place, there has been a great deal of speculation as to the exact whereabouts of Shambhala. (It is unlikely to be found at Körös's map coordinates.) While some esotericists believe that Shambhala is a real place with a concrete, physical presence in a secret location on Earth, others prefer to see it as existing on a higher spiritual plane, what might be called another dimension of space-time coterminous with our own. Alternatively, Shambhala might be considered as a state of mind, comparable to the terms in which some consider the Holy Grail. As with the Grail, Shambhala may be a state within ourselves, in which we may gain an insight into the higher spirituality inherent in the Universe, as distinct from the mundane world of base matter in which we normally exist.

Having said this, it should be noted that there are certain cases on record in which Westerners have experienced visions of a place bearing a striking resemblance to the fabled Shambhala. Victoria Le Page cites a particularly intriguing case in her book *Shambhala: The Fascinating Truth Behind the Myth of Shangri-la*. The case was investigated by a Dr Raynor Johnson who, in the 1960s, gathered together several hundred first-hand accounts of mystical experiences. It involved a young Australian woman who claimed to have psychic abilities, and who was referred to simply as L. C. W.

L. C. W. wrote that at the age of 21 she began to attend a place she came to know as 'Night-School'. At night she would fly in her sleep to this place, the location of which she had no idea. Once there she would join other people in dance exercises which she later recognised as being similar to the dervish exercises taught by George Gurdjieff. After several years, she graduated to a different class, where she was taught spiritual lessons from a great book of wisdom. It was only years later, when L. C. W. began to take an interest in mystical literature, that she realised the true location of Night-School must have been Shambhala.

L. C. W. had other visions in which she saw what appeared to be a gigantic mast or antenna, extending from Earth deep into interstellar space. The base of this antenna was in the Pamirs or Tien Shan Mountains, regions which are traditionally associated with Shambhala. She was taken towards this antenna by an invisible guide, and saw that it was a pillar of energy whose branches were actually paths leading to other worlds, marked by geometrical figures such as circles, triangles and squares.

According to L. C. W., this 'antenna' was nothing less than a gateway to other times, other dimensions and other regions of this Universe. In addition to the antenna serving as a gateway for souls from Earth to travel to other times and places, 'she believed souls from other systems in space could enter the earth sphere by the same route, carrying their own spiritual influences with them'.[8] L. C. W. also maintained that the antenna could be controlled directly by the mind of the voyager, and would extend a branch or 'pseudopod' in response to a single thought. This branch then became a 'trajectory of light' along which the soul would travel; in her case, she found herself in China 30 years in the future. The spiritual being who was guiding her explained that the earth was in the process of being purified, and that a 'great rebirth' was about to occur. She also witnessed the apparent falling of a cluster of 'stars' that represented the arrival of 'high souls [that] were now coming down to help in the special event'.[9]

Our knowledge of the Shambhalic tradition in the West has come mainly from Orientalist scholars such as Helena Blavatsky, René Guénon, Louis Jacolliot, Saint-Yves d'Alveydre and Nicholas Roerich. Since we have already spent some time with Madame Blavatsky, we may turn our attention to the work of the others, notably Nicholas Roerich (1874–1947), poet, artist, mystic and humanist, and perhaps the most famous and respected of the esotericists who brought news of this fabulous realm to Westerners.

Born in St Petersburg, Russia in 1874, Nicholas Roerich came from a distinguished family whose ability to trace its origins to the Vikings of the tenth century inspired his early interest in archaeology. This interest led in turn to a lifelong fascination with art, through which, in the words of K. P. Tampy, who wrote a monograph on Roerich in 1935, he became 'possessed of a burning desire to get at the beautiful and make use of it for his brethren'.[10] After attending the St Petersburg Academy of Fine Art, Roerich went to Paris to continue his studies. In 1906, he won a prize for his design of a new church, and was also rewarded with the position of Director of the Academy for the Encouragement of Fine Arts in Russia. However, the Russian Revolution occurred while he was on a visit to America, and he found himself unable to return to his motherland.

Roerich's profound interest in Buddhist mysticism led to his proposing an expedition in 1923 that would explore India, Mongolia and Tibet. The Roerich Expedition of 1923–26 was made across the Gobi Desert to the Altai Mountains. It was during this expedition that Roerich's party had a most unusual experience – one of the many experiences that seem to offer strange and puzzling connections between apparently disparate elements of the paranormal and that make it such a complex and fascinating field of human enquiry. In the summer of 1926, Roerich had set up camp with his son, Dr George Roerich, and several Mongolian guides in the Shara-gol valley near the Humboldt Mountains between Mongolia and Tibet. Roerich had just built a white *stupa* (or shrine), dedicated to Shambhala. The shrine was consecrated in August, with the ceremony witnessed by a number of invited lamas.

Two days later, the party watched as a large black bird wheeled through the sky above them. This, however, was not what astonished them, for far beyond the black bird, high up in the cloudless sky, they clearly saw a golden spheroidal object moving from the Altai Mountains to the north at tremendous speed. Veering sharply to the south-west, the golden sphere disappeared rapidly beyond the Humboldt Mountains. As the Mongolian guides shouted to one another in the utmost excitement, one of the lamas turned to Roerich and informed him that the fabulous golden orb was the sign of Shambhala, meaning that the lords of that realm approved of his mission of exploration.

Later, Roerich was asked by another lama if there had been a perfume on the air. When Roerich replied that there had been, the lama told him that he was guarded by the King of Shambhala, Rigden Jye-Po, that the black vulture was his enemy, but that he was protected by a 'Radiant form of Matter'. The lama added that anyone who saw the radiant sphere should follow the direction in which it flew, for in that direction lay Shambhala.

The exact purpose of this expedition (aside from exploration) was never made entirely clear by Roerich, but many writers on esoteric subjects have claimed that he was on a mission to return a certain sacred object to the King's Tower at the centre of Shambhala. According to Andrew Tomas, the sacred object was a fragment of the Chintamani stone, the great mass of which lies in the Tower. Astonishingly, the stone is said to have been brought to Earth originally by an extraterrestrial being.

According to tradition, a chest fell from the sky in AD 331; the chest contained four sacred objects, including the Chintamani stone. Many years after the casket was discovered, five strangers visisted King Tho-tho-ri Nyan-tsan to explain the use of the sacred objects. The Chintamani stone is said to come from one of the star systems in the constellation of Orion, probably Sirius. The main body of the stone is always kept in the Tower of Shambhala, although small pieces are sometimes transferred to other parts of the world during times of great change.

It is rumoured that the fragment of Chintamani which Roerich was returning to the Tower had been in the possession of the League of Nations, of which Roerich was a highly respected member.

The Caves Beneath the Himalayas

The concept of a subterranean realm (which we will discuss in much greater detail in Chapter Seven) is common throughout the world's religions and mythologies. With regard to the present study, we can identify a powerful antecedent to the legends and rumours still extant today in the mythology of Tibet. In his 1930 book *Shambhala*, Roerich describes his attempts to understand the origins of underworld legends 'to discover what memories were being cherished in the folk-memory'.[11] In commenting on the ubiquity of subterranean legends, he notes that the more one examines them, the greater the conviction that they are all 'but chapters from the one story'.[12] An examination of the folklores of 'Tibet, Mongolia, China, Turkestan, Kashmir, Persia, Altai, Siberia, the Ural, Caucasia, the Russian steppes, Lithuania, Poland, Hungary, Germany, France'[13] will yield tales of dwellers beneath the earth. In many places, the local people can even guide the curious traveller to cave entrances in isolated places, which are said to lead to the hidden world of the subterraneans.

Central Asia is home to legends of an underground race called the Agharti; the Altai Mountains are the dwelling place of the Chud. In *Shambhala*, Roerich states that the name 'Chud' in Russian has the same origin as the word 'wonder'. His guide through the Altai Mountains told him that the Chud were originally a powerful but peaceful tribe who flourished in the area in the distant past. However, they fell prey to marauding bands of warriors, and could only escape by leaving their fertile valley and departing into the earth to continue their civilisation in subterranean realms.

Roerich's guide continued that at certain times the Chud could be heard singing in their underground temples. Elsewhere in the Altai Mountains, on the way to Khotan, Roerich reports that the hoofs of their horses sounded hollow upon the ground, as though they were riding over immense caves. Other members of the caravan called to Roerich: 'Do you hear what hollow subterranean passages we are crossing? Through these passages, people who are familiar with them can reach far-off countries.'[14] (The significance of this claim will become more apparent in Chapter Seven.) The caravaneers continued: 'Long ago people lived there; now they have gone inside; they have found a subterranean passage to the subterranean kingdom. Only rarely do some of them appear again on earth. At our bazaar such people come with strange, very ancient money, but nobody could even remember a time when such money was in usage here.' When Roerich asked if he, too, could see such people, his companions replied: 'Yes, if your thoughts are similarly high and in contact with these holy people, because only sinners are upon earth and the pure and courageous people pass on to something more beautiful.'[15]

In the region of Nijni Novgorod there is a legend of a subterranean city called Kerjenetz that sank into a lake. In Roerich's time, local people still held processions through the area, during which they would listen for the bells of invisible churches.

Roerich's party went on to discover four more groups of menhirs, and several tombs, taking the form of a square outlined by large stones. To the people of the Himalayas, those who built these monuments, although now departed, are not to be found anywhere on the Earth's surface: 'all which has disappeared, has departed underground'.[16]

Dr Ferdinand Ossendowski, whom we shall meet again in a little while, was told by lamas in Mongolia of fabulous

civilisations existing before recorded history. To Ossendowski's astonishment, the lamas claimed that when the
homelands of these civilisations in the Atlantic and Pacific
were destroyed by natural cataclysms some of their
inhabitants survived in previously prepared subterranean
shelters, illuminated by artificial light. Andrew Tomas
speculates that the Celtic legend of 'the Lordly Ones in the
hollow hills' is a folk memory of the survivors of the
destruction of the Atlantic continent.[17]

In India, legends tell of a race of beings called the Nagas.
Serpent-like and extremely intelligent, the Nagas live in vast
caverns illuminated by precious stones. Although reptilian,
the Nagas have human faces and are incredibly beautiful.
Able to fly, they intermarried with kings and queens from the
surface world, although they remain shy of surface dwellers
and keep well away from all but the most spiritually
advanced. Their capital city is called Bhogawati, and is said to
be covered with rubies, emeralds and diamonds.[18]

Tomas writes that many Hindus and Tibetans have
entered the caves of the Nagas, which stretch for hundreds of
miles inside the mountains.

The inhabitants of this region speak of large lotus flowers
floating on the surface of the Manasarawar Lake in the
western part of the Tsang Po Valley. Radiant figures have also
been seen near this extremely cold fresh-water lake.

The Realm of Agartha

Despite its inclusion in many popular books on Eastern
mysticism, the name 'Agartha' is unknown in Asiatic
mythology. In fact, one of the many variations on the name,
'Asgaard', was first used by the French writer Ernest Renan
in the 1870s. Although clearly inspired by Nordic mythology,
Renan placed his Asgaard in Central Asia, while another
French writer, Louis Jacolliot (1837–1890), was writing at the
same time about a city of Asgartha.[19] A magistrate in
Chandernagor, India, Jacolliot wrote a number of books on
the relationship between Indian mythology and Christianity.

He was allegedly told the legend of Asgartha by a group of local Brahmins, who allowed him to consult various sacred texts, such as the *Book of Historical Zodiacs*.

According to Jacolliot, Asgartha was a prehistoric 'City of the Sun', home of the Brahmatma, the visible manifestation of God on Earth.[20] Asgartha existed in India in 13,300 BC, where the Brahmatma lived in an immense palace; he was invisible, and only appeared to his subjects once a year. Interestingly, Jacolliot stated that this high prehistoric culture existed long before the Aryans, who conquered Asgartha around 10,000 BC. The priests of Asgartha then managed to form an alliance with the victorious Aryan Brahmins, which resulted in the formation of the warrior caste of Kshatriyas. About 5,000 years later, Asgartha was destroyed by the brothers Ioda and Skandah, who came from the Himalayas. Eventually driven out by the Brahmins, the brothers travelled north – and later gave their names to 'Odin' and 'Scandinavia'.[21]

Ferdinand Ossendowski (1876–1945) was another early writer on the legend of Agartha. Although born in Vitebsk, Poland, he spent most of his early life in Russia, attending the University of St Petersburg. For much of the 1890s, he travelled extensively in Mongolia and Siberia, developing his interest in and knowledge of Buddhist mysticism. He returned to Europe in 1900 and gained a doctorate in Paris in 1903, before returning to Russia and working as a chemist for the Russian Army during the Russo-Japanese War of 1905. He then became president of the 'Revolutionary Government of the Russian Far East', before being taken prisoner by the Russian Government for his anti-Tsarist activities.[22]

After two years' imprisonment in Siberia, he taught physics and chemistry in the Siberian town of Omsk, until the Bolshevik Revolution forced him to flee Russia with a small group of fellow White Russians. Together they travelled across Siberia and into Mongolia, and he wrote of their adventures in his best-selling book *Beasts, Men and Gods* (1923). While in Mongolia, Ossendowski made the acquaintance of a fellow Russian, a priest named Tushegoun Lama who claimed to be a friend of the Dalai Lama. Tushegoun

Lama told Ossendowski of the subterranean kingdom of Agartha, home of the King of the World. Intrigued by this reference, Ossendowski asked his friend for further information on this mysterious personage. 'Only one man knows his holy name. Only one man now living was ever in [Agartha]. That is I. This is the reason why the Most Holy Dalai Lama has honoured me and why the Living Buddha in Urga fears me. But in vain, for I shall never sit on the Holy Throne of the highest priest in Lhasa nor reach that which has come down from Jenghis Khan to the Head of our Yellow Faith. I am no monk. I am a warrior and avenger.'[23]

Several months later, while continuing across Mongolia with some guides left behind by Tushegoun Lama (who had since gone his own way), Ossendowski was startled when his companions suddenly halted and dismounted from their camels, which immediately lay down. The Mongols began to pray, chanting: 'Om! Mani padme Hung!' Ossendowski waited until they had finished praying before asking them what was happening. One of the Mongol guides replied thus:

'Did you not see how our camels moved their ears in fear? How the herd of horses on the plain stood fixed in attention and how the herds of sheep and cattle lay crouched close to the ground? Did you notice that the birds did not fly, the marmots did not run and the dogs did not bark? The air trembled softly and bore from afar the music of a song which penetrated to the hearts of men, animals and birds alike. Earth and sky ceased breathing. The wind did not blow and the sun did not move. At such a moment the wolf that is stealing up on the sheep arrests his stealthy crawl; the frightened herd of antelopes suddenly checks its wild course; the knife of the shepherd cutting the sheep's throat falls from his hand; the rapacious ermine ceases to stalk the unsuspecting *salga*. All living beings in fear are involuntarily thrown into prayer and waiting for their fate. So it was just now. Thus it has always been whenever the "King of the World" in his subterranean palace prays and searches out the destiny of all peoples on the earth.'[24]

Later, Ossendowski met an old Tibetan, Prince Chultun Beyli, living in exile in Mongolia, who furnished him with more details of the subterranean realm of Agartha and the King of the World. Agartha, he said, extends throughout all the subterranean passageways of the world. The inhabitants owe allegiance to the 'King of the World'. They can cultivate crops due to a strange light that pervades the underground realm. Some of the inhabitants of these regions are extremely strange: one race has two tongues, enabling them to speak in two languages at the same time. There are also many fantastic animals, including tortoises with sixteen feet and one eye.

At this point, Ossendowski was approaching the Chinese border. It was his intention to take a train to Peking, from which he might find passage to the West. In the town of Urga he met an old lama, who provided him with yet more information on the King of the World. The King's influence on the activities of the world's apparent leaders was profound. If their plans were pleasing before God, then the King of the World would help them to realise them; but if they displeased God, then the King would surely destroy them. His power came from the 'mysterious science of "Om"', which is the name of an ancient Holyman who lived more than 300,000 years ago, the first man to know God.

When Ossendowski asked him if anyone had ever seen the King of the World, the old lama replied that during the solemn holidays of the ancient Buddhism in Siam and India the King appeared five times in a 'splendid car drawn by white elephants'.[25] He wore a white robe and a red tiara with strings of diamonds that hid his face. When he blessed the people with a golden apple surmounted by the figure of a lamb, the 'blind received their sight, the dumb spoke, the deaf heard, the crippled freely moved and the dead arose, wherever the eyes of the "King of the World" rested'.[26]

Ossendowski then asked the lama how many people had been to Agartha. He replied that very many had, but that they never spoke about what they had seen there. He continued that, when the Olets destroyed Lhasa, one of their detachments found its way into the outskirts of Agartha, where they learned some of the lesser mysterious sciences. This is the reason for the magical skills of the Olets and Kalmucks.

Another of Ossendowski's informants, a lama named Turgut, told him that the capital of Agartha is surrounded by the towns of the high priests and scientists, somewhat in the way that the Potala palace of the Dalai Lama in Lhasa is surrounded by monasteries and temples. The throne on which the King of the World sits is itself surrounded by millions of incarnated gods, the Holy Panditas. The King's palace is surrounded by the palaces of the Goro, who possess fantastic power, and who would easily be able to incinerate the entire surface of the Earth, should humankind be unwise enough to declare war on them. (As we shall see in Chapter Seven, the legend of the King of the World would serve as the inspiration for one of the most enduring technological myths of the twentieth century.)

The legend of Agartha was discussed at length by another writer, the self-educated Christian Hermeticist Saint-Yves d'Alveydre (1842–1909), whose marriage into money enabled him to indulge his yearning for mystical understanding. In 1885 he began to take lessons in Sanskrit from one Haji Sharif (1838–?), about whom very little is known save that he left India at the time of the Sepoy Revolt of 1857 and worked as a bird-seller at Le Havre.[27] The manuscripts of d'Alveydre's lessons are preserved in the library of the Sorbonne in Paris. In them, Sharif refers to the 'Great Agarthian School' and the 'Holy Land of Agarttha' (one of the many alternative spellings of the name).

Sharif claimed that the original language of humanity, called Vattan or Vattanian, derived from a 22-letter alphabet. Although he was unable physically to visit Agartha, d'Alveydre found an ingenious alternative: through disengaging his astral body, he was able to visit the fabulous realm in spirit form (see pages 108–110). His astral adventures resulted in a series of books (*Mission des Souverains*, *Mission des Ouvriers*, *Mission des Juifs* and *Mission de l'Inde*), which he published at his own expense. Interestingly, he destroyed the entire edition of the last work, *Mission de l'Inde*, for fear that he had revealed too many secrets of Agartha and might be made to pay for his transgression with his life. Only two copies survived: one that he kept himself and one that was hidden by the printer.[28]

He might well have been concerned, for *Mission de l'Inde* contains a detailed account of Agartha, which lies beneath the surface of the Earth somewhere in the East and is ruled over by an Ethiopian 'Sovereign Pontiff' called the Brahmatma. The realm of Agartha was transferred underground at the beginning of the Kali-Yuga, about 3200 BC. The Agarthians possess technology that was impressive in d'Alveydre's day, including railways and air travel. They know everything about the surface-dwellers, and occasionally send emissaries. Agartha contains many libraries in which all the knowledge of Earth is recorded on stone tablets in Vattanian characters, including the means by which the living may communicate with the souls of the dead.

D'Alveydre states that, although many millions of students have tried to possess the secrets of Agartha, very few have ever succeeded in getting further than the outer circles of the realm.

Like Bulwer-Lytton, who wrote of the Vril-ya in his fictional work *The Coming Race* (discussed in the previous chapter), d'Alveydre speaks of the Agartthians as being superior to humanity in every respect, the true rulers of the world. A certain amount of controversy arose when Ossendowski published his *Beasts, Men and Gods*: it displayed such similarities to d'Alveydre's work that he was accused by some of plagiarism only imperfectly masked by an alteration in the spelling of Agartha. Ossendowski denied the charge vehemently, and claimed never to have heard of d'Alveydre before 1924. René Guénon defended Ossendowski, and claimed that there were many tales of subterranean realms told throughout Central Asia. In fact, Guénon's work would later be heavily criticised by his translator Marco Pallis, who called his book *Le Roi du Monde* (*The King of the World*) 'disastrous' in conversation with Joscelyn Godwin, on the grounds that Ossendowski's sources were unreliable, and Guénon had allowed himself to enter the realms of the sensational.[29]

The Nazis and Tibetan Mysticism

The legends surrounding the realms of Agartha and Shambhala are confusing to say the least, and their frequently contradictory nature does nothing to help in an understanding of their possible influence on the hideous philosophy of the Third Reich. As we have seen, some writers claim that Agartha and Shambhala are physical places, cities lying miles underground with houses, palaces, streets and millions of inhabitants. Others maintain that they are altogether more rarefied places, existing on some other level of reality but apparently coterminous with our physical world. With regard to their exact location, Childress offers a short summary of their many possible locations: 'Shambhala is sometimes said to be north of Lhasa, possibly in the Gobi Desert, and other times it is said to be somewhere in Mongolia, or else in northern Tibet, possibly in the Changtang Highlands. Agharta is said to be south of Lhasa, perhaps near the Shigatse Monastery, or even in Northeast Nepal beneath Mount Kanchenjunga. Occasionally it is said to be in Sri Lanka. Both have been located inside the hollow earth [see Chapter Seven].'[30]

Adding to this confusion is the frequently made assertion that the two power centres are opposed to each other, with Agartha seen as following the right-hand path of goodness and light, and Shambhala following the left-hand path of evil and darkness (a dichotomy also expressed as spirituality versus materialism). There is, needless to say, an opposing view that holds that Agartha is a place of evil and Shambhala the abode of goodness.

There have been a number of rumours concerning practitioners of black magic operating in Tibet and referring to themselves as the Shambhala or the Agarthi.[31] Although apparently outlawed by Tibetan Buddhists, they are said to continue their activities in secret. One writer who claimed to have encountered them was a German named Theodore Illion who spent the mid-1930s travelling through Tibet. In his book *Darkness Over Tibet* (1937), he describes how he discovered a deep shaft in the countryside. Wishing to gauge its depth, he dropped several stones into it and waited for them to strike the bottom; he was rewarded only with silence. He was told by an initiate that the shaft was 'immeasurably deep' and that only the highest initiates knew where it ended. His companion added: 'Anyone who would find out where it leads to and what it is used for would have to die.'[32]

Illion claimed to have gained access to a subterranean city inhabited by monks, whom he later found to be 'black yogis' planning to control the world through telepathy and astral projection. When he discovered that the food he was being given contained human flesh, he decided to make a break for it and fled across Tibet with several of the monks after him. After several weeks on the run, he managed to escape from Tibet and returned to the West with his bizarre and frightening tale.[33]

There have also been persistent rumours that the Nazi interest in Tibet (itself a documented historical fact) was actually inspired by a desire to contact the black adepts of Shambhala and/or Agartha and to enlist their aid in the conquest of the world (see Chapter Three). One of the most vocal proponents of this idea was the British occult writer Trevor Ravenscroft, whose claims we shall examine in greater detail in the next chapter. The schism between Shambhala and Agartha is described by René Guénon, who relates in Le Roi du Monde how the ancient civilisation in the Gobi Desert was all but destroyed by a natural cataclysm, and the 'Sons of Intelligences of Beyond' retreated to the caverns beneath the Himalayas and re-established their civilisation. There followed the formation of two groups: the Agarthi, who followed the way of spirituality, and the Shambhalists, who followed the way of violence and materialism.

Guénon claimed (as would Illion several years later) that the denizens of the subterranean world sought to influence the lives and actions of the surface dwellers through various occult means, including telepathic hypnosis and mediumship. Childress finds it intriguing that Hitler sent expeditions to Tibet in the late 1930s, soon after the publication of Illion's book Darkness Over Tibet, and suggests that their true objective was to make contact with the occult groups.[34]

This crypto-historical scenario continues with Hitler making the acquaintance of a mysterious Tibetan monk who told him that Germany could conquer the world by forging an alliance with the 'Lords of Creation'. While the victorious Russians were picking their way through the ruins of Berlin (and, according to some, discovering the bodies of several Tibetan monks, as we saw in Chapter Three), it is claimed by the crypto-historians that Hitler was flying out of the city's Tempelhof Airfield to a rendezvous with the U-boat (possibly U-977) that would take him either to Argentina or Antarctica. There is, however, a variation on this theme that has the Führer escaping to Tibet to be hidden by those whose alliance he had sought. According to an article in the May 1950 issue of the pro-Nazi *Tempo Der Welt*, that magazine's publisher, Karl Heinz Kaerner, claimed to have met with Martin Bormann in Morocco the previous year. If the story is to be believed (which would be extremely unwise), Bormann informed Kaerner that Hitler was alive in a Tibetan monastery, and that one day he would be back in power in Germany!

In addressing the question of whether such black magicians really lived (or still live) in Tibet, Childress reminds us that in her book *Initiations and Initiates in Tibet*, the French writer, explorer and authority on Tibetan mysticism Alexandra David-Neel (1868–1969) describes an encounter with a man who could hypnotise and kill from a distance. Nicholas Roerich also mentions the occultists of the ancient Bön religion, who were at war with the Buddhists of Tibet.

As Childress notes:

Shambhala draws strong similarities to the Land of the Immortals (Hsi Wang Mu) in that it is said to be a wonderful, lush valley in the high mountains with a tall, ornate solid jade tower from which a brilliant light shines. Like in the Kun Lun Mountains, Agharta and Shambhala have a cache of fantastic inventions and artifacts from distant civilizations in the past.

In contrast to the Valley of the Immortals in the Kun Lun Mountains, the cave communities with their incredible sights were part illusion, say Illion and Ravenscroft. At the Valley of the Immortals, perhaps there really were ancient artifacts of a time gone by watched over by Ancient Masters. Yet, it is unlikely that any person not chosen specifically by those who are the caretakers of this repository would be allowed inside. Nor would those who had entered (such as possibly Nicholas Roerich) ever reveal the location or what they had seen there.[35]

While certainly intriguing, the claims of crypto-historians regarding Nazi involvement with the black magicians of Tibet suffer from a paucity of hard evidence in the form of documentation and testimony from surviving witnesses. (We have already noted [see page 99] that the much-quoted Hermann Rauschning is considered by some serious historians, such as Ian Kershaw, to be extremely unreliable.) As is so often the case in the field of occultism, the way is left open to those who are quite content to rely on spurious sources and hearsay in their creation of a tantalising but incredible vision of history. One of the most famous of these crypto-historians is Trevor Ravenscroft, and it is to his claims that we now must turn.

5 Talisman of conquest

The Spear of Longinus

A S WE NOTED IN THE INTRODUCTION, a number of writers on the occult have turned their attention over the years to the baffling catastrophe of Nazism and have added their own attempts to explain the terrifying mystery of its true origin by attempting to fit Nazi Germany into an occult context. Perhaps unsurprisingly, these writers have paid close attention to an intriguing statement Hitler is known to have made – 'Shall we form a chosen band, made up of those who really know? An order: a brotherhood of the Knights of the Holy Grail, around the Holy Grail of Pure Blood' – and have attempted to use this statement as a point of connection between the Nazis and the occult. Although serious historians accept that occult and folkloric concepts played a significant role in the development of Nazi ideas and doctrine, it has been left largely to writers on 'fringe' subjects to push the envelope (wisely or otherwise) and claim that the Nazis were motivated by *genuine* occult forces: in other words, that there actually exist in the Universe malign, nonhuman intelligences that seek ways to influence the destiny of humanity for their own ends and that used the Nazis as conduits through which these influences might work. According to this scheme of history, the Nazis were, quite literally, practising Satanists and black magicians. This is certainly an intriguing notion, but how useful is it as a means to explain the loathsome existence of Nazism?

The Holy Lance and its Influence on Nazi Occultism

In 1973 Trevor Ravenscroft, historian and veteran of the Second World War, published a book that would cause more controversy than any other dealing with the subject of Nazism and that is still the subject of heated debate today. Entitled *The Spear of Destiny*, the book chronicles the early career of the man who would stain the twentieth century with the blood of millions and whose name would become a synonym for cruelty of the most repulsive kind: Adolf Hitler. Hailed by some as a classic of occult history and derided by others as no more than a work of lurid fiction, *The Spear of Destiny* is still in print today and, whatever its merits or demerits, it remains one of the most important texts in the field of Nazi occultism. (It should be noted here that, such is the murky and bizarre nature of this field, to make such a claim for a book is by no means equivalent to defending its historical accuracy.)

Ravenscroft was a Commando in the Second World War, and spent four years in German POW camps after allegedly participating in an attempt to assassinate Field Marshal Rommel in North Africa in 1941. He made three escape attempts but was recaptured each time. While imprisoned, Ravenscroft claims to have experienced a sudden apprehension of 'higher levels of consciousness', which led him to study the legend of the Holy Grail 'and to research into the history of the Spear of Longinus and the legend of world destiny which had grown around it'.[1]

The spear in question is the one said to have been used by the Roman centurion Gaius Cassius to pierce the side of Christ during the crucifixion. Cassius suffered from cataracts in both eyes, which prevented him from battle service with his Legion, so he was sent to Jerusalem to report on events there. When the Nazarene was crucified, Cassius was present.

Isaiah had prophesied of the Messiah, 'A bone of Him shall not be broken.' Annas, the aged advisor to the Sanhedrin, and Caiaphas, the High Priest, were intent on mutilating the body of Christ to prove to the masses of the people that Jesus was not the Messiah, but merely a heretic and potential usurper of their own power.

The hours were passing and this presented the excuse they needed. For Annas was an authority on the Law, and the Jewish Law decreed that no man should be executed on the Sabbath Day. Straightaway, they petitioned Pontius Pilate for the authority to break the limbs of the crucified men so that they should die before dusk on that Friday afternoon.[2]

When the Temple Guard arrived to mutilate the bodies of Christ and the two thieves, Cassius decided to protect the Nazarene's body in the only way possible. He rode his horse towards the Cross and thrust his spear into Jesus's torso, between the fourth and fifth ribs. The flowing of the Saviour's blood completely restored the centurion's sight.

Gaius Cassius, who had performed a martial deed out of the compassionate motive to protect the body of Jesus Christ, became known as Longinus The Spearman. A convert to Christianity, he came to be revered as a great hero and saint by the first Christian community in Jerusalem, and a prime witness of the shedding of the Blood of the New Covenant for which the Spear became the symbol . . .

The legend grew around it, gaining strength with the passing of the centuries, that whoever possessed it and understood the powers it served, held the destiny of the world in his hands for good or evil.[3]

Ravenscroft informs us that, by rights, the man who should have written *The Spear of Destiny* (and would surely have done so, had he not died in 1957) was a Viennese philosopher and wartime British secret agent named Walter Johannes Stein (b. 1891). An Austrian Jew, Stein had emigrated from Germany to Britain in 1933. His association with Ravenscroft came about as a result of a book Stein had written, entitled

The Ninth Century: World History in the Light of the Holy Grail (1928). Ravenscroft was greatly impressed by the book, which asserts that the medieval Grail Romances and their description of the quest for the Holy Grail 'veiled a unique Western path to transcendent consciousness'.[4] It was clear to Ravenscroft that Dr Stein had conducted his historical research along rather unorthodox lines, relying on occult methods of mind expansion to apprehend data rather than the more traditional means of consulting extant medieval texts. In view of his own experience of higher levels of consciousness, and his resulting fascination with the Grail legends, Ravenscroft decided to call on Stein at his home in Kensington.

During this meeting, Ravenscroft voiced his belief that Stein had utilised some transcendent faculty in his research for *The Ninth Century*, adding that he believed a similar faculty had inspired Wolfram von Eschenbach to write the great Grail romance *Parsival* (c. 1200). According to Stein, von Eschenbach based *Parsival* on the key figures of the ninth century, who served as models for the characters in the romance. The Grail king Anfortas corresponded to King Charles the Bald, grandson of Charlemagne; Cundrie, the sorceress and messenger of the Grail, was Ricilda the Bad; Parsival himself corresponded to Luitward of Vercelli, the Chancellor to the Frankish Court; and Klingsor, the fantastically evil magician who lived in the Castle of Wonders, was identified as Landulf II of Capua who had made a pact with Islam in Arab-occupied Sicily and whom Ravenscroft calls the most evil figure of the century.[5]

Stein had first read *Parsival* while taking a short, compulsory course on German literature at the University of Vienna. One night, he had a most unusual extrasensory experience: 'He awoke . . . to discover that he had been reciting whole tracts of the . . . romantic verses in a sort of pictureless dream!'[6] This happened three times in all. Stein wrote down the words he had been speaking and, on comparing them with von Eschenbach's romance, found them to be virtually identical. To Stein this strongly implied the existence of some preternatural mental faculty, a kind of 'higher memory' that could be accessed under certain circumstances.

His subsequent researches into the Grail Romances led to his discovery, one August morning in 1912 in a dingy bookshop in Vienna's old quarter, of a tattered, leather-bound copy of *Parsival* whose pages were covered with annotations in a minute script. Stein bought the book from the shop assistant and took it to Demel's Cafe in the Kohlmarkt, where he began to pore over its pages. As he read, he became more and more uneasy at the nature of the annotations.

> This was no ordinary commentary but the work of somebody who had achieved more than a working knowledge of the black arts! The unknown commentator had found the key to unveiling many of the deepest secrets of the Grail, yet obviously spurned the Christian ideals of the [Grail] Knights and delighted in the devious machinations of the Anti-Christ.
>
> It suddenly dawned on him that he was reading the footnotes of Satan![7]

Stein was repelled yet fascinated by the vulgar racial fanaticism displayed in the annotations, by the 'almost insane worship of Aryan blood lineage and Pan-Germanism'.

> For instance, alongside the verses describing the Grail Procession and the Assembly of Knights at the High Mass in the Grail Castle, there appeared an entry written in large letters scrawled across the printed page: 'These men betrayed their pure Aryan Blood to the dirty superstitions of the Jew Jesus – superstitions as loathsome and ludicrous as the Yiddish rites of circumcision.'[8]

To Stein, the annotations represented the workings of a brilliant but utterly hideous mind, a mind that had inverted the traditional idea of the quest for the Grail as a gradual and immensely difficult awakening to wider spiritual reality, turning it into its antithesis: the opening of the human spirit, through the use of black magic, to the power and influence of Satan himself.

Shaken by what he had read in the annotated pages of the book, Stein glanced up for a moment through the café window and found himself looking into a dishevelled, arrogant face with demoniacal eyes. The apparition was shabbily dressed and was holding several small watercolours that he was trying to sell to passers-by. When Stein left the café late that afternoon, he bought some watercolours from the down-and-out painter and hurried home. It was only then that he realised that the signature on the watercolours was the same as that on the copy of *Parsival* he had bought: Adolf Hitler.

According to Ravenscroft, by the time Stein found the annotated copy of *Parsival* Adolf Hitler had already paid many visits to the Weltliches Schatzkammer Museum (Habsburg Treasure House) in Vienna, which held the Lance of St Maurice (also known as Constantine's Lance) used as a symbol of the imperial power of Holy Roman emperors at their coronations.[9] Having failed to gain entry to the Vienna Academy of Fine Arts and the School of Architecture, and growing more and more embittered and consumed with an increasing sense of his own destiny as dominator of the world, Hitler had thrown himself into an intense study of Nordic and Teutonic mythology and folklore, German history, literature and philosophy. While sheltering from the rain in the Treasure House one day, he heard a tour guide explaining to a group of foreign politicians the legend associated with the Lance of St Maurice: that it was actually the spear that Gaius Cassius had used to pierce the side of Christ during the Crucifixion, and that whoever succeeded in understanding its secrets would hold the destiny of the world in his hands for good or evil. 'The Spear appeared to be some sort of magical medium of revelation for it brought the world of ideas into such close and living perspective that human imagination became more real than the world of sense.'[10]

Intent on meeting the man who had written so perceptively and frighteningly in the battered copy of *Parsival*, Stein returned to the dingy bookshop and this time encountered the owner, an extremely unsavoury-looking man named Ernst Pretzsche. Pretzsche told him that Hitler pawned many of his books in order to buy food, and redeemed them with money earned from selling his paintings. (Apparently, the shop assistant had made a mistake in selling *Parsival* to Stein.) Pretzsche showed Stein some of Hitler's other books, which included works by Hegel, Nietzsche and Houston S. Chamberlain, the British fascist and advocate of German racial superiority who frequently claimed to be chased by demons.

In the conversation that ensued, Pretzsche maintained that he was a master of black magic and had initiated Hitler into the dark arts. After inviting Stein to come and consult him on esoteric matters at any time (which Stein had no intention of doing, such was the loathsomeness of the man), Pretzsche gave him Hitler's address in Meldemannstrasse.

Hitler was extremely irate when Stein walked up to him and told him of his interest in the annotations in the copy of *Parsival* he had bought. He cursed Pretzsche for selling one of the books he had pawned. However, once Stein had told him of his own researches into the Holy Grail and the Spear of Longinus, Hitler became more amicable, apparently regarding the young university student as a possible ally in the Pan-German cause. They decided to pay a visit to the Schatzkammer together to look at the Holy Lance. As they stood before the display, the two men responded to it in very different ways.

> For some moments [Stein] was almost overcome by the powerful emotions which filled his breast and flowed like a river of healing warmth through his brain, evoking responses of reverence, humility and love. One message above all seemed to be inspired by the sight of this Spear which held within its central cavity one of the nails which had secured the body of Jesus to the Cross. It was a message of compassion which had been so wonderfully expressed in the motto of the Grail Knights: '*Durch Mitleid wissen.*' A call from the Immortal Self of Man resounding in the darkness of confusion and doubt

within the human soul: Through Compassion to Self-Knowledge.[11]

As Stein glanced at his companion, it seemed to him that Hitler was responding in a way which was diametrically opposite to his own.

> Adolf Hitler stood beside him like a man in a trance, a man over whom some dreadful magic spell had been cast. His face was flushed and his brooding eyes shone with an alien emanation. He was swaying on his feet as though caught up in some totally inexplicable euphoria. The very space around him seemed enlivened with some subtle irradiation, a kind of ghostly ectoplasmic light. His whole physiognomy and stance appeared transformed as if some mighty Spirit now inhabited his very soul, creating within and around him a kind of evil transfiguration of its own nature and power.[12]

The inscrutable occult processes that were set in motion by Hitler's discovery of the Holy Lance were consolidated on 14 March 1938, when Hitler arrived in Vienna to complete the *Anschluss* of Austria. While the Viennese people cheered the German forces' arrival, the Jews and opponents of the Nazi regime faced a persecution that, while utterly appalling, was but a pale foreshadowing of the horrors to come. Seventy-six thousand people were arrested when the Nazis arrived, with a further 6,000 people dismissed from key ministries in the Austrian Government.[13] Jews of all ages, whether they were religious or not, were ordered to scrub anti-Nazi slogans from the streets; the water they were given was mixed with acid that burned their hands. Hitler's SS Death's Head squads and members of the Hitler Youth urinated on Jews and forced them to spit in each other's faces; others were forced to dance on Torah scrolls. In less than a month, the deportation of Jews to the concentration camps would begin.[14]

While these atrocities were being perpetrated, Hitler (according to Ravenscroft) went to the Habsburg Treasure

House to claim the Holy Lance. With him were Heinrich Himmler and Wolfram Sievers, whom he ordered to leave him alone with the object of his diabolical desire.

> Although ... the Spear of Longinus had been the inspiration of his whole life and the key to his meteoric rise to power, it was more than a quarter of a century since he had last seen it, and nearly thirty years since he first beheld it and heard of its unique legend.
>
> Whatever Hitler's visions on this occasion, the scene of the German Führer standing there before the ancient weapon must be regarded as the most critical moment of the twentieth century until the Americans claimed the Spear in Nuremberg in 1945, and, while holding it in their possession, inaugurated the Atomic Age by dropping their atom bombs on Hiroshima and Nagasaki.[15]

Problems with Ravenscroft's Account

Joscelyn Godwin has called *The Spear of Destiny* 'a bloodcurdling work of historical reinvention',[16] and in spite of the breathless praise it has received from occult writers and reviewers over the years, it is difficult to disagree with his judgement. This view is also taken by the Australian author and journalist Ken Anderson, whose book *Hitler and the Occult* (1995) is a powerful and well-argued critique of Ravenscroft, Stein and *The Spear of Destiny*. For the rest of this chapter, we must therefore turn our attention to the problems inherent in Ravenscroft's account, as he learned it from Stein, of Hitler's desire to claim this allegedly most powerful of magical talismans. To be sure, these problems are manifold and display clear inconsistencies both with what we know of the history of the Third Reich and the wider context of European history.

For instance, we are told in *Spear* that the Holy Lance had been prized by many great warriors through the centuries, including Napoleon Bonaparte, who had demanded the lance

after the Battle of Austerlitz of December 1805. 'Just before
the battle began, the lance had been smuggled out of
Nuremberg and hidden in Vienna to keep it out of the French
dictator's hands.'[17] However, as Anderson comments, it would
have been a rather stupid decision to hide the lance in
Vienna, since the French had already occupied the city the
previous month. 'Why would anyone want to smuggle
anything into an occupied city if the purpose in so doing was
to keep it out of the hands of the head of the occupying
force?'[18] Moreover, historical records prove that the lance was
taken from Nuremberg to Vienna in 1800 and *placed in the
museum on full display*. Had he wanted the lance, Napoleon
could have acquired it at any time.

And what of the spear itself, which, claims Ravenscroft,
was the very one used by the Roman centurion to pierce the
side of Christ? We are told that Hitler

> found little difficulty in sorting out the merits of the
> various Spears, purporting to be the weapon of the
> Roman Centurion Longinus, which were scattered
> around the palaces, museums, cathedrals and churches
> of Europe . . . Adolf Hitler was excited to find one Spear
> which appeared to have been associated with a legend
> of world destiny throughout its entire history. This
> Spear, *dating back to the Third Century*, had apparently
> been traced by numerous historians right through to the
> tenth century to the reign of the Saxon King Heinrich I,
> the 'Fowler', where it was last mentioned in his hands
> at the famous battle of Unstrut in which the Saxon
> Cavalry conquered the marauding Magyars.[19] [Emphasis
> added.]

At this point, a question will doubtless have occurred to
the reader: how could a weapon dating back only to the third
century have been used to pierce the side of Christ? It is a
question Ravenscroft does not answer.[20] The existence of a
lance which was supposedly used to stab Christ is first
recorded in the sixth century by the pilgrim St Antonius of
Piacenza, who claims to have seen it in the Mount Zion

Basilica in Jerusalem. When Jerusalem fell to the Persians in
AD 615, the shaft of the lance was captured by the victors,
while the lance-head was saved and taken to Constantinople
where it was incorporated into an icon and kept in the Santa
Sophia Church. More than six centuries later, the point found
its way into the possession of the French King Louis and was
taken to the Sainte-Chapelle in Paris. The lance-head disappeared (and was possibly destroyed) during the French
Revolution. The shaft of the lance was sent to Jerusalem in
about AD 670 by the Frankish pilgrim Arculf, and only
reappears in history in the late ninth century, turning up in
Constantinople. It was captured by the Turks in 1492, who
sent it as a gift to Rome. It has remained in St Peter's since
then, although its authenticity has never been established
beyond doubt.[21]

However, archaeologists have established that this lance,
first mentioned in the sixth century, is *not* the one Hitler
found in the Habsburg Treasure House. This lance is known
as the Lance of St Maurice, or Constantine's Lance, which
was made in the eighth or ninth century.[22]

Anderson writes: 'It would take much research to examine
each one of Ravenscroft's claims concerning the possessors of
the Maurice Lance and its affect on them and on world
history.'[23] And in fact, such a task lies well beyond the scope
of this book also. He goes on:

Besides, we do not have the unique facility Ravenscroft
had [i.e. techniques of psychic mind expansion] in
tracing its owners where there is no written record, for
example its progression from the time it left the hands
of Heinrich I and turned up many years later in the
possession of his son Otto the Great. Ravenscroft says
Hitler's henchman SS head Heinrich Himmler put the
finest scholars in Germany to work on bridging the gap
but they were unable to do so. However, Ravenscroft's
mentor, Dr Walter Stein, 'by means of a unique method
of historical research involving "Mind Expansion" was
able to discover Heinrich had sent the lance to the
English King Athelstan.' (Athelstan [895–940] was the

grandson of Alfred the Great. Crowned King in 925, he was the first ruler of all England.) Stein 'found' that the lance was present at the Battle of Malmesbury in which the Danes were defeated on English soil. It was subsequently returned as a gift for Otto's wedding to Athelstan's sister Eadgita.[24]

Anderson spots a crucial mistake in this account of the lance (and one which certainly casts doubt on Stein's unorthodox methods of historical 'research'.) According to William of Malmesbury, the *sword* of Constantine the Great was sent by Hugh the Good, King of the Franks, to King Athelstan to persuade him to give his daughter's hand in marriage.[25]

It so happens that historical inaccuracies are also to be found in Ravenscroft's account of his own exploits in the Second World War, in which he claims to have been taken prisoner by the Germans after the attempted assassination of Rommel. Born in 1921, Ravenscroft attended Repton Public School and then Sandhurst Military College. Six months later, in December 1939, he received his commission in the Royal Scots Fusiliers. He then trained as a commando and joined the Special Services.[26] According to the cover blurb on various editions of *The Spear of Destiny*: 'He was captured on a raid which attempted to assassinate Field Marshal Rommel in North Africa and was a POW in Germany from 1944 to 1945, escaping three times but each time being recaptured.'

Although the raid on Rommel certainly took place on 13–14 November 1941 (with all but two of the party being captured), Ravenscroft is not mentioned in records as being present in the 28-man team who conducted the operation. Anderson reports that when he made enquiries of former Commando Sergeant Jack Terry, the ex-soldier insisted that Ravenscroft was not a member of the party.[27] 'In any case Ravenscroft's service record shows he was "missing at sea" on 24 October 1941, well before the raid. He was subsequently taken prisoner of war on an unspecified date.'[28]

There also appear to be inconsistencies in Ravenscroft's account of how he came to meet Walter Stein. A few years after the war, Ravenscroft read Stein's book *World History in the Light of the Holy Grail* and came to the conclusion that much of the material in the book had been accessed by Stein through occult means of mind expansion, perhaps similar to those he himself had employed while a prisoner of war. Paying Stein a visit in Kensington, London, Ravenscroft informed him of his belief, and also of his belief that Wolfram von Eschenbach had employed the same talents in composing his Grail romance *Parsival* in the twelfth century.

> Ravenscroft quoted to Stein this extract from Eschenbach's work: 'If anyone requests me to [continue the story] let him not consider it as a book. I don't know a single letter of the alphabet.' Ravenscroft says that the reason Eschenbach was stressing that he did not know a letter of the alphabet was to make it clear that he had not gathered the material for the book from his contemporaries, traditional folklore, or any existing written work. Rather, he was saying his so-called Grail romance was an 'Initiation Document' of the highest order.[29]

Stein was impressed enough by his visitor's argument that he invited him to stay to lunch, and the two men remained friends and colleagues from then until Stein's death. Ravenscroft himself died of cancer in January 1989 in Torquay, England.

Anderson interviewed Ravenscroft's brother, Bill, in January 1995. A former King's Own Borderers officer, Bill Ravenscroft stated that his brother met Walter Stein not by paying an unannounced visit to his Kensington home but rather through Stein's wife, Yopi, while Trevor Ravenscroft was teaching at the Rudolf Steiner school in East Grinstead, England just after the war.[30] According to Bill Ravenscroft, Trevor learned of Stein's impressive library through Yopi and was given permission by her to consult the books in the library in order to complete *The Spear of Destiny*. Trevor Ravenscroft makes no mention whatsoever of Yopi in his book. Anderson asks: why? 'Was Bill's memory of events incorrect? Was it because the symbiotic relationship that supposedly developed between Trevor and the man he claims was his mentor never happened?'[31]

If *The Spear of Destiny* is to be believed, the moment Hitler entered the Habsburg Treasure House upon the annexation of Austria in 1938 and stood before the holy artefact he had coveted for so long humanity in the twentieth century was lost, locked into an irrevocable collision course with disaster. And yet there are more problems with this pivotal point in the book. Ravenscroft writes: 'When Hitler was driven down the Ringstrasse to the Ring and on to the Heldenplatz to the reviewing stand in front of the Hofburg, the tumultuous jubilation of the crowds reached near-delirium. How could the citizens of Vienna have known that the ecstasy on the face of Adolf Hitler was the twisted ecstasy of revenge!'[32]

Joachim Fest, one of the greatest authorities on Hitler and the Third Reich offers a slightly different account of the Führer's moment of triumph at the 'reunion' of Germany and Austria: 'All the aimlessness and impotence of those years were now vindicated, all his furious craving for compensation at last satisfied, when he stood on the balcony of the Hofburg and announced to hundreds of thousands in the Heldenplatz the "greatest report of a mission accomplished" in his life . . .'[33] If Fest's academic credentials are insufficient, there are also photographs to prove that Hitler faced the Viennese crowds from the balcony of the Hofburg, *not* on a 'reviewing stand' in front of it.

Ravenscroft goes on to claim that after reviewing the Austrian SS and giving his permission for the founding of a new SS regiment, Hitler refused an invitation for a tour of the city. Instead, he 'left the Ring to drive directly to the Imperial Hotel where the most luxurious suite in the city awaited him'.[34] Arrangements for a civic dinner and reception were cancelled because Hitler was 'terrified that an attempt would be made to kill him'[35] and remained in his suite. Anderson asks a pertinent question: if Hitler was terrified that an attempt would be made on his life, why did he arrive in Vienna in an open car that passed through the cheering crowds, then stand in full view outside the Hofburg, and then go out onto the balcony of his hotel suite several times at the insistence of the Viennese people?[36]

In spite of this, Ravenscroft has Hitler leaving the Imperial Hotel 'long after midnight' to head for the Habsburg Treasure House and the Holy Lance. According to Anderson:

> . . . Hitler arrived in Vienna at 5 p.m. on 14 March and the mass welcome in the Heldenplatz took place the next day – the fifteenth. If Ravenscroft has meant us to understand that the rally in the square he speaks of was on the fifteenth, then there is a further problem: Hitler stayed in Vienna less than twenty-four hours! He was not there on the night of the fifteenth.
>
> After attending a military parade at the Maria-Theresa monument at two o'clock that afternoon – the same parade which Ravenscroft says Hitler attended before going on to the Imperial – Hitler flew out in his Junkers aircraft as the twilight settled on an enervated Vienna.[37]

It is also difficult to imagine how Hitler could have left his hotel and gone to the Treasure House without being seen by anyone in the seething crowds that remained in the streets. It would surely have been easier for him to order the Holy Lance to be brought from the museum to his hotel suite.[38] On reflection, it must be said that the only things in the Habsburg Treasure House Hitler coveted were the Habsburg Crown Jewels (which were sent to Nuremberg immediately following the *Anschluss*), not to mention the Austrian gold and currency deposits that would aid a German economy stressed by preparations for war. Hitler was motivated more by financial than occult concerns, as the transfer of Austrian gold and currency reserves to Germany amply demonstrates.[39]

It will, one hopes, be apparent from this all too brief overview of the problems inherent in *The Spear of Destiny* that, while the book may be a fascinating – if somewhat lurid – read, in the Dennis Wheatley mould of occult ripping yarns, as a serious historical work it is completely unsatisfactory. It is, of course, conceivable that Trevor Ravenscroft was well aware that he was penning a work of almost total fiction; however, this is mere conjecture and is absolutely not proven. Even assuming that he wrote the book in good faith, believing its revelations regarding Hitler and the Holy Lance to be accurate, it is crippled by the research methods on which he appears to rely: namely, the use of occult techniques to enhance the powers of the mind and thus gain access to historical information that has not been preserved in any conventional way. In the final analysis, we must dismiss *The Spear of Destiny* on the grounds that when information gathered through psychic processes conflicts with what has been established through documentary evidence or the testimony of first-hand witnesses we have no serious alternative but to abandon it in favour of what can be verified by those who do not possess these psychic talents.

Before moving on, we must say a few words about the claims of many occult writers that Hitler was involved in black magic practices, having been initiated into the dark arts by Dietrich Eckart and Karl Haushofer. (Eckart, Alfred Rosenberg and Rudolf von Sebottendorff were said to have conducted horrific seances, in which a naked female medium exuded ectoplasm from her vagina and through whom contact was established with the seven Thulist hostages who had been murdered by the Communists in April 1919 [see page 56]. The ghosts predicted that Hitler would claim the Holy Lance and lead Germany into global conflagration.)[40] There is no evidence whatsoever to link Hitler directly with black magic practices of any description. While it is of course beyond question that the Nazi Party arose out of the National Socialist German Workers' Party, which in turn began as the Thule Society (a group founded on occult and racist principles), there is no evidence that Hitler himself was an occultist – and considerable evidence that he wasn't.

Speer, for instance, recalls Hitler's contempt for the woolly-headed mysticism of Heinrich Himmler:

What nonsense! Here we have at last reached an age that has left all mysticism behind it, and now he wants to start all over again. We might just as well have stayed with the church. At least it had tradition. To think that I may some day be turned into an SS saint! Can you imagine it? I would turn over in my grave . . .[41]

Hitler was also scornful of Himmler's attempts to establish archaeological links between modern Germans and the ancient Aryan descendants of Atlantis:

Why do we call the whole world's attention to the fact that we have no past? It isn't enough that the Romans were erecting great buildings when our forefathers were still living in mud huts; now Himmler is starting to dig up these villages of mud huts and enthusing over every potsherd and stone axe he finds. All we prove by that is that we were still throwing stone hatchets and crouching around open fires when Greece and Rome had already reached the highest stage of culture. We really should do our best to keep quiet about this past. Instead Himmler makes a great fuss about it all. The present-day Romans must be having a laugh at these revelations.[42]

In truth, those who subscribed to occultist or pseudo-religious notions were indeed something of a laughing stock in the high echelons of the Third Reich. Himmler's beliefs about the original prehistoric Germanic race were considered absurd by both Hitler and Goebbels, the propaganda minister. 'When, for example, the Japanese presented [Himmler] with a samurai sword, he at once discovered kinships between Japanese and Teutonic cults and called upon scientists to help him trace these similarities to a racial common denominator.'[43]

As for the belief that Hitler was deeply interested in astrology and kept in constant touch with astrologers who advised him on the various courses of action he should take, this too is completely fallacious. According to the former Office of Strategic Services (OSS) officer Walter Langer:

All of our informants who have known Hitler rather intimately discard the idea [of Hitler's belief] as absurd. They all agree that nothing is more foreign to Hitler's personality than to seek help from outside sources of this type.

The Führer had never had his horoscope cast, but in an indicative move Hitler, some time before the war, forbade the practice of fortune-telling and star-reading in Germany.[44]

As we have just seen, while Hitler was contemptuous of mysticism and pseudoreligion, Himmler was another matter entirely, and it is to him that we must now turn our attention.

6 Ordinary madness

Heinrich Himmler and the SS

MANY WRITERS ON THE OCCULT have suggested that the notorious SS (*Schütz Staffeln* or Defence Squads) was actively engaged in black-magic rites designed to contact and enlist the aid of evil and immensely powerful trans-human powers, in order to secure the domination of the planet by the Third Reich. While conventional historians are contemptuous of this notion, it nevertheless holds some attraction for those struggling with the terrible mystery at the heart of Nazism, who have come to believe that only a supernatural explanation can possibly shed light on the movement's origins and deeds. Goodrick-Clarke, one of the very few serious historians to have explored the subject of the occult inspiration behind Nazism, stresses that although *völkisch* occultists such as Guido von List and Lanz von Liebenfels undoubtedly contributed to the 'mythological mood of the Nazi era' (with its bizarre notions of pre-historic Aryan superhumans inhabiting vanished continents), 'they cannot be said to have directly influenced the actions of persons in positions of political power and responsibility'.[1]

As Goodrick-Clarke concedes, however, the one exception is a man named Karl Maria Wiligut (1866–1946), who exerted a profound influence upon Reichsführer-SS Heinrich Himmler. Before turning our attention to the SS itself, therefore, we must pause to examine the life and thought of Wiligut, and the reasons for his intellectual hold over the leader of the most powerful organisation in the Third Reich.

The Man Behind Himmler

Wiligut was born in Vienna into a military family and followed his grandfather and father into the Austrian army, joining the 99th Infantry at Mostar, Herzegovina in late 1884 and reaching the rank of captain by the time he was 37. Throughout his years in the army, he maintained his interest in literature and folklore, writing poetry with a distinctly nationalistic flavour. In 1903, a book of his poems entitled *Seyfrieds Runen* was published by Friedrich Schalk, who had also published Guido von List. Although his studies in mythology had led him to join a quasi-Masonic lodge called the Schlarraffia in 1889, Wiligut does not seem to have been active in the *völkisch* or Pan-German nationalist movements at this time.[2]

During the First World War, Wiligut saw action against the Russians in the Carpathians and was later transferred to the Italian front; by the summer of 1917, he had reached the rank of colonel. Decorated for bravery and highly thought of by his superiors, Wiligut was discharged from the army in January 1919, after nearly 35 years of exemplary service.

At around this time, the Viennese occult underground began to buzz with rumours concerning Wiligut and his alleged possession of an 'ancestral memory' that allowed him to recall the history of the Teutonic people all the way back to the year 228,000 BC. According to Wiligut, his astonishing clairvoyant ability was the result of an uninterrupted family lineage extending thousands of years into the past. He claimed to have been initiated into the secrets of his family by his father in 1890. Goodrick-Clarke has identified the source of this information about Wiligut as Theodor Czepl, who knew of Wiligut through his occult connections in Vienna, which included Wiligut's cousin, Willy Thaler, and various members of the Order of the New Templars (ONT). Czepl paid several visits to Wiligut at his Salzburg home in the winter of 1920, and it was during these visits that Wiligut claimed that the Bible had been written in Germany, and that the Germanic god Krist had been appropriated by Christianity.[3]

According to Wiligut's view of prehistory, the Earth was originally lit by three suns and was inhabited by various mythological beings, including giants and dwarves. For many tens of thousands of years, the world was convulsed with warfare until Wiligut's ancestors, the Adler-Wiligoten, brought peace with the foundation of the 'second Boso culture' and the city of Arual-Jöruvallas (Goslar, the chief shrine of ancient Germany) in 78,000 BC. The following millennia saw yet more conflicts involving various now-lost civilisations, until 12,500 BC, when the religion of Krist was established. Three thousand years later, an opposing group of Wotanists challenged this hitherto universal Germanic faith, and crucified the prophet of Krist, Baldur-Chrestos, who nevertheless managed to escape to Asia. The Wotanists destroyed Goslar in 1200 BC, forcing the followers of Krist to establish a new temple at Exsternsteine, near Detmold.[4]

The Wiligut family itself was originally the result of a mating between the gods of air and water, and in later centuries fled from persecution at the hands of Charlemagne, first to the Faroe Islands and then to Russia. Wiligut claimed that his family line included such heroic Germanic figures as Armin the Cherusker and Wittukind. As Goodrick-Clarke notes: 'It will be evident from this epic account of putative genealogy and family history that Wiligut's prehistorical speculations primarily served as a stage upon which he could project the experiences and importance of his own ancestors.'[5] In addition, Peter Levenda makes the salient point that Wiligut's 'cross-eyed thesis' was based on a spurious amalgamation of genuine cultural traditions (such as those described in the *Eddas*) and Theosophical belief systems that have little or no provenance in the actual history of mythology.[6]

In Wiligut's view, the victimisation of his family that had been going on for tens of thousands of years was continuing at the hands of the Catholic Church, the Freemasons and the

Jews, all of whom he held responsible for Germany's defeat in the First World War. His already somewhat precarious mental health was further undermined when his infant son died, thus destroying the male line of the family. This placed a great strain on his relationship with his wife, Malwine, who in any event was not particularly impressed with his claims of prehistoric greatness for his family. His home life continued to deteriorate, until his violence, threats to kill Malwine and bizarre occult interests resulted in his being committed to the mental asylum at Salzburg in November 1924. Certified insane, he was confined there until 1927.

In spite of this, Wiligut maintained contact with his colleagues in various occult circles, including the ONT and the Edda Society. Five years after his release from the asylum, Wiligut decided to move to Germany and settled in Munich. There he was fêted by German occultists as a fount of priceless information on the remote and glorious history of the Germanic people.

Wiligut's introduction to Heinrich Himmler came about through the former's friend Richard Anders, who had contributed to the Edda Society's *Hagal* magazine and who was now an officer in the SS. Himmler was greatly impressed with the old man's ancestral memory, which implied a racial purity going back much further than 1750 (the year to which SS recruits had to be able to prove their Aryan family history[7]). Wiligut joined the SS in September 1933, using the name 'Karl Maria Weisthor'. He was made head of the Department for Pre- and Early History in the SS Race and Settlement Main Office in Munich, where he was charged with the task of recording on paper the events he clairvoyantly recalled. His work evidently met with the satisfaction of the Reichsführer-SS, who promoted him to SS-Oberführer (lieutenant-brigadier) in November 1934.[8]

As if his own ravings were not enough, Weisthor introduced Himmler to another occultist, a German crypto-historian and List Society member named Günther Kirchhoff (1892–1975) who believed in the existence of energy lines crossing the face of the Earth. Weisthor took it upon himself to forward a number of Kirchhoff's essays and dissertations on ancient Germanic tradition to Himmler, who gave instructions to the *Ahnenerbe* (the SS Association for Research and Teaching on Heredity) to study them. One such dissertation concerned a detailed survey undertaken by Kirchhoff and Weisthor in the region of the Murg Valley near Baden-Baden in the Black Forest. After exhaustively examining 'old half-timbered houses, architectural ornament (including sculpture, coats-of-arms, runes, and other symbols), crosses, inscriptions, and natural and man-made rock formations in the forest',[9] the two occultists concluded that the region had been a prehistoric centre of the Krist religion.

Unfortunately for Kirchhoff, even the *Ahnenerbe* came to think of him as a crackpot who understood nothing of scholarly prehistorical research (quite an indictment, coming from that particular organisation). When Kirchhoff accused them, along with the Catholic Church, of conspiring against him, the *Ahnenerbe* responded by describing his work as 'rubbish' and him as a 'fantasist of the worst kind'.[10] In spite of this, Himmler continued to instruct the *Ahnenerbe* to take seriously Kirchhoff's unscholarly rantings, until the outbreak of the Second World War forced him firmly into the background.

Weisthor, on the other hand, would make one further important contribution to Himmler's SS. While travelling through Westphalia during the Nazi electoral campaign of January 1933, Himmler was profoundly affected by the atmosphere of the region, with its romantic castles and the mist- (and myth-) shrouded Teutoburger Forest. After deciding to take over a castle for SS use, he returned to Westphalia in November and viewed the Wewelsburg castle, which he appropriated in August 1934 with the intention of turning it into an ideological-education college for SS officers. Although at first belonging to the Race and Settlement Main Office, the Wewelsburg castle was placed under the control of Himmler's Personal Staff in February 1935.

It is likely that Himmler's view of the Wewelsburg castle was influenced by Weisthor's assertion that it 'was destined to become a magical German strongpoint in a future conflict between Europe and Asia'.[11] Weisthor's inspiration for this prediction was a Westphalian legend regarding a titanic future battle between East and West. Himmler found this particularly interesting, in view of his own conviction that a major confrontation between East and West was inevitable – even if it were still a century or more in the future. In addition, it was Weisthor who influenced the development of SS ritual (which we shall examine later in this chapter) and who designed the SS *Totenkopfring* that symbolised membership of the order. The ring design was based on a death's head, and included a swastika, the double sig-rune of the SS and a *hagall* rune.

In 1935, Weisthor moved to Berlin, where he joined the Reichsführer-SS Personal Staff and continued to advise Himmler on all aspects of his Germanic pseudo-history. Eyewitnesses recollect that this was a period of great activity, during which Weisthor travelled widely, corresponded extensively and oversaw numerous meetings. According to Goodrick-Clarke: 'Besides his involvement with the Wewelsburg castle and his land surveys in the Black Forest and elsewhere, Weisthor continued to produce examples of his family traditions such as the Halgarita mottoes, Germanic mantras designed to stimulate ancestral memory . . . and the design for the SS *Totenkopfring*.'[12] In recognition of his work, Weisthor was promoted to SS-Brigadeführer (brigadier) in Himmler's Personal Staff in September 1936.

While in Berlin, Weisthor worked with the author and historian Otto Rahn (1904–1939), who had a profound interest in medieval Grail legends and the Cathar heresy. In 1933, Rahn published a romantic historical work entitled *Kreuzzug gegen den Gral* (*Crusade Against the Grail*), which was a study of the Albigensian Crusade, a war between the Roman Catholic Church and the Cathars (or Albigensians), an ascetic religious sect that flourished in southern France in the twelfth and thirteenth centuries. The Cathars believed that the teachings of Christ had been corrupted by the Church – and, indeed, that Christ was exclusively a being of spirit who had never been incarnated in human form. This belief arose from their conviction that all matter was the creation of an evil deity opposed to God. Thus they claimed that the dead would not be physically resurrected (since the body was made of matter and hence evil) and that procreation itself was evil, since it increased the amount of matter in the Universe and trapped souls in physicality.[13] The Cathars were eventually destroyed by Catholic armies on the orders of Pope Innocent III in the first decade of the thirteenth century.

As Levenda notes, Catharism held a particular fascination and attraction for Himmler and other leading Nazis. 'After all, the very word "Cathar" means "pure," and purity – particularly of the blood as the physical embodiment of spiritual "goodness" – was an issue of prime importance to the SS.'[14] Just as the Cathars had despised the materialism of the Catholic Church, so the Nazis despised Capitalism, which they equated with the 'excesses of the Jewish financiers that – they said – had brought the nation to ruin during the First World War and the depression that followed'.[15] The Cathar belief that the evil god who had created the material Universe was none other than Jehovah provided additional common ground with Nazi anti-Semitism.

Ritual suicide was also practised by the Cathars. Known as the *endura*, it involved either starving oneself to death, self-poisoning or strangulation by one's fellow Cathars. Levenda makes another interesting point about the Nazi fascination with Catharism:

> [T]he Cathars were fanatics, willing to die for their cause; sacrificing themselves to the Church's onslaught they enjoyed the always-enviable aura of spiritual underdogs. There was something madly beautiful in the way they were immolated on the stakes of the Inquisition, professing their faith and their hatred of Rome until the very end. The Nazis could identify with the Cathars: with their overall fanaticism, with their contempt for the way vital spiritual matters were commercialized (polluted) by the Establishment, and with their passion for 'purity'. It is perhaps inevitable that the Cathars should have made a sacrament out of suicide, for they must have known that their Quest was

doomed to failure from the start. They must have wished for death as a release from a corrupt and insensitive world; and it's entirely possible that, at the root of Nazism, lay a similar death wish. Hitler was surrounded by the suicides of his mistresses and contemplated it himself on at least one occasion before he actually pulled the trigger in Berlin in 1945. Himmler and other captured Nazi leaders killed themselves rather than permit the Allies to do the honors for them. . . . [L]ike the Cathars whom they admired, the Nazis saw in suicide that consolation and release from the world of Satanic matter promised by this most cynical of Cathar sacraments.[16]

The thesis of Rahn's book was that the Cathar heresy and Grail legends constituted an ancient Gothic Gnostic religion that had been suppressed by the Catholic Church, beginning with the persecution of the Cathars and ending with the destruction of the Knights Templar a century later. From 1933, Rahn lived in Berlin and his book and his continued researches into Germanic history came to the attention of Himmler. In May 1935, Rahn joined Weisthor's staff, joining the SS less than a year later. In April 1936, he was promoted to the rank of SS-Unterscharführer (NCO).

His second book, *Luzifers Hofgesinde* (*Lucifer's Servants*), which was an account of his research trip to Iceland for the SS, was published in 1937. This was followed by four months of military service with the SS-Death's Head Division 'Oberbayern' at Dachau concentration camp, after which he was allowed to pursue his writing and research full time. In February 1939, Rahn resigned from the SS for unknown reasons, and subsequently died from exposure the following month while walking on the mountains near Kufstein.[17]

As with Rahn's resignation from the SS, the reasons for Weisthor leaving the organisation are uncertain. One possible reason is that his health was badly failing; although he was given powerful drugs intended to maintain his mental faculties, they had serious side effects, including personality changes that resulted in heavy smoking and alcohol consumption. Also at this time his psychological history – including his committal for insanity – which had been a closely guarded secret became known, causing considerable embarrassment to Himmler. In February 1939, Weisthor's staff were informed that he had retired because of poor health, and that his office would be dissolved.[18] Although the old occultist was supported by the SS during the final years of his life, his influence on the Third Reich was at an end. He was given a home in Aufkirchen, but found it to be too far away from Berlin and he moved to Goslar in May 1940. When his accommodation was requisitioned for medical research in 1943, he moved again, this time to a small SS house in Carinthia where he spent the remainder of the war with his housekeeper, Elsa Baltrusch, a member of Himmler's Personal Staff. At the end of the war, he was sent by the British occupying forces to a refugee camp where he suffered a stroke. After their release, he and Baltrusch went first to his family home at Salzburg, and then to Baltrusch's family home at Arolsen. On 3 January 1946, his health finally gave out and he died in hospital.[19]

Heinrich Himmler

The man who was so deeply impressed with the rantings of Wiligut, who would become most closely associated with the terror of the SS and an embodiment of evil second only to Adolf Hitler himself, was born in Munich on 7 October 1900. Himmler's father was the son of a police president and had been a tutor to the princes at the Bavarian court, and thus applied suitably authoritarian principles on his own family.[20] As Joachim Fest notes: 'No doubt it would be going too far to see in the son's early interest in Teutonic sagas, criminology and military affairs the beginnings of his later development, but the family milieu, with its combination of "officialdom, police work and teaching", manifestly had a lasting effect on him.'[21]

Himmler was not blessed with a robust physical constitution, and this hampered his family's initial intention that he should become a farmer. Nevertheless, the ideal of the noble peasant remained with him and heavily influenced his later ideology and plans for the SS. After serving very briefly at the end of the First World War, Himmler joined Hitler's NSDAP. In 1926 he met Margerete Boden, the daughter of a West Prussian landowning family, and married her two years later. A fine example of the Germanic type (tall, fair-haired and blue-eyed), she was also seven years older than Himmler and is said to have inspired his interest in alternative medicine such as herbalism and homeopathy.[22]

Himmler was appointed head (Reichsführer) of the SS on 6 January 1929. At that time the organisation had barely 300 members, but such were Himmler's organisational skills that he increased its membership to over 50,000 in the next four years. In 1931 he established a special Security Service (SD) within the SS, which would oversee political intelligence. It was led by the psychopathic Reinhard Heydrich, 'the only top Nazi leader to fit the racial stereotype of being tall (six feet, three inches), blond, and blue-eyed'.[23] Himmler took control of the party's police functions in April 1934, and then took command of the Gestapo (*Geheime Staatspolizei* or Secret State Police). SS units were instrumental in Hitler's Blood Purge of 30 June 1934, which saw the end of the *Sturmabteilung* (SA), the brown-shirted and sadistic militia of the early Nazi Party, and its chief, Ernst Röhm. Members of the SS were required to correspond to special racial criteria (tall, blond, blue-eyed) and had to be able to trace their Aryan ancestry at least as far back as the year 1750. Initially, the SS membership included approximately 44 per cent from the working class; however, as its status increased following the Nazi rise to power, it attracted more members from the upper class.

By 1937, the three major concentration camps in Germany were staffed by the SS *Totenkopfverbände* (Death's Head Units), and the following year saw the formation of the *Verfügungstruppe* (Action Groups), which numbered 200,000 and which later became the *Waffen-SS* (Military SS). By the end of 1938, SS membership had reached nearly 240,000, a figure that would later rise to approximately one million.

According to the historian Joachim C. Fest:

[T]he aims of the enormous SS apparatus were ... comprehensive and concerned not so much with controlling the state as with becoming a state itself. The occupants of the chief positions in the SS developed step by step into the holders of power in an authentic 'collateral state', which gradually penetrated existing institutions, undermined them, and finally began to dissolve them. Fundamentally there was no sphere of public life upon which the SS did not make its competing demands: the economic, ideological, military, scientific and technical spheres, as well as those of agrarian and population policies, legislation and general administration. This development found its most unmistakable expression in the hierarchy of the Senior SS and Police Commanders, especially in the Eastern zones; the considerable independence that Himmler's corps of leaders enjoyed *vis-à-vis* the civil or military administration was a working model for a shift of power planned for the whole area of the Greater German Reich after the war. This process received its initial impetus following the so-called Röhm Putsch, and it moved towards its completion after the attempted revolt of 20 July 1944. The SS now pushed its way into 'the centre of the organizational fabric of the Wehrmacht', and Himmler, who had meanwhile also become Reich Minister of the Interior, now in addition became chief of the Replacement Army. On top of his many other functions he was thus in charge 'of all military transport, military censorship, the intelligence service, surveillance of the troops, the supply of food, clothing and pay to the troops, and care of the wounded'.[24]

The Ahnenerbe *and the Rituals of the SS*

It has been said of Himmler many times that his personality was a curious mixture of rationality and fantasy: that his capacity for rational planning, the following of orders and administrative detail existed alongside an idealist enthusiasm for utopianism, mysticism and the occult. This combination of the quotidian and the fantastic led to Himmler's conception of the ultimate role of the SS: 'his black-uniformed troops would provide both the bloodstock of the future Aryan master-race and the ideological élite of an ever-expanding Greater Germanic Reich'.[25]

From 1930, Himmler concentrated on the formulation of his plans for the SS, which included the establishment of the SS officers' college at the Wewelsburg castle in 1933. Two years later, he established the *Ahnenerbe* with the Nazi pagan ideologue Richard Walther Darré. The *Ahnenerbe* was the Ancestral Heritage Research and Teaching Society, and was initially an independent institute conducting research into Germanic prehistory, archaeology and occult mysticism. It was subsequently incorporated into the SS in April 1940, with its staff holding SS rank. Levenda thinks it likely that the inspiration for the *Ahnenerbe* came from a number of German intellectuals and occultists who had subscribed to the theories of the *völkisch* writers of the late nineteenth century, as well as from the adventures of a number of explorers and archaeologists, including the world-famous Swedish explorer Sven Hedin.[26]

Born in Stockholm in 1865, Hedin left Sweden at the age of twenty and sailed to Baku on the Caspian Sea. This was the first voyage of a man who would travel through most of Asia, and whose exploits would be recorded in the book *My Life as an Explorer* (1925). Hedin's voyages and tales of fabulous Asian cities did much to consolidate the European and American publics' fascination with the mysterious Orient – a fascination that had already been kindled by Madame Blavatsky and the Theosophical Society.[27]

Levenda writes:

There is evidence to suggest that the *Ahnenerbe* itself was formed as a private institution by several friends and admirers of Sven Hedin, including Wolfram Sievers (who would later find justice at the Nuremberg Trials) and Dr Friedrich Hielscher who, according to the records of the Nuremberg Trial of November 1946, had been responsible for recruiting Sievers into the *Ahnenerbe*. In fact, there was a Sven Hedin Institute for Inner Asian Research in Munich that was part of the *Ahnenerbe* and as late as 1942 Hedin himself (then about seventy-seven years old) was in friendly communication with such important *Ahnenerbe* personnel as Dr Ernst Schäfer from his residence in Stockholm. Moreover, on January 16, 1943, the Sven Hedin Institute for Inner Asian (i.e. Mongolian) Research and Expeditions was formally inaugurated in Munich with 'great pomp,' a ceremony at which Hedin was in attendance as he was awarded with an honorary doctorate for the occasion.[28]

It is possible that Hedin may have met Karl Haushofer (whom we discussed in Chapter Three) while in the Far East, since Hedin was an occasional ambassador for the Swedish Government and Haushofer was a German military attaché. 'Given Haushofer's excessive interest in political geography and his establishment of the *Deutsche Akademie* all over Asia (including China and India, Hedin's old stomping grounds), it would actually be odd if the two hadn't met.'[29] Indeed, the *Deutsche Akademie* and the *Ahnenerbe*, whose director was Wolfram Sievers, were run along very similar lines. Dr Walther Wüst, the Humanities chairman of the *Ahnenerbe* who carried the SS rank of *Oberführer*, was also acting president of the *Deutsche Akademie*. Both organisations conducted field research at Dachau concentration camp.[30]

Himmler's vision of the SS required its transformation from Hitler's personal bodyguard to a pagan religious order with virtually complete autonomy, answerable only to the Führer himself. As we have seen, Himmler chose as the headquarters for his order the castle of Wewelsburg, near Paderborn in Westphalia and close to the stone monument known as the Exsternsteine where the Teutonic hero Arminius was said to have battled the Romans.

The focal point of Wewelsburg, evidently owing much to the legend of King Arthur and the Knights of the

Round Table, was a great dining hall with an oaken table to seat twelve picked from the senior Gruppenführers. The walls were to be adorned with their coats of arms; although a high proportion lacked these – as of course did Himmler himself – they were assisted in the drafting of designs by Professor Diebitsch and experts from the *Ahnenerbe*.[31]

Beneath the dining hall was a circular room with a shallow depression reached by three stone steps (symbolising the three Reichs). In this place of the dead, the coat of arms of the deceased 'Knight' of the SS would be ceremonially burned. Each member of Himmler's Inner Circle of Twelve had his own room, which was dedicated to an Aryan ancestor. Himmler's own quarters were dedicated to King Heinrich I, the Saxon king who had battled Hungarians and Slavs and of whom Himmler was convinced he was the reincarnation,[32] although he also claimed to have had conversations with Heinrich's ghost at night.[33]

Inside the dining hall, Himmler and his Inner Circle would perform various occult exercises, which included attempts to communicate with the spirits of dead Teutons and efforts to influence the mind of a person in the next room through the concentration of will-power.

There was no place for Christianity in the SS, and members were actively encouraged to break with the Church.

New religious ceremonies were developed to take the place of Christian ones; for instance, a winter solstice ceremony was designed to replace Christmas (starting in 1939 the word 'Christmas' was forbidden to appear in any official SS document), and another ceremony for the summer solstice. Gifts were to be given at the summer solstice ceremony rather than at the winter solstice . . . (A possible, though by no means documented, cause for this switch of gift-giving to the summer solstice is the death of Hitler's mother on the winter solstice and all the grief and complex emotions this event represented for Hitler. It's understandable that Hitler – as the Führer and at least nominally in charge of the direction the new state religion would take – would have wanted to remove every vestige of 'Christmas' from the pagan winter solstice festival. As a means of denying his grief? Or as an act of defiance against the god whose birth is celebrated on that day, a god who robbed Hitler of his beloved mother? It's worthwhile to note in this context that for a national 'Day of the German Mother' Hitler chose his own mother's birthday.)[34]

Besides Christmas, weddings and christenings were also replaced by pagan rituals, and pagan myths, as we saw earlier in this chapter, influenced Himmler's choice of Wewelsburg as the SS-order castle. The meticulous work of Peter Levenda in unearthing previously unpublished documents from the period allows us to consider the pagan world view of the *Ahnenerbe* and the SS. The files of the *Ahnenerbe* contained an article by A. E. Müller originally published in a monthly journal called *Lower Saxony* in 1903, which describes the celebration of the summer solstice at the Exsternsteine monument near the Wewelsburg in the mid-nineteenth century.

[They are] like giants from a prehistoric world which, during the furious creation of the Earth, were placed there by God as eternal monuments ... Many of our *Volk* are known to have preserved the pagan belief and its rituals, and I remember that some sixty years ago, in my earliest childhood days ... the custom was to undertake a long, continuous journey that lasted for whole days and which only ended on St John's Day, to see those ancient 'Holy Stones' and to celebrate there, with the sunrise, the Festival of the Summer Solstice.[35]

The town of Paderborn itself also had considerable pagan significance, as demonstrated by a letter from a man named von Motz to the head of the *Ahnenerbe*, Wolfram Sievers, which is quoted in Levenda's hugely informative book *Unholy Alliance*:

I am sending to you now ... six photographs with explanatory text. Maybe these can appear in one of the next issues of [the official SS magazine] *Schwarze Korps* in order to show that it is to some extent a favored practice of the church on images of its saints and so forth to illustrate the defeat of adversaries by [having them] step on them.

The referenced essay also mentioned that there are depictions of the serpent's head, as the symbol of original sin, being stepped on [by the saints].

These depictions are quite uncommonly prevalent. It is always Mary who treads on original sin.

Now these pictures appear to me particularly interesting because the serpent refers to an ancient symbol of Germanic belief. At the Battle of Hastings the flag of the Saxons shows a golden serpent on a blue field ...

The Mary Statue at Paderborn was erected in the middle of the past century in the courtyard of the former Jesuit College. As professor Alois Fuchs related several times before in lectures concerning the Paderborn art monuments, the artist that created the Mary Statue must have been a Protestant. This is for me completely proven because the face in the moon-sickle in every case represents Luther.

It is well known that Rome and Judah, preferring thus to take advantage of their own victims, created victory monuments for them.[36]

As Levenda notes, these motifs are common in the *völkisch* underpinnings of Nazism, with the serpent, thought of as an archetype of evil in Christianity, considered sacred by the Aryans. In addition, '"Rome and Judah" shamelessly exploited the suffering of their own people by depicting them as heroes or as vanquishers of evil through their agonies (thus reinforcing weak, non-Aryan suicidal tendencies among the oppressed populations of Europe).'[37]

As we have noted, the *Ahnenerbe* received its official status within the SS in 1940, and while other occult-oriented groups such as the Freemasons, the Theosophists and the Hermetic Order of the Golden Dawn were being suppressed, the *Ahnenerbe* was given free rein to pursue its own line of mystical and occult enquiry, with the express purpose of proving the historical validity of Nazi paganism. Its more than 50 sections covered every aspect of occultism and paganism, including Celtic studies, the rituals surrounding the Exsternsteine monument, Scandinavian mythology, runic symbolism, the World Ice Theory of Hans Hörbiger (which will be discussed in Chapter Seven), and an archaeological research group that attempted to prove the geographical ubiquity of the ancient Aryan civilisation. In addition, at the door of the *Ahnenerbe* must lie the ineradicable iniquity of the medical experiments conducted at Dachau and other concentration camps, since it was this organisation that commissioned the unbelievably hideous programme of 'scientific research' on living human subjects.

The mental ambiguity of Heinrich Himmler – rational, obedient and totally desirous of security on the one hand; immersed in the spurious fantasy of Aryan destiny on the other – was demonstrated most powerfully in the final phase of the Nazi regime, when it became obvious that Germany would lose the war and the 'Thousand-year Reich' would become dust. From 1943 onward, Himmler maintained loose contacts with the Resistance Movement in Germany, and in the spring of 1945 he entered into secret negotiations with the World Jewish Congress. (By September 1944 he had already given orders for the murder of Jews to be halted, in order to offer a more 'presentable' face to the Allies, an order that was not followed.[38])

Himmler's actions at this time indicate what Fest calls 'an almost incredible divorce from reality', one example being his suggestion to a representative of the World Jewish Congress that 'it is time you Jews and we National Socialists buried the hatchet'.[39] He even assumed, in all seriousness, that he might lead a post-war Germany in an alliance with the West against the Soviet Union. When the reality of the Third Reich's defeat finally overwhelmed his fantasies and sent them to oblivion, and the idea of disguise and escape finally presented itself to him, Himmler adopted perhaps the worst false identity he could have chosen: the uniform of a sergeant-major of the Secret Military Police, a division of the Gestapo. Such was his 'divorce from reality', even then, that it did not occur to him that any Gestapo member would be arrested on sight by the Allies. This indeed occurred on 21 May 1945.

Like their master, many SS men took their own lives in 1945, appalled less at Himmler's betrayal of Hitler through his attempts to negotiate with the Allies than at his betrayal of the SS itself and of the ideals that had given meaning (at least to them) to the destruction they had wrought upon their six million victims. The collapse of this SS ideal 'left only a senseless, filthy, barbaric murder industry, for which there could be no defence'.[40]

7 The secret at the heart of the world

Nazi Cosmology and Belief in the Hollow Earth

F OR READERS ENCOUNTERING THE FIELD of Nazi occultism (and its unholy spawn, contemporary belief in genuine Nazi occult power) for the first time, the Hollow Earth Theory may well prompt a sigh of exasperation. We have already examined a number of esoteric concepts that may be more or less unpalatable to the modern mind; the realm we are about to enter, however, may be considered both the most ridiculous and the most sinister yet, since it constitutes both a synthesis and a further development of the strange ideas promulgated by the *völkisch* occultists and, later, by the philosophers and pseudo-scientists of the Third Reich. As we shall see in this chapter, the concept of the hollow Earth – and the related notion of vast, inhabited caverns within a solid Earth – have come to occupy a central position in the fields of ufology, conspiracy theory, fringe science and Nazi-survival theories. Indeed, the relevance of these subjects to the belief systems that define late-twentieth-century popular occultism may come as a surprise to many readers.

The Provenance of the Hollow Earth Theory

Of all the strange and irrational beliefs held by the Nazis, the most bizarre is surely the idea that our planet is not a sphere floating in the emptiness of space, but rather is a hollow bubble, with everything – people, buildings, continents, oceans and even other planets and stars – existing on the inside. The origin of this curious notion, which would be developed and accepted in the twentieth century by people such as Peter Bender, Dr Heinz Fisher and many members of the German Admiralty, can be traced back to the seventeenth century and the writings of the Jesuit Athanasius Kircher (1602–1680), who speculated on conditions beneath the surface of the Earth in a treatise written in 1665 entitled *Mundus Subterraneus* (*The Subterranean World*). In this work, Kircher draws on the theories and speculations of various medieval geographers about the unexplored north and south polar regions. As Joscelyn Godwin notes, Kircher paid particular attention to the thirteenth-century friar Bartholomew of England, who maintained that 'at the North Pole there is a black rock some 33 leagues in circumference, beneath which the ocean flows with incredible speed through four channels into the subpolar regions, and is absorbed by an immense whirlpool'.[1] Having entered this whirlpool, the waters then travel through a myriad 'recesses' and 'channels' inside the planet and finally emerge in the ocean at the South Pole (the continent of Antarctica had yet to be discovered).

Kircher's justification for his ideas was ingenious, if utterly flawed. He claimed that the polar vortices must exist, otherwise the northern and southern oceans would be still and would thus become stagnant, releasing noxious vapours that would prove lethal to life on Earth. In addition, he believed that the movement of water through the body of the Earth was analogous both to the recently discovered circulation of the blood and to the animal digestive system, with elements in sea water extracted for the production of metals and the waste voided at the South Pole.[2] This likening of the Earth to a single, living entity will doubtless call to mind certain New Age concepts, in particular the so-called 'Gaia Hypothesis'. (While New Ageism might appear to be nothing but benign, concerned as it is with the spiritual evolution of humanity, it does contain certain aspects that are more sinister and potentially dangerous.)

The seventeenth-century writer Thomas Burnet (1635?–1715) also suggested that water circulated through the body of the Earth, issuing from an opening at the North Pole. In 1768, this idea was further developed by Alexander Colcott, who added an interesting and portentous twist: Godwin suggests that he may have been the first to theorise that, once inside the Earth, the water joined a vast, concave ocean – in other words, that the Earth was actually a hollow globe.[3]

In the eighteenth century, the Hollow Earth Theory carried far more intellectual currency than it does now: even the illustrious Sir Edmund Halley (1656–1742), discoverer of the comet that carries his name, proposed in the Philosophical Transactions of the Royal Society of 1692 that the Earth was a hollow sphere containing two additional concentric spheres, at the centre of which was a hot core, a kind of central sun. The Swiss mathematician Leonhard Euler (1707–1783) concurred and, indeed, went somewhat further, stating that there 'was a center sun inside the Earth's interior, which provided daylight to a splendid subterranean civilization'.[4]

The apparent credibility of these theories resulted in a brand new subgenre of fantastic literature. Godwin provides a brief rundown, based on the work of the French author Michel Lamy, of the most significant of these tales:

> While medieval theology, as celebrated in Dante's *Divine Comedy*, had found the interior of the earth to be a suitable location for Hell, later writers began to imagine quite the contrary. The universal philosopher Guillaume Postel, in his *Compendium Cosmographicum* (1561) and the topographer Georg Braun, in his *Urbium praecipuarum totius mundi* (1581), suggested that God had made the Earthly Paradise inaccessible to mankind by stowing it beneath the North Pole. Among the early novels on the theme of a Utopia beneath the surface of the earth are the Chevalier de Mouhy's *Lamékis, ou les voyages extraordinaires d'un Egyptien dans la Terre intérieure* (*Lamékis, or the extraordinary voyages of an Egyptian in the inner earth*, 1737), and Ludvig Baron von

Holberg's *Nicholas Klim* (1741), the latter much read in Holberg's native Denmark. Giovanni Jacopo Casanova, the adventurer and libertine, also situated Paradise inside the earth. In *Icosameron* (1788), a work supposedly translated by him from the English, he describes the twenty-one years passed by his heroes Edward and Elizabeth among the 'megamicros,' the original inhabitants of the 'protocosm' in the interior of our globe. One way into this realm is through the labyrinthine caves near Lake Zirchnitz, a region of Transylvania. The megamicros issue from bottomless wells and assemble in temples, clad in red coats. Their gods are reptiles, with sharp teeth and a magnetic stare.[5]

The literature of the Romantic era, needless to say, is rich in fantasies of polar mysteries and lands within the earth. The best known works are probably George Sand's *Laura ou le voyage dans le crystal* (*Laura, or the voyage in the Crystal*); Edgar Allen Poe's *The Narrative of Arthur Gordon Pym*; Alexander Dumas's *Isaac Laquédem*; Bulwer Lytton's *The Coming Race* [see Chapter Three]; Jules Verne's *Voyage au centre de la terre* (*Voyage to the Centre of the Earth*) and *Le Sphinx des glaces* (*The Sphinx of the Ice*). Novels by later and less distinguished authors include William Bradshaw's *The Goddess of Atvatabar* (1892), Robert Ames Bennet's *Thyra, a Romance of the Polar Pit* (1901), Willis George Emerson's *The Smoky God* (1908), and the Pellucidarian stories of Edgar Rice Burroughs, creator of Tarzan.[6]

In view of the exciting potential of the Hollow Earth Theory, not to mention the literary vogue for such romantic fictions, it was only a matter of time before someone had the bright idea of actually searching for the entrances to the mysterious world apparently lying beneath humanity's feet. Such a man was John Cleves Symmes (1780–1829), who spent a good portion of his life trying to convince the world not only that the Earth was hollow, but that it would be worthwhile to finance an expedition, under his leadership, to find a way inside.

'I Declare the Earth is Hollow . . .'

A native of New Jersey, Symmes enlisted in the United States Army where he distinguished himself for bravery in the French and Indian Wars. Evidently a man of considerable personal integrity, he married a widow named Mary Anne Lockwood in 1808, and ensured that her inheritance from her husband was used to raise her five children (he had five of his own). In 1816, he retired with the rank of Captain and became a trader in St Louis.[7] Two years later, Symmes first announced his beliefs to the world, thus:

CIRCULAR

Light gives light to discover – ad infinitum

St Louis, Missouri Territory, North America
April 10, AD 1818

To all the World:

I declare the earth is hollow and habitable within; containing a number of solid concentric spheres, one within the other, and that it is open at the poles twelve or sixteen degrees. I pledge my life in support of this truth, and am ready to explore the hollow, if the world will support and aid me in the undertaking.

Jno. Cleves Symmes
Of Ohio, late Captain of Infantry.

N.B. – I have ready for the press a treatise on the principles of matter, wherein I show proofs of the above positions, account for various phenomena, and disclose Dr. Darwin's 'Golden Secret.'

My terms are the patronage of THIS and the NEW WORLDS.

I dedicate to my wife and her ten children.

I select Dr. S. L. Mitchell, Sir H. Davy, and Baron Alexander Von Humboldt as my protectors.

I ask one hundred brave companions, well equipped, to start from Siberia, in the fall season, with reindeer and sleighs, on the ice of the frozen sea; I engage we will find a warm and rich land, stocked with thrifty vegetables and animals, if not men, on reaching one degree northward of latitude 82; we will return in the succeeding spring.

J. C. S.[8]

Of all the academic societies in America and Europe to which Symmes sent his circular, only the French Academy of Sciences in Paris bothered to respond – and that was to say, in effect, that the theory of concentric spheres inside the Earth was nonsense. Undaunted by the total lack of academic interest in his ideas, Symmes spent the next ten years travelling around the United States, giving lectures and trying to raise sufficient funds to strike out for the interior of the planet. He petitioned Congress in 1822 and 1823 to finance his expedition, and even secured 25 votes the second time.[9] Ultimately, the strain of constant travelling and lecturing took its toll on Symmes's health. He died at Hamilton, Ohio on 29 May 1829. His grave in the Hamilton cemetery is marked by a stone model of the hollow Earth, placed there by his son, Americus.

Symmes's theory of the hollow Earth is described principally in two books: *Symmes's Theory of Concentric Spheres* (1826) by James McBride, and *The Symmes Theory of Concentric Spheres* (1878) by Americus Symmes.[10] (Symmes himself wrote a novel, under the pseudonym 'Captain Adam Seaborn', entitled *Symzonia: A Voyage of Discovery*, published in 1820.) As Martin Gardner notes, in these books, 'Hundreds of reasons are given for believing the earth hollow – drawn from physics, astronomy, climatology, the migration habits of animals, and the reports of travelers. Moreover, a hollow planet, like the hollow bones of the body, would be a sturdy and economical way for the Creator to arrange things.'[11]

As we have noted, the Hollow Earth Theory attracted the attention of many writers of fiction. Aside from the best-known mentioned above, a number of minor authors explored the topic. In 1871, for instance, Professor William F. Lyon published *The Hollow Globe, or the World's Agitator or Reconciler* that included many bizarre speculations on open polar seas, the electro-magnetic origin of earthquakes (which were thought impossible unless the world were hollow) and the theory of gravitation (which needed considerable reworking in view of the drastically reduced mass of a hollow planet). The text of the book was apparently received during mediumistic trances by a Dr Sherman and his wife, with Professor Lyon transcribing the material. Among the many curious revelations in this book is the 'great fact that this globe is a hollow or spherical shell with an interior as well as an exterior surface, and that it contains an inner concave as well as outer convex world, and that the inner is accessible by an extensive spirally formed aperture, provided with a deep and commodious channel suited to the purposes of navigation for the largest vessels that float, and that this aperture may be found in the unexplored open Polar Sea'.[12]

The Reverend Dr William F. Warren, President of Boston University, published his book *Paradise Found* in 1885, in which he argued for the origin of the human race at the North Pole. While Warren did not claim that the Earth was hollow, his book nevertheless added to the speculation on the significance of the polar regions, and the idea that the solution to the mystery of humanity's origin might lie there.[13]

In 1896, John Uri Lloyd published his book *Etidorhpa* (the title is 'Aphrodite' reversed). One of the strangest books on the subject, *Etidorhpa* tells the story of one Llewellyn Drury, a Mason and seeker after mystery, who encounters a telepathic humanoid creature without a face. The creature takes Drury into a deep cave in Kentucky, and the two emerge on the inner surface of the Earth, where the adventurer is taught to levitate beneath the rays of the central sun.[14]

A Single Bubble in Infinite Nothingness

In 1870, perhaps the strangest of all alternative cosmological theories was formulated by Cyrus Teed: the theory that not only is the Earth hollow but *we* are the ones living on the inside. Born in 1839 in Delaware County, New York, Teed received a Baptist upbringing. After a spell as a private with the United States Army, he attended the New York Eclectic Medical College in Utica, New York. (Eclecticism was an alternative form of medicine that relied on herbal treatments.) It seems that Teed was greatly troubled by the concept of infinite space, which he could not reconcile with the well-ordered Universe of the Scriptures. While he accepted that the Earth was round (he had little choice, since it had been circumnavigated), he found the notion of a ball of rock floating endlessly through an infinite void so unsettling that he set about attempting to formulate an alternative structure for the observable Cosmos.

The answer apparently came to him in a vision in his alchemical laboratory in Utica at midnight one night in 1869. A beautiful woman appeared before him, telling him of the previous lives he had lived, how he was destined to become a messiah, and about the true structure of the Universe. Under the pseudonym Koresh (the Hebrew for Cyrus), Teed published two works: *The Illumination of Koresh: Marvellous Experience of the Great Alchemist at Utica, N. Y.* and *The Cellular Cosmogony*. In his splendid book *Fads and Fallacies in the Name of Science*, Martin Gardner summarises the key points of Teed's outrageous cosmology:

The entire cosmos, Teed argued, is like an egg. We live on the inner surface of the shell, and inside the hollow are the sun, moon, stars, planets, and comets. What is outside? Absolutely nothing! The inside is all there is. You can't see across it because the atmosphere is too dense. The shell is 100 miles thick and made up of seventeen layers. The inner five are geologic strata, under which are five mineral layers, and beneath that, seven metallic ones. A sun at the center of the open space is invisible, but a reflection of it is seen as our sun. The central sun is half light and half dark. Its rotation causes our illusory sun to rise and set. The moon is a reflection of the earth, and the planets are reflections of 'mercurial discs floating between the laminae of the metallic planes'. The heavenly bodies we see, therefore, are not material, but merely focal points of light, the nature of which Teed worked out in great detail by means of optical laws . . .

The earth, it is true, seems to be convex, but according to Teed, it is all an illusion of optics. If you take the trouble to extend a horizontal line far enough, you will always encounter the earth's upward curvature. Such an experiment was actually carried out in 1897 by the Koreshan Geodetic Staff, on the Gulf Coast of Florida. There are photographs in later editions of the book showing this distinguished group of bearded scientists at work. Using a set of three double T-squares – Teed calls the device a 'rectilineator' – they extended a straight line for four miles along the coast only to have it plunge finally into the sea [thus proving the Earth to be a concave sphere]. Similar experiments had been conducted the previous year on the surface of the Old Illinois Drainage Canal.[15]

As Gardner observes, Teed was undoubtedly a pseudo-scientist and displayed all the paranoia and obfuscation associated with that fascinating and infuriating group. His explanations of the structure of the Universe (the ways in which planets and comets are formed, for instance) were couched in impossible-to-understand terms such as 'cruosic force', 'coloric substance' and 'afferent and efferent fluxions of essence'. In addition, he bitterly attacked orthodox science, which sought to impose its erroneous view of reality on a 'credulous public'. He likened himself '(as does almost every pseudo-scientist) to the great innovators of the past who found it difficult to get their views accepted'.[16]

Teed's scientific pronouncements were combined with apocalyptic religious elements, as demonstrated in the following prophetic announcement:

We are now approaching a great biological conflagration. Thousands of people will dematerialize, through a biological electro-magnetic vibration. This will be brought about through the direction of one mind, the only one who has a knowledge of the law of this bio-alchemical transmutation. The change will be accomplished through the formation of a biological battery, the laws of which are known only to one man. This man is Elijah the prophet, ordained of God, the Shepherd of the Gentiles and the central reincarnation of the ages. From this conflagration will spring the sons of God, the biune offspring of the Lord Jesus, the Christ and Son of God.[17]

Unfortunately for Teed, his revelations did not prove of any great interest to the natives of Utica, who took to calling him the 'crazy doctor' and sought their medical advice elsewhere. With his medical practice facing ruin and his wife already having left him, Teed decided to take to the road to spread his curious word. As a travelling orator, he was a spectacular success (he is said to have earned $60,000 in California alone[18]). He was particularly popular in Chicago, where he settled in 1886 and founded first the College of Life and later Koreshan Unity, a small communal society.

In the 1890s, Teed bought a small piece of land just south of Fort Meyers, Florida, and built a town called Estero. He referred to the town as 'the New Jerusalem', predicted that it would become the capital of the world, and told his followers to expect the arrival of eight million believers. The actual number who arrived was something of a disappointment, being closer to 200; nevertheless, the happy, efficient and hard-working community seems to have functioned extremely well. Their strange ideas notwithstanding, the members, male and female alike, were treated as equals, which is no bad thing.[19]

Teed died in 1908 after being beaten by the Marshal of Fort Meyers. He had claimed that after his death he would be taken up into Heaven with his followers. They dutifully held a prayer vigil over his body, awaiting the event that, unsurprisingly, did not take place. As Teed's body started to decompose, the county health officer arrived and ordered Teed's burial. He was finally interred in a concrete tomb on an island off the Gulf Coast. In 1921 a hurricane swept the tomb away: Teed's body was never found.[20]

As we shall see shortly, in Germany a theory comparable to Teed's was developed by an aviator named Peter Bender. Although Bender himself would die in a Nazi prison camp, his Hollow Earth Doctrine (*Hohlweltlehre*) found many followers in the Third Reich, including some naval leaders who thought that it might be possible to spy on British naval movements by pointing their radar beams up! As with the more conventional (!) Hollow Earth Theory, there are many people who still fervently believe that we are living on the inside of a hollow sphere.

The Hollow Earth in the Twentieth Century

Instead of going the way of other strange notions about the nature of the Universe and collapsing in the face of empirical science, the Hollow Earth Theory survived the end of the nineteenth century, refusing to be banished to the realm of the defunct and disproved. Indeed, in spite of its utter erroneousness, its elegance, romance and air of fantastic mystery ensured it a place in the hearts of those who felt dismayed by the arrogance of orthodox science, not to mention the arrogance of the world's leaders. As we shall see, its very simplicity enabled (and still enables) believers to use it as a template for all manner of esoteric 'truths', conspiracy theories and 'proofs' of the secret nefarious activities of governments. This will become especially apparent when we examine the corollary to the Hollow Earth Theory which, for want of a better expression, we might term the Subterranean Cavern Theory. The idea that the planet is honeycombed with vast cave systems, many of which are inhabited by highly advanced beings and monstrous creatures, developed through the combination of Eastern mysticism (see Chapter Four) with Hollow Earth beliefs, and resulted in a frighteningly paranoid and bizarre scenario that includes the machinations of a secret, one-world government, clandestine alien occupation of our planet, and attempts to perfect mind-control of Earth's population. We will examine these subjects, together with the perceived involvement of the

Nazis in their development, a little later; but for now, let us return to the status of the Hollow Earth Theory at the opening of the twentieth century.

The first important book of the twentieth century to deal with the theory was *The Phantom of the Poles* by William Reed, published in 1906. This book was the first serious attempt to gather evidence for a hollow Earth, the 'phantom' of the title being a reference to the poles' existence only as locations in space, and not points on the Earth's surface. The only major alteration Reed made to earlier versions of the theory was to reduce the size of the openings at the North and South Poles to a few hundred miles instead of several thousand. The reason for this was that expeditions had been pushing further and further into the polar regions, without finding any evidence of vast openings into the Earth's interior. This refinement notwithstanding, Reed reiterated the beliefs of earlier theorists: 'The earth is hollow. The Poles, so long sought, are phantoms. There are openings at the northern and southern extremities. In the interior are vast continents, oceans, mountains and rivers. Vegetable and animal life are evident in the New World, and it is probably peopled by races unknown to dwellers on the Earth's surface.'[21]

In 1913, William Gardner published his book *A Journey to the Earth's Interior: or, Have the Poles Really Been Discovered?* The book contained the now-famous illustration of the Earth with half of its northern hemisphere cut away to reveal the continents and oceans within. According to Gardner, the central sun was 600 miles in diameter, and its surface was 2,900 miles from the inner surface of the Earth. The polar openings were 1,400 miles wide, and the planetary shell was 800 miles thick. Like Reed and others before him, Gardner believed that conditions within the Earth were extremely pleasant, akin to some semi-tropical paradise. Like Symmes, he attempted to gather sufficient funds for an expedition, without success. At the end of *A Journey to the Earth's Interior*, Gardner wrote of his hope that one day, with the aid of airships, the openings would be proved to exist.[22] Of course, the advent of routine manned flight proved his theory wrong, although, as we shall see later in this chapter, the words of one famous explorer who flew over the poles have been twisted by hollow Earth believers to imply things he never intended.

Hörbiger's World Ice Theory

While not proposing that the Earth is hollow, the World Ice Theory (*Welteislehre*, or WEL) of Hans Hörbiger (1860-1931) amply demonstrates how outrageously inaccurate cosmological models can be used for political and propaganda purposes. Such was the case with Hörbiger's *Glazial-Kosmogonie*, which the Viennese mining engineer wrote in collaboration with an amateur astronomer and which Martin Gardner calls 'one of the great classics in the history of crackpot science'.[23] Although ridiculed by astronomers in Germany – and by just about everyone else in the rest of the world – the World Ice Theory was to gain a fanatical following in Nazi Germany, where it was seen as a brilliant refutation of the orthodox materialistic science personified by the Jewish scientist Albert Einstein. Indeed, according to the rocket scientist Willy Ley (whom we have already met in Chapter Three and will meet again in the next chapter), supporters of this theory acted very much like a miniature political party, issuing leaflets, posters and circulars, and publishing a monthly journal, *The Key to World Events*.[24] Pauwels and Bergier offer a revealing snapshot of their behaviour:

> [Hörbiger] seemed to have considerable funds at his disposal, and operated like a party leader. He launched a campaign, with an information service, recruiting offices, membership subscriptions, and engaged propagandists and volunteers from among the Hitler Youth. The walls were covered with posters, the newspapers filled with announcements, tracts were distributed and meetings organized. When astronomers met in conference their meetings were interrupted by partisans shouting: 'Down with the orthodox scientists!' Professors were molested in the streets; the directors of

scientific institutes were bombarded with leaflets: 'When we have won, you and your like will be begging in the gutter.' Businessmen and heads of firms before engaging an employee made him or her sign a declaration saying: 'I swear that I believe in the theory of eternal ice.'[25]

Hörbiger was deeply fascinated by the origin and behaviour of moons, believing that they held the key to the way in which the Universe functions. For example, our present moon, Luna, is not the only satellite that the Earth has had: there have been at least six others, all of which crashed into the Earth, causing massive geological upheavals, so Hörbiger believed. According to Hörbiger, too, space is not a vacuum but is filled with hydrogen, which has the effect of slowing down celestial bodies in their courses, causing them to spiral in gradually towards their parent body. This, he maintained, is the ultimate fate of the Solar System, with all of the planets falling into the Sun. As they head inexorably towards their parent star, smaller planets occasionally are captured by larger worlds, becoming temporary satellites.

The Austrian engineer's theories were taken up and developed after his death by a British mythologist named Hans Schindler Bellamy, who wrote a book entitled *Moons, Myths and Man* based on the World Ice Theory.[26] Martin Gardner provides us with an admirably condensed summary of his odd beliefs. Bellamy concentrated his research on the period in which the pre-Lunar moon orbited Earth: since humanity was present at this time, it was able to preserve a record of the moon's cataclysmic collision with the Earth in the form of myths and legends. Bellamy refers to this satellite as the 'tertiary moon'. As it spiralled closer and closer to the Earth, its gravitational field pulled the world's oceans into a 'girdle tide', a gigantic, raised belt of water rising up from the equator. Humanity was forced by the resulting planet-wide glaciation to live in mountainous regions on either side of the girdle tide. As the tertiary moon drew closer, its orbital velocity increased until it was circling the Earth six times every day, its scarred and pitted surface apparently giving rise to the legends of dragons and other flying monsters.

When the moon reached a certain distance from the Earth, the planet's stronger gravitational field tore the satellite apart. The result was planet-wide rains and hail storms (all moons having thick coatings of ice on their surfaces), followed by bombardments of gigantic rocks and boulders as the moon finally disintegrated. With the moon gone, the girdle-tide of water collapsed, resulting in the Biblical Deluge.

Eventually, the Earth recovered from its titanic bruising, and this period of tranquillity gave rise to the legends of a Golden Age and earthly Paradise. However, with the arrival of the present moon, Luna, about 13,500 years ago, chaos reigned once again, with earthquakes, axial shifts and glaciation disfiguring the face of the planet. According to Bellamy, the Atlantean civilisation was destroyed in this cataclysm. He also believed that the *Book of Revelation* is actually a historical account of the destruction of the tertiary moon, and *Genesis* a description of the Earth's recovery following the collision.

For his own part, Hörbiger claimed that Luna is covered with a coating of ice 140 miles thick, and that ice also covers Mercury, Venus and Mars. In fact, the famous 'canals' on Mars (now known to be an optical illusion) are, in Hörbiger's warped cosmology, cracks on the surface of a 250-mile-deep frozen sea on the Martian surface. The Universe, Hörbiger maintained, was packed with gigantic blocks of ice, the action of which accounted for the majority of astronomical events. The Milky Way, for instance, was actually a ring of enormous blocks of ice, not hundreds of millions of stars as the doctored photographs of orthodox astronomy implied. Like moons, the blocks of ice also encounter resistance from the hydrogen with which space is filled, and also spiral into the Sun, causing sunspots when they hit.

Of course, the fact that a theory was idiotic was no barrier to its success in the Third Reich, and the World Ice Theory was eagerly embraced and disseminated by the Propaganda Ministry. Willy Ley records some of the statements made by representatives of the cult of WEL in its literature:

Our Nordic ancestors grew strong in ice and snow; belief in the World Ice is consequently the natural heritage of Nordic Man.

Just as it needed a child of Austrian culture – Hitler! – to put the Jewish politicians in their place, so it needed an Austrian to cleanse the world of Jewish science.

The Führer, by his very life, has proved how much a so-called 'amateur' can be superior to self-styled professionals; it needed another 'amateur' to give us complete understanding of the universe.[27]

Gardner, writing in the 1950s, ends his discussion of Hörbiger with the amusing comment (from our present perspective) that 'the Cosmic Ice Theory will find disciples until the first spaceship lands on the cratered surface of an iceless moon'.[28] He was certainly correct, and Hörbiger was certainly incorrect. However, it is difficult to resist the temptation to note the recent discovery of large ice deposits at the lunar poles, and the theory that they are the result of cometary impacts – comets being, of course, gigantic lumps of ice . . .

The Phantom Universe

The island of Rügen in the Baltic was the site of one of the most bizarre and misguided strategies of the Second World War. In April 1942, an expedition under the leadership of the infra-red ray specialist Dr Heinz Fisher and equipped with state-of-the-art radar sets landed on Rügen and began to make a series of observations. Fisher ordered the radar sets to be pointed at an angle of $45°$ into the sky, a position they maintained for several days. The reason for this peculiar experiment was to prove that the Earth is not a sphere floating in space but is actually a bubble set in an infinity of rock. With the radar pointed upwards at a $45°$ angle, it was hoped that the beams would be reflected back from objects at some distance along the internal surface of the bubble. It was also hoped that the radar would provide Fisher's team with an image of the British Fleet at Scapa Flow.[29]

According to Professor Gerard S. Kuiper of the Mount Palomar Observatory, who wrote several articles on the

Hollow Earth Theory: 'High officials in the German Admiralty and Air Force believed in the theory of a hollow Earth. They thought this would be useful for locating the whereabouts of the British Fleet, because the concave curvature of the Earth would facilitate long-distance observation by means of infra-red rays, which are less curved than visible rays.'[30]

Although they are not the most reliable of sources, Pauwels and Bergier nevertheless make a good point in their occult classic *The Morning of the Magicians* when they note that if our modern civilisation is unified by anything, it is by the fundamental agreement we reach over cosmology – in other words, we are at least able to agree that the Earth is a near-spherical object drifting in an immense void several billion light years in radius. It is one of the many indicators of the baffling and terrifying perversity of the Nazis that so many of them believed in this ridiculous inversion of reality:

The defenders of the Hollow Earth theory, who organized the famous para-scientific expedition to the island of Rügen, believed that we are living inside a globe fixed into a mass of rock extending to infinity, adhering to its concave sides. The sky is in the middle of this globe; it is a mass of bluish gas, with points of brilliant light which we mistake for stars. There are only the Sun and the Moon – both infinitely smaller than the orthodox astronomers think. This is the entire Universe. We are all alone, surrounded by rock.[31]

The origin of this idea, as applied in Nazi Germany, can be traced to 1918 and a young German aviator, Peter Bender, who came upon some old copies of Cyrus Teed's periodical, *The Sword of Fire*. Bender developed and 'refined' the theory (if such a term can be used) into what he called the *Hohlweltlehre* (Hollow World Theory), also enlisting the strange ideas of Marshall B. Gardner who had claimed that the Sun is actually inside the Earth on whose surface we are kept not by gravity but by the pressure of sunlight.[32] Bender claimed that the hollow bubble of the Earth was the same size as we believe our spherical Earth to be, with solar radiation keeping everything pressed to the concave surface. Beneath our feet is an infinite mass of rock; above our heads the atmosphere stretches to 45 miles, beyond which there is a hard vacuum. At the centre of this vacuum there are three objects: the Sun, the Moon and the Phantom Universe, which is a globe of blue gas containing the shining points of light astronomers mistake for stars.

> It is night over a part of this concave Earth when the blue mass passes in front of the Sun, and the shadow of this mass on the Moon produces eclipses . . . This theory of Bender's became popular round about the 1930s. The rulers of Germany and officers of the Admiralty and Air Force High Command believed that the Earth is hollow.[33]

The Rügen experiment was, of course, a miserable failure. The Nazi hierarchy turned their backs on the *Hohlweltlehre* and on Peter Bender himself, who was sent to his death in a concentration camp. Hörbiger's *Welteislehre*, with its equally ridiculous doctrine of the eternal conflict between ice and fire in an infinite Universe, won the day.

The Much-abused Admiral Byrd

Few twentieth-century personalities have been more closely connected with the Hollow Earth Theory – not to mention the theory that UFOs are man-made and are based in Antarctica – than the great Arctic and Antarctic explorer Rear Admiral Richard E. Byrd. As we shall see in this section, and in the final chapter of this book, Admiral Byrd's exploits in the fastness of the South Polar regions have become the stuff of legend, not only in the history of the exploration of our world but also in the fields of ufology, crypto-history and paranoiac conspiracy theory.

Born into an illustrious family at Winchester, Virginia in 1888, Byrd enrolled at the United States Naval Academy at the age of twenty, and received his commission four years later, in 1912. He learned to fly in the First World War, and retained a love of and fascination with flight for the rest of his life. Following the war of 1914–1918, he conducted a number of experiments in flight over water and out of sight of land (and thus without any landmarks by which to navigate), using various scientific instruments such as bubble sextants and drift indicators. His pioneering work with this aspect of navigation led to his being appointed by the US Navy to plan the first transatlantic flight in 1919. The trip was made by the US Navy Flying Boats NC1, NC3 and NC4 (the NC4 being the first plane to complete the flight, via Newfoundland and the Azores, in May of that year).[34]

Seven years later, in 1926, Byrd and Floyd Bennett became the first men to fly over the North Pole. Byrd had been appointed navigator on the proposed transpolar flight from Alaska to Spitzbergen of the US Navy dirigible *Shenandoah*; but the flight was cancelled by President Coolidge. Upon their return to New York, Byrd was asked by Roald Amundsen what his next objective would be. His response was matter-of-fact: to fly over the South Pole.

Byrd's first Antarctic Expedition (1928–1930) was the first to utilise aircraft, aerial cameras and snowmobiles. With his three planes – a Ford Tri-motor monoplane, a Fokker Universal and a Fairchild K3 monoplane – Byrd became the first explorer to combine aerial reconnaissance with ground surveys (making his expedition more important than that of Sir Hubert Wilkins, who had flown in Antarctica ten weeks previously).

The Second Byrd Antarctic Expedition (1933–1935) was, like the first, privately financed, thanks to the continuing American fascination with polar exploration. For most of the winter of 1934, Byrd remained alone in a meteorological hut some 120 miles into the Antarctic interior, conducting observations of the weather and aurora. These observations were the first of their kind, and nearly cost Byrd his life: he was rescued from the hut by other expedition members when he fell victim to carbon monoxide poisoning.

The United States Antarctic Service Expedition (1939–1941) was led by Byrd, but financed by the US Government.

Its objectives were contained within an order from President Roosevelt in November 1939, which was received by Byrd five days later on board his ship, the *North Star*, in the Panama Canal Zone. Roosevelt wanted two bases to be established: East Base would be set up near Charcot Island or Alexander I Land; West Base would be built near King Edward VII Land or on the Bay of Whales. The principal objective of the expedition was the mapping of the Antarctic coastline between meridians 72°W and 148°W, with additional mapping to be undertaken on the west coast of the Weddell Sea between Cape Eielson and the Luitpold Coast.

The expedition was a great success, with most of the mapping (700 miles of coastline) being achieved, and the establishing of two bases 1,600 miles apart by air. In addition, numerous scientific observations were made on the summit of the Antarctic Peninsula, including seismic, cosmic ray, auroral, biological, tidal and magnetic surveys. The bases were evacuated with the outbreak of the Second World War, during which Byrd returned to active service as the Chief of Naval Operations.

In the early post-war years, Byrd contributed to the organisation of the US Navy Antarctic Developments Project of 1946–1947, also known as 'Operation Highjump'. The project was one of the first military events of the Cold War, and was designed to offer US personnel experience of operating in polar conditions. Operation Highjump deployed 4,700 men, 33 aircraft, 13 ships and 10 caterpillar tractors, and also saw the first use of helicopters and icebreakers in Antarctica. Since Operation Highjump has become one of the most notorious and significant events in the crypto-history of post-war Nazi activities, we must leave an in-depth examination for the final chapter. For now, let us turn our attention to the reasons for Richard Byrd being so closely identified with the concept of a hollow Earth.

The blame can be laid firmly at the doors of three central figures in the Hollow Earth debate: Amadeo Giannini, Raymond Bernard and Ray Palmer. All three made astonishing claims regarding Rear Admiral Byrd's voyage over the North Pole in 1947 – a voyage that did not, in fact, take place: we have already seen that he was not in the Arctic in 1947 but in Antarctica. (Giannini got around this inconvenient fact by claiming that Byrd made a secret trip to the Arctic in 1947.) Before we meet these three fascinating characters, we must pause to consider their claims that, regardless of their veracity, have become central in the argument for a hollow Earth and which are still cited by proponents of this bizarre theory.

The claims arise from certain comments made by Byrd about the North Polar regions. In February 1947, Byrd reportedly said: 'I'd like to see that land beyond the Pole. That area beyond the Pole is the centre of the great unknown.' This was followed by his mythical flight in that year, which took him 1,700 miles beyond the North Pole. During this flight, he is said to have reported by radio that he saw vast areas of ice-free land with mountains, forests, lakes, rivers and lush vegetation. He even saw a large animal, resembling a mammoth, lumbering through the undergrowth![35] Nine years later, in January 1956, Byrd is said to have made similarly monumental discoveries during a United States expedition to Antarctica, during which they 'accomplished a flight of 2,700 miles from the base at McMurdo Sound, which is 400 miles west of the South Pole, and penetrated a land extent of 2,300 miles beyond the Pole'.[36] Upon his return, Byrd stated that the expedition had 'opened up a vast new land'. Shortly before his death in 1957, Byrd referred to 'that enchanted continent in the sky, land of everlasting mystery'.[37]

For believers in the hollow Earth, these statements were a godsend: apparently corroborative testimony from a highly respected explorer. The interpretation was straightforward: the Earth really does have a vast opening at each Pole, leading to the hollow interior, and it was into these openings that Byrd had flown. The 'vast new land' was actually the lip of the South Polar opening, the curvature of which was so gradual that Byrd did not realise he was well on his way into the inner Earth. The 'enchanted continent in the sky' was none other than the fabulous Rainbow City, home of the hidden super-civilisation that operated the UFOs.[38]

As the more responsible commentators on this subject state (often with noticeable relish), there is absolutely no evidence that the Earth is a hollow globe, and the statements attributed to Rear Admiral Byrd do not refer to journeys (witting or unwitting) into the Polar openings. As W. A. Harbinson and Joscelyn Godwin state, the 'great unknown' and the 'land beyond the Pole' are merely descriptions of those parts of Antarctica that had yet to be explored; the 'enchanted continent in the sky' was 'no more than a description of a phenomenon common in Antarctic conditions: the mirage-like reflection of the land below'.[39]

Harbinson continues with his sweeping away of the nonsense that has developed around Byrd's exploratory flights:

[W]hat, precisely, did Rear Admiral Byrd say? In extracts from his journal, published in the *National Geographic* magazine of October 1947, he wrote: 'As I write this, we are circling the South Pole . . . The Pole is approximately 2500 feet [760 metres] below us. On the other side of the Pole we are looking into that vast unknown area we have struggled so hard to reach.'

Did Byrd claim to have flown 1,700 miles (2,750 kilometres) beyond the North Pole in February 1947? No. Describing his flight beyond the South Pole on 16 February 1947 he wrote: 'We flew to approximately latitude 88°30' south, an estimated 100 miles [160 kilometres]. Then we made approximately a right-angle turn eastward until we reached the 45th east meridian, when we turned again, this time on the way back to Little America.'

Did Byrd report seeing on his journey, not ice and snow, but land areas consisting of mountains, forests, green vegetation, lakes and rivers: and, in the under-growth, a strange animal that resembled a mammoth? No. According to his journal: 'Altogether we had surveyed nearly 10,000 square miles [25,900 square kilometres] of "the country beyond the Pole". As was to be expected, although it is somewhat disappointing to report, there was no observable feature of any significance beyond the Pole. There was only the rolling white desert from horizon to horizon.'[40]

It is a fundamental feature of 'paranormal' debate that believers will always find a way around sceptics' arguments, and also, of course, that sceptics will always find a way to rubbish the evidence provided by believers. The Hollow Earth theory is no exception, and Rear Admiral Byrd's voyages of Polar discovery continue to be presented as incontrovertible proof of the existence of the Polar openings and the fabulous lands and creatures within, in spite of the fact that those voyages, epoch-making as they were, revealed little more than ice. As we shall now see, Byrd's flights served as the inspiration for ever more elaborate variations on the basic Hollow Earth theme.

Amadeo Giannini and the Physical Continuity of the Universe

The first writer to appropriate Rear Admiral Byrd's polar experiences (real or otherwise) in support of his own cosmological theories was Amadeo Giannini, who had had a kind of extrasensory revelation about the structure of the Earth and the surrounding Universe while walking through a forest in New England in October 1926. Like Symmes before him, Giannini spent many years attempting to gain both official recognition for his theory from orthodox scientists and astronomers and adequate funds to mount an expedition to the Polar regions to prove it. Again like Symmes, he was frustrated in both endeavours.

In 1959 he produced a book entitled *Worlds Beyond the Poles* that was published by the New York vanity publisher Vantage Press at a cost to Giannini of $3,000 and that set out, in confusing and badly written prose, his argument concerning what he called the 'Physical Continuity of the Universe'. The theory was bizarre even by the standards of the Hollow Earth thinking that had spawned Bender's

Hohlweltlehre. According to Giannini, our belief that the Earth is a sphere floating in space is the result of an optical illusion: the Earth is actually physically connected to the rest of the Universe at the Poles.

In Giannini's view, Byrd, in flying beyond the Poles, had managed to reach the lands connecting this world to the next. Indeed, according to David Hatcher Childress, Giannini was the first to quote the great explorer's words about the 'land beyond the pole' and the 'great unknown'. Giannini stated: 'It must be conceded that the land beyond to which Admiral Byrd referred had to be land beyond and out of bounds of theoretic Earth extent. If it had been considered part of the mathematized Earth it would not have been referred to as the "center of the great unknown." '[41] As we have already noted, it is a considerable leap of logic to take a poetic description of an unexplored land and claim that it connotes a hollow or infinitely extensive planet.

Ray Palmer, Richard Shaver and the Horror Beneath Our Feet

Anxious that his revolutionary theory should reach as wide an audience as possible, Giannini sent a copy of *Worlds Beyond the Poles* to the man most likely to give it a sympathetic reading: Raymond Palmer. Born in Milwaukee, Wisconsin in 1910, Palmer would become something of a Renaissance man in the fields of the bizarre and unusual, writing science fiction stories, editing pulp magazines and founding *Fate*, the world's longest-running journal of the paranormal.

It has to be said that life did not deal him the best of hands: at the age of seven he was run over by a truck and his back was broken; two years later, a failed spinal operation left him with a hunchback, and this, combined with a growth-hormone deficiency, resulted in an adult height of just four feet. Understandably enough, this led him to become something of a loner, with a voracious appetite for reading, particularly the fantastic romances that were becoming increasingly popular in the 1920s and 1930s. Palmer was also a great fan of Hugo Gernsback's pulp science fiction magazine *Amazing Stories*, the first of its kind. (The term 'pulp' comes from the low-grade paper on which these popular magazines were printed.) Palmer organised the first-ever science fiction fan club, the Science Correspondence Club, and founded the first SF fanzine, *The Comet*, in 1930. Over the next few years, he wrote a number of stories for the pulps before becoming editor of *Amazing Stories* in 1938. At that time, the magazine was in serious difficulties, but Palmer turned it around with an emphasis on romantic, suspenseful and picaresque adventures. Under his editorship, the magazine's circulation rose by several tens of thousands.[42]

The principal reason for the improvement in the fortunes of *Amazing Stories* was Palmer's knack of spotting what his reading public wanted and giving it to them, in spite of criticism from many of the 'hard' SF fans who later deserted him for John W. Campbell's *Astounding Science Fiction*, which published the technology-orientated fiction of people like Robert Heinlein, Isaac Asimov and A. E. van Vogt. However, the success or failure of magazines depends very much on their performance at the news-stands, and by that criterion *Amazing* was doing just fine. Palmer noticed that his readers seemed fascinated by the idea of lost civilisations – not to mention the paintings of nubile young women in skintight costumes that frequently graced the magazine's covers. This sexual imagery, combined with cosmic mysticism, seemed to Palmer a potentially lucrative mixture, and it did not escape his notice that *Amazing* always seemed to jump in circulation whenever it featured a story about Atlantis or Lemuria. This led Palmer to wonder how best he might capitalise on this curious interest among his readers. In late 1943, he found the answer in the form of a strange letter from a man named Richard Shaver.

Born in Berwick, Pennsylvania in 1907, Richard Sharpe Shaver was very fond of playing pranks on people, which earned him a somewhat dubious reputation. As a child, he had had two imaginary companions, one good, the other evil, who became more real to him than the living people around him.[43] After graduating from high school he worked for a meat packer and then a tree surgeon before moving to Detroit and enrolling in the Wicker School of Art. In 1930, Shaver joined a communist group called the John Reed Club (named after the American correspondent who had reported on the Russian Revolution).[44] Like just about everyone else, Shaver fell on hard times with the arrival of the Depression, but managed to eke out a living as a part-time art instructor at the Wicker Art School, supplementing his meagre income by going to a park and selling sketches of passers-by for 25 cents each.

In 1933, Shaver married a fellow art student named Sophie Gurivinch who had come originally from Kiev in the Ukraine. They had a daughter the same year, and Shaver took a job as a welder in Highland Park, Michigan. He continued in this job for about a year until he suffered heat stroke, lost the power of speech and was admitted to the Ypsilanti State Hospital for two weeks. In February 1934, Shaver's brother Tate, to whom he had been very close, died. His brother's death affected Shaver very badly and he became increasingly depressed and paranoid, claiming that people were following him. However, as Childress notes,[45] as a known communist, Shaver may well have been genuinely under surveillance.

Shaver received another blow when his wife Sophie died in a mysterious accident in her apartment (they were living separately at the time). While Shaver returned to his welding job, their daughter went to live with Sophie's parents (who apparently told her that her father, too, was dead).[46] For the next few years, Shaver travelled around North America, finding the odd job here and there and marrying again. The marriage was short-lived, his wife leaving him when she found papers indicating that he had been in a sanitarium. Shaver moved back to Pennsylvania and married for a third time.

In 1936, he came across an article in *Science World* magazine. Entitled 'The True Basis of Today's Alphabet' and written by a man named Albert F. Yeager, the article claimed that there were six letters in our alphabet that represented concepts in addition to sounds. These six letters could thus be used as a key to unlock the hidden meanings in words. In response to this article, Shaver wrote to *Science World*, claiming that he understood the hidden concepts behind *all* the letters of the alphabet. He called this conceptual language 'Mantong'.

After several years of work with the Mantong language, Shaver wrote the following letter to *Amazing Stories* in September 1943:

> Sirs:
> Am sending this in hopes you will insert it in an issue to keep it from dying with me. It would arouse a lot of discussion. Am sending you the language so that some time you can have it looked at by someone in the college or a friend who is a student of antique times. The language seems to me to be definite proof of the Atlantean legend.
> A great number of our English words have come down intact as romantic – ro man tic – 'science of man life patterning by control.' Trocadero – t ro see a dero – 'good one see a bad one' – applied now to theatre. This is perhaps the only copy of this language in existence and it represents my work over a long period of years. It is an immensely important find, suggesting the god legends have a base in some wiser race than modern man; but to understand it takes a good head as it contains multi-thoughts like many puns on the same subject. It is too deep for ordinary man – who thinks it is a mistake. A little study reveals ancient words in English occurring many times. It should be saved and placed in wise hands. I can't, will you? It really has an immense significance, and will perhaps put me right in your thoughts again if you will really understand this.
> I need a little encouragement.
> –R. S. Shaver, Barto, Pennsylvania[47]

Enclosed with this letter was the Roman alphabet together with its associated Mantong concepts, which Childress reprints in his excellent book *Lost Continents and the Hollow Earth*:

A – Animal (used AN for short)

B – Be (to exist – often command)

C – See

D – (also used DE) Disintegrant energy; Detrimental (most important symbol in language)

E – Energy (an all concept, including motion)

F – Fecund (use FE as in female – fecund man)

G – Generate (used GEN)

H – Human (some doubt on this one)

I – Self; Ego (same as our I)

J – (see G) (same as generate)

K – Kinetic (force of motion)

L – Life

M – Man

N – Child; Spore; Seed

O – Orifice (a source concept)

P – Power

Q – Quest (as question)

R – (used as AR) Horror (symbol of dangerous quantity of dis force in the object)

S – (SIS) (an important symbol of the sun)

T – (used as TE) (the most important symbol; origin of the cross symbol) Integration; Force of growth (the intake of T is cause of gravity; the force is T; tic meant science of growth; remains as credit word)

U – You

V – Vital (used as VI) (the stuff Mesmer calls animal magnetism; sex appeal)

W – Will

X – Conflict (crossed force lines)

Y – Why

Z – Zero (a quantity of energy of T neutralized by an equal quantity of D)[48]

By applying these strange hidden meanings behind the letters of the alphabet, one can perceive even stranger hidden meanings behind various words. Childress supplies a number of examples, but we need only detain ourselves with a couple. The word BAD, for instance, can be interpreted as 'Be a de', to be a destructive force. LADY is interpreted as 'Lay de', a complimentary term meaning to allay depression. The reader will note that in both of these examples, the letter D (DE) is used, meaning unpleasant, destructive and detrimental. The letters D and T were of great importance to Shaver, as we shall see shortly.

At this point, it is worth noting a peculiar similarity between Shaver's strange interpretation of the alphabet and the spurious power and significance perceived by Rudolf John Gorsleben, the Edda Society and Karl-Maria Wiligut in the runes of Norse mythology (see Chapters One and Six). In each case, a hidden history of humanity was to be discovered by careful examination of the components of written language – with the aid, that is, of an overheated imagination. It must be added, however, that in Shaver's case the result was harmless, if somewhat lurid entertainment; while the historical and linguistic fantasising of the Edda Society and its members became one of the motivators of racial hatred.

Shaver's letter landed on the desk of *Amazing*'s associate editor Howard Browne. Perhaps unsurprisingly, he threw it into his waste basket as soon as he had finished reading it, dismissing Shaver as a crackpot.[49] Palmer, however, was intrigued and decided to publish both the letter and the accompanying alphabet in the December 1943 issue of *Amazing Stories*. Alongside Shaver's material was a caption that read: 'We present this interesting letter concerning an ancient language with no comment, except to say that we applied the letter-meaning to the individual letters of many old root words and proper names and got an amazing "sense" out of them. Perhaps if readers interested were to apply his formula to more of these root words, we will [sic] be able to discover if the formula applies . . .'[50]

Palmer proved more perspicacious than his colleague Howard Browne: the December issue prompted hundreds of people to write in claiming that the Mantong alphabet really did release the hidden meanings of words. Encouraged by this response, Palmer wrote to Shaver asking for more information on the Mantong language and how his understanding of it had developed. Shaver responded by sending a 10,000-word manuscript evocatively entitled 'A Warning to Future Man'. Palmer felt that this was the circulation-booster he had been looking for: the article detailed the hidden history of the Earth, complete with ancient spacefaring civilisations, lost continents, sex, violence and high adventure. Shaver's writing style, however, was not as impressive as his subject matter, and Palmer decided to rewrite 'A Warning to Future Man', turning it into a 31,000-word story which he retitled 'I Remember Lemuria!' and published in the March 1945 issue of *Amazing Stories*.[51]

In this story and the many others that followed it (all of which were billed as true), Shaver painted a terrifying picture of a world honeycombed with vast caverns and tunnel systems containing enormous cities and advanced technology. Shaver's awareness of this world had begun while he was a welder in Highland Park in 1932. He realised that one of the welding guns was somehow allowing him to read the thoughts of his fellow workers in the factory. As if this were not bizarre enough, he also began to pick up the thoughts of evil creatures living far underground – creatures that apparently had the power to kidnap surface people and subject them to unthinkable tortures in their secret underground caverns. 'The voices came from beings I came to realize were not human; not normal modern men at all. They lived in great caves far beneath the surface. These alien minds I listened to seemed to know that they had great power, seemed conscious of the fact they were evil.'[52] This realisation proved too much for Shaver: he quit his job and embarked on the aimless wanderings through North America mentioned earlier. During this time he was tormented by invisible, deleterious rays projected at him by the evil subterraneans. Eventually, however, he was contacted by a beautiful young woman named Nydia who was a member of another subterranean group opposed to the evil ones. Needless to say, they became lovers and with her help Shaver was able to gain entry into the underworld and access the 'thought records' that contained the fantastic history of the Earth.

According to the thought records, the Sun was originally a huge planet whose coal beds were ignited by a meteor strike, transforming it into a star. Since this star burned coal(!), it radiated clean, positive energy. The Earth was then colonised by two spacefaring civilisations, the Titans and the Atlans, who possessed marvellous technological devices 'such as the ben-ray, which broadcast healing energies; the stim-ray, which prolonged and heightened sexual pleasure; the telesolidograph, which could broadcast three-dimensional images; the penetray, used to observe events from vast distances; and the telepathic augmenter or telaug, which transmitted thought.'[53]

The Atlans and Titans called the Earth Lemuria, and lived in Utopian bliss until 20,000 years ago, when the Sun's outer shell was destroyed and it entered its current phase, producing harmful radiation, called d, de or dis. This disintegrant energy is the opposite of t or te, the integrative, formative energy in Shaver's dualistic world view. Their immortality under threat, the Atlans and Titans excavated gargantuan caverns and tunnels far below Lemuria/Earth's surface, in which they built fantastically huge cities, the largest of which would dwarf New York or London. These subterranean realms shielded the entire Titan and Atlan population, some 50 billion individuals. However, the underground cities did not prove a permanent solution and 12,000 years ago Lemuria/Earth was abandoned in favour of younger star systems.[54]

Many Lemurians had already fallen victim to the debilitating effects of the Sun's harmful radiation and were forced to remain on Earth. Some of them moved to the surface (the reader will not be surprised to learn that these were the ancestors of *Homo sapiens*), while the ones who remained in the subterranean realms degenerated into a race of disfigured, idiotic and very malicious beings known as the 'dero'. This word is a contraction of 'abandondero', and is based on the Mantong words 'de' (meaning negative or destructive) and 'ro' (meaning subservient). Hence the deros were, literally, controlled by negative forces. The group to which Shaver's exotic girlfriend belonged are known as the 'tero', or integrative ro, 'te' denoting positive or constructive energy. The tero, who somehow managed to avoid contamination by the Sun's radiation, are locked in a constant struggle with their unpleasant cousins.

According to Shaver, the fiendish, sadistic and perverted dero kidnap thousands of hapless surface-dwellers every year, and take them into their cavern cities where they are tortured, sexually abused, used as slave labour or eaten. Although fundamentally stupid and brutal, the dero nevertheless know how to use the fabulous machinery left behind by the Lemurians and are able to spread evil and destruction throughout the world by means of dis rays. As Bruce Lanier Wright wryly notes: 'If you doubt this, you may be suffering from brain damage. Vast numbers of surface worlders – you, me, and most certainly Richard Shaver – have been slyly lobotomised by rays projected from the caverns.'[55]

The response to 'I Remember Lemuria!' was astonishing. Not only did the March 1945 issue of *Amazing* sell out but Palmer received a torrent of mail, numbering thousands of letters, many of which were from people claiming to have had bizarre experiences with the denizens of the fabulous subterranean world. One letter, from an ex-Air Force captain, read in part:

> For heaven's sake drop the whole thing! You are playing with dynamite. My companion and I fought our way out of a cave with submachine guns. I have two 9-inch scars on my left arm . . . [M]y friend has a hole the size of a dime in his right biceps. It was scarred inside. How we don't know. But we both believe we know more about The Shaver Mystery than any other pair . . . [D]on't print our names. We are not cowards, but we are not crazy.[56]

While the above may or may not be true (Childress suggests that Palmer himself may have fabricated it), there is no doubt that many thousands of people were deeply affected by 'the Shaver Mystery', and wrote to Palmer to tell him so. Many had tales of encounters with strange people who may have been deros, while others complained that they, too, were hearing bizarre voices in their heads. Some even claimed to have visited the cavern-world itself.

By now, the phrase 'paranoid schizophrenia' will surely have suggested itself to the reader. To be sure, Shaver's claims sound very much like he was suffering from this condition: the voices in the head experienced in connection with a mechanical device (the welding gun) are classic symptoms, as is the belief that unpleasant influences are being projected at the victim through air ducts, pipes and so on. As Peebles notes, paranoid schizophrenics 'commonly believe a death ray is causing health problems, destroying their brain, or causing them to hear voices'.[57] This sounds remarkably like what the hapless Shaver was apparently going through, and yet it falls far short of explaining why the number of letters to *Amazing Stories* jumped from 50 per month before the Shaver Mystery to 2,500 per month during and after, virtually all of which maintained that something sinister and terrifying really was going on beneath the Earth's surface.

Palmer himself was reluctant to commit himself on the veracity of Shaver's claims. While he invariably supported Shaver, he also suggested that the dero caverns might not exist as physical locations in this dimension, but rather on the astral plane. However, Palmer did make the perhaps inevitable claim that he himself had heard the voices of the cavern dwellers while visiting Shaver and his last wife, Dorothy, at their Pennsylvania home. Palmer claimed that he heard five disembodied voices discussing the dismemberment of a human being in a cavern four miles below. For his part, Shaver maintained that the deros and teros did not live on some astral plane but were solid, flesh-and-blood beings, and that the cavern world was a real place.

Despite its huge popularity with the readers of *Amazing Stories*, the Shaver Mystery prompted a powerful backlash among diverse groups, including hard science fiction fans who objected to a pornographic fantasy being marketed as truth (and who organised a campaign to boycott the magazine) and various occult groups who criticised Palmer for releasing information that would surely prove lethal to anyone inexperienced or foolish enough to attempt an exploration of the caverns. At the end of 1948, the Ziff-Davis Publishing Company, which published *Amazing*, decided that enough was enough, and the Shaver Mystery was dropped from the magazine, in spite of the fact that Shaver's 'revelations' had virtually doubled its readership and enabled it to move from quarterly to monthly publication.[58]

Palmer would later claim that the Shaver Mystery had been suppressed by a publisher 'too sedate' for material of this nature. However, Wright notes that Palmer's relations with Ziff-Davis had become rather strained, possibly as a result of his launching *Fate* magazine. (Palmer left *Amazing* in 1949 to concentrate on his new publication.)[59] According to Jim Probst in his book *Shaver: The Early Years*: 'The Queens Science Fiction League of New York passed a resolution that the Shaver stories endangered the sanity of their readers, and brought the resolution before the Society for the Suppression of Vice. A fan conference in Philadelphia was rocked by threats to draw up a petition to the Post Office, asking that *Amazing Stories* be banned from the mail.'[60]

This was not the end of the Shaver Mystery, however; it would later inspire a number of people to start their own publications. Richard Toronto published *Shavertron* between 1979 and 1985. Subtitled 'The Only Source of Post-Deluge Shaverania', the magazine reported on the continuing activities of the nefarious dero, such as the time they apparently interfered with Toronto's car while it was parked on a steep hillside and he was standing in front of it (Toronto barely managed to avoid being run over and killed).[61]

The Hollow Hassle was published by Mary Le Vesque between 1979 and 1983 and featured a regular column by the Rev Charles A. Marcoux, a fascinating and colourful character who claimed to have hunted the deros during his many cave explorations. In the August 1981 issue of *The Hollow Hassle* he wrote (in typically muddled syntax): 'My experiences in the cavern world began at a very young age with astral experiences in the caverns ever since my birth, and in other worlds from other dimensions too. I joined R. A. Palmer and R. S. Shaver's group in January of 1945, and I am one of the few original members left. I still "SEARCH FOR THE PORTALS," and as far as I know, am the only original member who does.'[62]

The Hollow Earth Insider ran for a few years in the early 1990s. Edited by Dennis Crenshaw, the journal included reprinted material by Shaver, in addition to news clippings and conspiracy theories, such as government (and dero) mind control. As Childress notes, the concept of mind control was central to the Shaver Mystery and adds the intriguing speculation that Shaver himself may well have been a victim. (We will take a closer look at the subject of mind control in the next chapter.)

Palmer made a last effort to perpetuate the Shaver Mystery in the early 1960s with *The Hidden World*, a trade paperback series that contained reprints of the original Shaver stories, together with yet more tales from people claiming to have encountered and been victimised by the fiendish deros. Unfortunately, *The Hidden World* was not particularly successful and publication ceased in 1964. Shaver himself claimed to have discovered pictorial records of the Titans and Atlans hidden within the rocks and stones of the Wisconsin prairies in the 1950s, and for the rest of his life tried in vain to persuade various scientists that they constituted final proof of the reality of the cavern world. He died of a heart attack in 1975. Palmer continued to publish journals, although none even approached the success of *Amazing Stories* and *Fate*. He died in 1977.

Before we continue, we must pause to examine what Palmer and many others considered to be the most impressive evidence for the Hollow Earth Theory, and which is still cited as proof that we are indeed living on the surface of a hollow sphere. In view of the ease with which this 'evidence' can be dismissed (and has been by a number of the more responsible commentators on this subject), it is surprising that so many writers still cling to it with such misguided tenacity.

In 1970, the Environmental Science Service Administration of the US Department of Commerce made public a collection of photographs taken by their weather satellite ESSA-7 in November 1968. Several of these photographs contained, at first sight, an absolutely extraordinary image: an enormous dark area where the Earth's North Pole should have been. When Palmer saw the photographs, he had no hesitation in reproducing them in his magazine *Flying Saucers*, with an accompanying article stating that here, at last, was the proof – and from an official source – that there was indeed a gigantic opening at the North Pole, leading to the hollow interior of the planet.

The true reason for the dark area in the photographs was nowhere near as romantic and exciting as the Hollow Earthers would have their readers believe. The ESSA-7 photographs were actually photomosaics containing many hundreds of elements, rather than single exposures. Due to the satellite's orbital trajectory, the area at and immediately around the Pole had not been included in these photomosaics – they had simply not been photographed, and thus showed up as dark areas on the images. Unfortunately, this explanation has not dissuaded certain sensationalist writers from citing the ESSA-7 pictures, even to this day, as conclusive proof that the Earth is hollow.[63]

There is perhaps some truth in Peebles's assertion that the Shaver Mystery constituted, in effect, a modern mythology that served a number of functions, including escapism from post-war reality and the incipient threat of the Cold War; an answer to the question of why there was so much evil and suffering in the world; and, of course, an exciting corollary to the perceived menace of Communism: a new enemy whose very existence could be used to define the contrasting, positive attributes of the American Way. Palmer himself was a clever manipulator (if that is not too strong a word) of the public need both for escapism and for an explanation of the violence and evil that seemed to characterise life on Earth (it was all the fault of the deros). This was further illustrated by his reaction to the rise of the UFO mystery, which came to the world's attention with Kenneth Arnold's sighting of nine crescent-shaped objects over Mount Rainier in Washington State on 24 June 1947. Arnold's sighting was followed by a torrent of reports of strange objects flitting through the skies. In the pages of *Fate* magazine, Palmer instantly provided the answer to the puzzle: some of the UFOs were indeed alien spacecraft, but most were vessels piloted by the denizens of the cavern world. (We will look much more closely at the UFO mystery, which has become intimately connected to the idea of Nazi survival, in the next chapter.) Whatever the underlying truth (if any) of the claims of Shaver, Palmer and others about the strange and frightening drama constantly being played out beneath our feet, the Shaver Mystery has come to define the Hollow Earth Theory in the twentieth century and now occupies a central position in the complex network of rumours, speculations, crypto-historical inferences, anomalous events and genuine government violations of public trust that constitutes modern conspiracy theory.

Raymond Bernard and the 'Greatest Geographical Discovery in History'

Perhaps the most famous of all books published on the subject of the hollow Earth is entitled (unsurprisingly) *The Hollow Earth* and is subtitled (unbelievably) 'The Greatest Geographical Discovery in History'. Its author was yet another colourful and far from trustworthy personality named Walter Siegmeister, although he also went under other names, for reasons that will become clear.

Siegmeister was born in New York in 1901. His father's occupation as a doctor perhaps had something to do with the boy's intense fascination with sexual reproduction and the male and female reproductive anatomy (he was particularly interested in menstruation).[64] After completing his education at Columbia University and New York University (he gained a bachelor's degree from Columbia in 1924 and a master's degree and doctorate from NYU in 1930 and 1932), Siegmeister moved to Florida in 1933 where he published a newsletter entitled *Diet and Health*, through which he promulgated his opinions on the benefits of raw food and a healthy lifestyle.

After a disastrous business partnership with a confidence trickster named G. R. Clements, during which they sold useless, waterlogged land to people wishing to grow crops, Siegmeister fled the United States and the legal action with

Heinrich Himmler (1900–1945) Reichsführer-SS, chief of the German Police
(*The Trustees of the Imperial War Museum, London*)

1·9·1·9

Thule-Gesellschaft

Madame Blavatsky, (1831–1891) founder of the Theosophical Society (*Fortean Picture Library*)

Thule Society emblem (*David Hatcher Childress*)

Plastic swastika badges. Each depicts the use of the swastika in antiquity – a subject dear to Himmler's heart (*Robin Lumsden*)

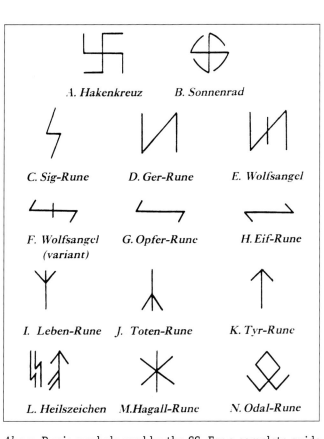

A. Hakenkreuz B. Sonnenrad

C. Sig-Rune D. Ger-Rune E. Wolfsangel

F. Wolfsangel (variant) G. Opfer-Rune H. Eif-Rune

I. Leben-Rune J. Toten-Rune K. Tyr-Rune

L. Heilszeichen M. Hagall-Rune N. Odal-Rune

Above Runic symbols used by the SS. For a complete guide to runic symbols as used by the SS, see Robin Lumsden's *Himmler's Black Order 1923–1945* (Sutton Publishing)

Above Karl-Maria Wiligut-Weisthor in 1936 (*Kreismuseum Wewelsburg*)

Below This oak shield, carved with runic symbols, was typical of the wall decorations hung in Wewelsberg castle (*Robin Lumsden*)

Various views of the 'totenkopf' or death's head ring, displaying runic symbols (*Robin Lumsden*)

Above Hitler speaking in the Reichstag (*The Trustees of the Imperial War Museum, London*)

Below A Nazi rally, 1936 (*The Trustees of the Imperial War Museum, London*)

Above The Externsteine in the Teutoburger Wald near Paderborn, Germany – a place of mythological significance in Aryan history (*Karl Aarsleff/Fortean Picture Library*)

Above A pseudo-pagan solstice celebration 1937, sponsored by the SS and held in the Berlin Olympic Stadium (*Robin Lumsden*)

Right Hitler in 'blood banner' ceremony. A feature of Nazi rallies was the dedication of new standards. This was always done by Hitler who held a corner of the banner in his hand and joined this with the banner that was to be dedicated. He then shook hands with the senior officer of the escort, in this case a Standarten-führer of the S.A. (*The Trustees of the Imperial War Museum, London*)

Edward G. E. L. Bulwer-Lytton (1803–1873), author of *The Coming Race* (*Mary Evans Picture Library*)

Pulp science fiction writer Richard Shaver's *Hidden World* series (*Fortean Picture Library*)

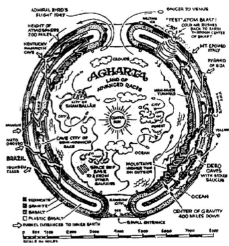

Above Map of the mythical realms of Agharta and Shambala (*SpiritWeb*)

Left German scientist Neupert's illustration of the 'hollow earth' 1935 (*Mary Evans Picture Library*)

Left Rear Admiral Richard Evelyn Byrd (1888–1957) flew Over the South Pole on 29 November 1929 with three companions and Igloo his pet terrier (*Fortean Picture Library*)

Above Emblem of the Deutsche Antarktische Expedition 1938–9 (*David Hatcher Childress*)

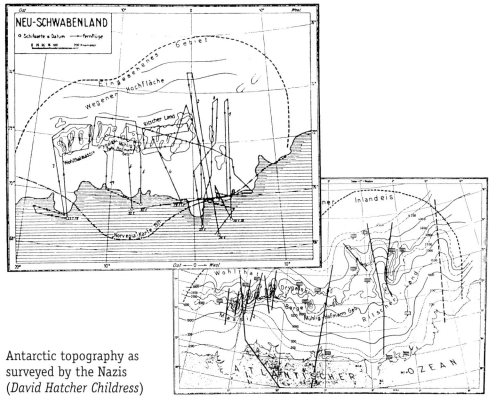

Antarctic topography as surveyed by the Nazis (*David Hatcher Childress*)

Above left Nazi Germany's wartime rocket chief Walter Dornberger seen here on the left with Werner von Braun in 1944 (*David Hatcher Childress*)

Above right Dornberger in 1954 after entering the United States under Project Paperclip. He went on to emerge as senior executive of the Bell Aerosystems Division of Textron (*David Hatcher Childress*)

Left Viktor Schauberger (1885–1958), Austrian inventor of a number of 'flying discs' who supposedly worked on a top secret project in Texas after the war. On his death bed he said over and over: 'They took everything from me. I don't even own myself.' (*David Hatcher Childress*)

Below left Artist's impression of a Schriever flying disc (©*Lee Krystek 1998*)

Below right Artist's impression of the Bellonzo Schriever-Miethe Disc (© *James H. Nichols 1991*)

which he was threatened, and went to Equador in 1941. There he met a friend, John Wierlo, who had moved from America the previous year, and together they conceived the idea of creating a new Utopia and a 'super-race' somewhere in the jungles in the east of the country. The 'Adam' of this scheme would be Wierlo (by all accounts an impressive example of manhood); the 'Eve' would be a 24-year-old woman named Marian Windish, a hermit who had apparently lived for two years in the Equadorian jungle.[65] The new Utopia, however, was not to be: Wierlo later claimed that he had no intention of creating a super-race, and it also transpired that Marian Windish was already married. Wierlo also accused Siegmeister of faking an ability to walk on water by means of a series of supports just below the surface. So outlandish were Siegmeister's claims of miraculous powers and meetings with Tibetan masters on Equadorian mountains (many of which appeared in the American press) that he was forbidden from using the US Mail Service and deported by the Equadorian Immigration Department.[66]

Upon his return to the United States, Siegmeister, now using the name Dr Robert Raymond, continued his promotion of a healthy diet by selling health foods and two books he had written, entitled *Are You Being Poisoned by the Food You Eat?* and *Super-Health thru Organic Super-Foods*. He then began travelling again throughout South America, selling his books through mail order, now under the name Dr Uriel Adriana, AB, MA, PhD. When his mother died in 1955, leaving him a substantial amount of money, he moved to Brazil and bought a large plot of land with the intention of continuing his efforts to create a super-race. In his 1955 book *Escape From Destruction*, which he again wrote under the pseudonym Raymond Bernard, he warned of a coming nuclear war, from which a few people would be saved by extraterrestrials who would take them to Mars.[67]

While in Brazil, Siegmeister came across an odd book entitled *From the Subterranean World to the Sky* by one O. C. Huguenin who seems to have held a high position in the Brazilian Theosophical Society. In common with Shaver, Huguenin claimed that the UFOs were the handiwork of an ancient civilisation (Huguenin claimed they were the Atlanteans) that had built them 12,000 years ago, just before the destruction of their continent. Some Atlanteans escaped the cataclysm by taking their craft through the Polar openings and re-establishing their fabulous civilisation in the inner Earth. The reason UFOs were being seen by so many surface dwellers was that the Atlanteans were concerned at humanity's use of nuclear energy (concerns that were also attributed to the so-called 'Space Brothers' by the American contactees of the 1950s – see Chapter Eight).

At this time, two Theosophist friends of Huguenin, Commander Paulo Strauss and Professor Henrique de Souza, were also actively promoting in Brazil the idea of the hollow Earth: Strauss by lecturing widely about a UFO base called Agharta, and de Souza by claiming that he was in contact with the Atlanteans.[68] Siegmeister also claimed to have met an Atlantean woman (who looked like an eighteen-year-old, but who was actually 70) at the Theosophical Society Headquarters in São Lourenço. At one of these meetings, de Souza told Siegmeister that Brazil contained a number of tunnels leading down to the inner Earth (Childress notes that one of the tunnels was supposed to be in the Roncador Mountains of the Matto Grosso, the region in which the famous explorer Colonel Percy Fawcett disappeared in 1925).[69] According to de Souza, Fawcett was still alive and well in an Atlantean city, although he was prevented from leaving in case the surface dwellers forced him to reveal its whereabouts. Although he claimed to have made many trips into the Roncador Mountains, Siegmeister never found any of the tunnel entrances.

When some friends in America sent him a copy of Ray Palmer's journal *Flying Saucers*, containing articles about Rear Admiral Byrd's flights and the Hollow Earth Theory, Siegmeister went into creative overdrive, writing *Agharta, The Subterranean World* and *Flying Saucers from the Earth's Interior*. At this time, 1960, Siegmeister received a letter from one Ottmar Kaub, who was a member of an organisation called UFO World Research based in St Louis, Missouri. Kaub was writing on behalf of the organisation's leader, Dr George

Marlo, who claimed to have visited the inner Earth on board a UFO, and who wished to live at Siegmeister's Brazilian colony. Dr Marlo claimed to know two beings called Sol-Mar and Zola, who lived in a city called Masars II, underneath South Africa. Sol-Mar and Zola described the inner Earth as a paradise with a perfect climate, giant fruits, beautiful birds with 30-foot wingspans, and where the people grew to over 12 feet tall.[70]

For the next few years, Marlo tantalised Siegmeister with promises of a meeting with Sol-Mar and Zola – meetings that were always unavoidably postponed for various reasons. Eventually, Siegmeister realised that Marlo was lying about his contacts with the Inner Earthers and decided to continue his researches alone.

In 1964, he managed to find a New York publisher for his last book, *The Hollow Earth*, which was largely a rewrite of *Flying Saucers from the Earth's Interior* and also borrowed heavily from Reed, Gardner and Giannini. The book sold well, but unfortunately Siegmeister did not live to enjoy its success: he died of pneumonia in 1965. Although *The Hollow Earth* contains a great deal of material from earlier writers, it is distinguished by its lengthy treatment of the idea that the governments of the world are well aware of the 'fact' that UFOs are spacecraft, and that they come from the inner Earth (it was one of the first books to pay serious attention to this idea). In addition, Siegmeister was one of the first writers to suggest that the US and Soviet Governments were secret allies in the face of the potential threat posed by the Inner Earth civilisation, a claim that has become an integral part of modern conspiracy theory.[71]

Siegmeister's greatest legacy, however, must be the identification of Brazil as the most significant location in the mythology of the hollow Earth. Not only is that country a hot spot for UFO activity and encounters with apparent 'aliens', it also contains possibly more subterranean tunnel networks and entrances to the inner Earth than any other country. Before moving on, we may cast a glance at some of the reports that have recently been coming out of Brazil concerning some rather unusual discoveries. For instance, the Brazilian organisation Sociedade de Estudos Extraterrestres (SOCEX) has spent the last few years investigating claims that an elaborate tunnel network exists in the mountains of Santa Catarina and Parana States, particularly around the town of Joinville about 190 miles south-west of São Paulo (which, oddly enough, was Siegmeister's base of operations in Brazil).[72]

In another SOCEX report, two men entered a tunnel near the city of Ponta Grossa, 250 miles south-west of São Paulo, in which they discovered a staircase leading further underground. Descending the staircase, the men found themselves in a small underground city, where they remained for five days with its 50 inhabitants. Many people have reported UFOs in the area, and some say they have heard singing, the voices apparently coming from underground.[73]

While these stories may be taken with a large grain of salt (their protagonists are invariably referred to by pseudonyms or just initials), the claim that Brazil, and indeed the rest of South America, is an important centre of UFO activity and of the belief in powerful subterranean civilisations is of considerable significance to the present study. In South America we find the nexus of the ideas we shall be discussing in the last two chapters of this book: firstly, that by the end of the Second World War the Nazis had begun to develop aircraft and weapons systems radically in advance of anything in use elsewhere at the time; and secondly, that Nazism as a potent political force did not cease to exist with the defeat of the Third Reich but continues in one or more secret locations, still exerting a powerful influence on world events.

As with most aspects of what may broadly be termed 'the paranormal', the concepts of Nazi occultism and genuine Nazi occult power (the former a verifiable historical fact, the latter an unsafe extrapolation based on rumour and hearsay) have merged into one another to such a degree that a clear line of dichotomy between the two has become virtually impossible to define. This will become especially apparent as we conclude this chapter on the hollow Earth and subterranean civilisations with a look at the tunnel system that is said to exist beneath South America. While legends of tunnels beneath South America have existed ever since the Spanish conquest of the continent, referring to the mysterious places where the Incas were said to have hidden most of their gold, there is some evidence for their actual existence. Some modern explorers even claim to have visited them.

Chief among these is David Hatcher Childress, who has written many books on the more unorthodox aspects of archaeology and who offers an account of one such adventure he undertook in his fascinating and informative study of the Shaver Mystery and the Hollow Earth Theory, *Lost Continents and the Hollow Earth*. Childress describes how he followed a lead provided in a letter sent to him by one of his South American readers, named Marli, who described an opening leading to a tunnel system near the small mountain town of São Tomé das Lettres, north of São Paulo.

Childress travelled to the town with Marli, and in a local restaurant they listened, together with about twenty others, to the owner as he told a strange story of a man-made tunnel extending far into the earth. Marli translated the restaurant owner's Portugese:

'The Brazilian army went into the tunnel one time to find out where it ends. After travelling for four days through the tunnel the team of Army explorers eventually came to a large room deep underground. This room had four openings to four tunnels, each going in a different direction. They had arrived in the room by one of the tunnels.

'They stayed in the room for some time, using it as their base, and attempted to explore each of the other three tunnels, but after following each for some time, turned back to the large room. Eventually they returned to the surface, here at São Tomé das Lettres.

'. . . [T]here is a man here in town who claims to know the tunnel and claims that he has been many weeks inside the tunnel. This man claims that the tunnel goes all the way to Peru, to Machu Picchu in the

Andes. This man claims that he went completely under South America, across Brazil and to Machu Picchu.[74]

The restaurant owner went on to tell how he himself had encountered a strange man near the tunnel entrance one morning. The man was dressed in traditional Andean Indian clothes, and was extremely tall, approximately seven feet. As soon as he saw the restaurant owner, the man walked away without saying anything.

Childress goes on to report that the following morning he, Marli and a fellow explorer named Carl Hart went to the tunnel entrance with the intention of exploring as far as they could. He continues:

> I was amazed at this ancient feat of engineering. We were descending down into the earth in a wide, gradually sloping tunnel that was dug into a red, clay-type dirt. It was not the smooth, laser-cut rock walls that Erich von Däniken had claimed to have seen in Equador in his book *Gold of the Gods*, but it was just as incredible.
>
> It wouldn't have taken some space-age device to make this tunnel, just simple tools; yet, it was clearly a colossal undertaking. Why would anyone build such a tunnel? Was it an ancient mine that went deep into the earth, searching for an elusive vein of gold or merely red clay for the long-gone ceramic kilns? Was it an elaborate escape tunnel used in the horrific wars that were said to have been fought in South America – and around the world – in the distant past? Or was it some bizarre subterranean road that linked up with other tunnels in the Andes and ultimately could be used to journey safely to such places as Machu Picchu, Cuzco or the Atacama Desert?[75]

In the event, the answers to these questions evaded the small party: after an hour, they arrived at a point where the floor dropped approximately one metre, and decided that this was a convenient place to turn back, since the tunnel seemed to continue endlessly on, and they were not equipped for a lengthy exploration. Although the group did not encounter any fabulous wonders of the subterranean realm, the very existence of the tunnel proves that the legends associated with South America have some basis in fact.

8 The cloud Reich

Nazi Flying Discs

S O FAR IN THIS BOOK we have looked at some extremely strange notions, many of which were held by the Nazis themselves and many by certain writers who have, over the years, attempted to prove that the Third Reich was ruled by men who were, quite literally, practitioners of Black Magic. We now come to a subject that, at first sight, might seem somewhat out of place in our survey, and yet the suggestion has been frequently made that the UFOs (unidentified flying objects) first reported in the late 1940s were the products of experimental aircraft designs that were developed towards the end of the Second World War. Most (if not all) serious historians would throw up their hands in horror at the very mention of such a seemingly ludicrous idea, particularly when one considers the associated claims that, since sightings of UFOs are still reported today by thousands of people around the world, these radical aircraft designs must have been captured, copied and further developed by the victorious powers; and, what is more, that some UFOs may even be piloted by escaped Nazis operating out of one or more hidden bases.

As will surely be apparent from the material we have examined so far, the Nazi occultist idea is both bizarre and complicated, not least because it encompasses several additional fields of arcane knowledge and speculation. We have already seen how the Nazi élite were fascinated by the concepts of the Holy Grail and the Knights Templar, by Eastern mysticism and the Hollow Earth theory, by odd cosmological concepts and the hidden legacies of fabulous, long-vanished civilisations. In fact, the notion of the secret transmission of esoteric information through history (as discussed in Chapter Three, concerning the story of the Knights Templar following their suppression) can also be applied to the Nazis themselves and their awful legacy of racial hatred. While many would think that this legacy is confined to the demented ravings of a few groups of neo-fascists in Europe and America, there is some evidence to suggest that the truth may be far more sinister and frightening. This evidence, which has been gathered and presented over the years by investigators of the UFO phenomenon, as well as by those with an interest in the more unusual German weapons designs of the Second World War, points to the possibility that some extremely advanced aircraft designs did actually reach the prototype stage in 1944 and 1945. Those researchers who have uncovered this evidence, and whom we shall meet in this chapter, have also taken the logical next step of suggesting that the Americans and Russians captured a number of designs at the end of the war and continued their development throughout the post-war years. In addition, they suggest that many leading Nazis (including, according to some accounts, Hitler himself) were able to escape the ruins of the Third Reich and continue their nefarious plans for world domination in the icy fastnesses of the Arctic and Antarctic.

Could there possibly be any truth to these incredible speculations? Could UFOs actually be man-made air- and spacecraft? Could some of them belong to a hidden 'Fourth Reich' that represents a cancer that was not, after all, cut from the body of humankind? To deal with these questions, we must, once again, enter the curious realm of crypto-history, where the line between reality and fantastic rumour becomes blurred and indistinct; in short, we must return to Pauwels's and Bergier's 'Absolute Elsewhere'. In this realm, science and occultism meet, as do theories of vast historical conspiracies and outrageous cosmological speculations. The claims about the survival of the Nazis are connected to all these fields, and depend to a great extent on the use of highly advanced technology and resources by secret forces.

The Mystery of the UFOs

Although human beings have been seeing strange things in the skies since the dawn of history, the idea that some of them are actually technological devices (called by some 'X Devices', although that term is now obsolete) is relatively recent. The first person to suggest that mysterious objects and lights in the sky might be machines from another planet was probably the great American anomalist Charles Fort (1874–1932); however, it was not until the late 1940s that the idea began to gain a wider currency, following the famous sighting by pilot Kenneth Arnold over the Cascade Mountains in Washington State on 24 June 1947.

The UFO mystery has never gone away, and has certainly never been explained to universal satisfaction: indeed, it is now more deeply ingrained in the public consciousness than ever before, and the 'flying saucer' can truthfully be described as one of the great cultural icons of the twentieth century. While sceptics would argue that the reason for this is a mixture of wishful thinking, the misidentification of mundane phenomena and out-and-out hoaxes, the truth of the matter is more subtle and complex. It is certainly true that approximately 95 per cent of sightings can be attributed to stars, planets, meteorites, satellites, aircraft and so on; yet there remains the tantalising five per cent that cannot be explained so easily.

In order to illustrate this fact, we can look very briefly at one of the classic UFO sightings from the early days of modern ufology. (Although there are many impressive sightings from the 1990s, they are still the subject of intense debate and I believe it is more prudent to choose a sighting that has stood the test of time and is still regarded as almost certainly genuine.) At about 7.45 on the evening of 11 May 1950, Mr and Mrs Paul Trent watched a large object fly over their farm near McMinnville, Oregon, USA. Mrs Trent had been out feeding their rabbits when she noticed the UFO. She called her husband, who was able to take two black-and-white photographs of it. The photographs show a circular object with a flat undersurface and a bevelled edge; extending from the upper surface of the object is a curious structure reminiscent of a submarine conning tower, which is offset slightly from the vertical axis.

The bright, silvery object was tilted slightly as it moved across the sky in absolute silence, and presently was lost to view. The Trents later said that they had felt a slight breeze from the underside of the UFO. The Trents sought no publicity following their sighting (in fact, they waited until they had used up the remainder of the camera's film before having the UFO photographs developed!); they mentioned the incident to only a few friends. However, news of the sighting quickly spread to a reporter from the local *McMinnville Telephone Register* who visited the Trents and found the photographic negatives under a writing desk where the Trent children had been playing with them.[1] A week later, the photographs appeared in *Life* magazine and became world-famous.

Seventeen years later, the McMinnville UFO sighting was investigated by William K. Hartmann and was included in the famous (and, in the UFO community, widely despised) *Condon Report* produced by the US Air Force-sponsored Colorado University Commission of Enquiry. The *Condon Report* (named after the enquiry's leader, the respected physicist Dr Edward U. Condon) was dismissive of the UFO phenomenon, which it considered to be of no interest to science. However, the report contained a number of cases that it conceded were not amenable to any conventional explanation. One of these cases was the McMinnville sighting. The photographs were submitted to extremely rigorous scientific analysis, after which Hartmann concluded:

This is one of the few UFO reports in which all factors investigated, geometric, psychological, and physical, appear to be consistent with the assertion that an extraordinary flying object, silvery, metallic, disk-shaped, tens of meters in diameter, and evidently artificial, flew within sight of two witnesses. It cannot be said that the evidence positively rules out a fabrication, although there are some physical factors such as the accuracy of certain photometric measures of the original negatives which argue against a fabrication.[2]

In the 50 or so years since the Trents had their strange encounter, the photographs have been repeatedly subjected to more and more sophisticated analyses, and have passed every test. This case is just one of a large number of sightings of highly unusual, apparently intelligently guided objects, seen both in the skies and on the ground, that have been occurring for decades. There are, of course, various theories to account for these sightings, aside from the sceptical notion that all are, without exception, hoaxes, illusions or misidentifications of ordinary phenomena.

The most widely accepted theory is, of course, the Extraterrestrial Hypothesis (ETH), which holds that genuine UFOs are spacecraft piloted by explorers from another planet. This theory has the greatest currency in the United States. In Europe, more credence is given to an alternative theory known as the Psychosocial Hypothesis, which suggests that encounters with UFOs and 'aliens' may be due to subtle and ill-understood processes occurring within the mind of the percipient. Inspired by the Swiss psychoanalyst Carl G. Jung, who examined UFOs in his book *Flying Saucers: A Modern Myth of Things Seen in the Sky* (1959), the psychosociologists see such encounters as similar to waking dreams that fulfil an undefined psychic need. (To Jung, the circular shape of the UFO suggested a psychic need for wholeness and unity, represented by the mandala, a circular symbol identified by Jung as one of the archetypes residing in humanity's collective unconscious.)

There are a number of secondary theories for UFOs, including the idea that they are time machines from the future, that they are actually living beings indigenous to interplanetary space, that they originate in other dimensions of existence and so on, all of which are beyond the scope of this book. The idea that UFOs are man-made, and based on plans captured by the Allies in the ruins of Nazi Germany at the end of the Second World War, has been put forward by a number of writers and researchers. Outlandish as it may sound, it is actually well worth examining the evidence for 'Nazi flying saucers'.

The Foo Fighters

Although it set the stage for the drama of modern ufology, Kenneth Arnold's 1947 sighting of nine anomalous objects flitting between the peaks of the Cascade Mountains was not the first twentieth-century UFO encounter. In the closing stages of the Second World War, Allied pilots on night-time bombing raids over Europe frequently reported strange flying objects. These objects were christened 'Foo Fighters', after a catchphrase in the popular *Smokey Stover* comic strip. 'Where there's foo, there's fire.' ('Foo' was also a play on the French word *feu*, meaning fire.) The aircrews suspected that the objects might be some kind of German secret weapon. On 2 January 1945, the New York *Herald Tribune* carried the following brief Associated Press release:

> Now, it seems, the Nazis have thrown something new into the night skies over Germany. It is the weird, mysterious 'Foo fighter' balls which race alongside the wings of Beaufighters flying intruder missions over Germany. Pilots have been encountering this eerie weapon for more than a month in their night flights. No one apparently knows what this sky weapon is. The 'balls of fire' appear suddenly and accompany the planes for miles. They seem to be radio-controlled from the ground, so official intelligence reports reveal.[3]

In their book *Man-Made UFOs* (1994), Renato Vesco (a pioneer of the Nazi-UFO hypothesis) and David Hatcher Childress cite the testimony of a former American flying officer who had worked for the intelligence section of the Eighth Air Force towards the end of the war. Wishing to remain anonymous, the officer said to the New York press:

'It is quite possible that the flying saucers are the latest development of a "psychological" anti-aircraft weapon that the Germans had already used. During night missions over western Germany I happened to see on several occasions shining discs or balls that followed our formations. It was well known that the German night fighters had powerful headlights in their noses or propeller hubs – lights that would suddenly catch the target, partly in order to give the German pilots better aim but mostly in order to blind the enemy tail gunners in their turrets. They caused frequent alarms and continual nervous tension among the crews, thereby lowering their efficiency. During the last year of the war the Germans also sent up a number of radio-controlled bright objects to interfere with the ignition systems of our engines or the operation of the on-board radar. In all probability American scientists picked up this invention and are now perfecting it so that it will be on a par with the new offensive and defensive air weapons.'[4]

Unfortunately, Vesco and Childress are not forthcoming with a detailed reference for this statement.

The British UFO investigators Peter Hough and Jenny Randles make the interesting point that the Second World War saw more people in the skies than any other prior period, and that it was therefore no great surprise that UFOs should have been spotted in abundance.[5] Of course, this statement carries the implication of a likely nonhuman origin of the objects, which advocates of the Nazi-UFO hypothesis hotly dispute: for them, the large number of Foo Fighter sightings, coupled with the obvious interest the objects showed in Allied aircraft, strongly implies that they were built specifically to interact in some way with those aircraft.

As is so often the case with the UFO mystery, genuine sightings generated various rumours of official interest in the phenomenon. For instance, there was, allegedly, a secret British government investigation into the Foo Fighter reports called the Massey Project. 'However,' write Hough and Randles, 'Air Chief Marshal Sir Victor Goddard – who was an outspoken believer in alien craft during the 1950s – flatly denied this and said that Treasury approval for such a minor exercise at a time when Britain was fighting for its survival would have been ludicrous.'[6]

Some encounters undoubtedly had mundane explanations. For example, during a bombing raid on a factory at Schweinfurt, Germany on 14 October 1943, flight crews of the American 384th Squadron observed a large cluster of discs, which were silver in colour, one inch thick and about three inches in diameter. They were floating gently down through the air directly in the path of the American aircraft, and one pilot feared that his B-17 Flying Fortress would be destroyed on contact with the objects. However, the bomber cut through the cluster of discs and continued on its way undamaged. It is quite possible that encounters such as this were actually with 'chaff', pieces of metal foil released by German Aphrodite balloons to confuse radar by returning false images.[7]

Nevertheless, many aircrews reported events that were not so easy to explain, including the harassment of their aircraft by small, glowing, disc-shaped and spherical objects that were highly manoeuvrable. On 23 November 1944, Lieutenant Edward Schlueter of the 415th US Night Fighter Squadron was flying a heavy night fighter from his base at Dijon towards Mainz. Twenty miles from Strasbourg, Lieutenant Fred Ringwald, an Air Force intelligence officer who was on the mission as an observer, glanced out of the cockpit and noticed about ten glowing red balls flying very fast in formation. Schlueter suggested that they might be stars, but this explanation was proved wrong when the objects approached the plane.

Schlueter radioed the American ground radar station, informing them that they were being chased by German night fighters, to which the station replied that nothing was showing on their scope. Schlueter's radar observer, Lieutenant Donald J. Meiers, checked his own scope, but could detect nothing unusual. Schlueter then decided to make for the objects at full throttle. The response from the Foo Fighters was instantaneous: their fiery red glow rapidly dimmed, until they were lost to sight. Less than two minutes later, however, they reappeared, although they seemed to have lost interest in the American aircraft and glided off into the night towards Germany.[8] Upon the objects' departure, the fighter's radar began to malfunction, forcing the crew to abandon their mission.

In an encounter of 27 November 1944 over Speyer, pilots Henry Giblin and Walter Cleary reported a large orange light flying at 250 mph about 1,500 feet above their fighter. The radar station in the sector replied that there was nothing else there. Nevertheless, a subsequent malfunction in the plane's radar system forced it to return to base. An official report was made – the first of its kind – which resulted in many jokes at the pilots' expense.[9] After the 27 November encounter, pilots who saw the Foo Fighters decided not to include them in their flight reports.

This self-imposed censorship was broken by two pilots named McFalls and Baker of the 415th, who submitted a flight report on their mission of 22 December 1944. In part, the report reads:

> At 0600, near Hagenau, at 10,000 feet altitude, two very bright lights climbed toward us from the ground. They leveled off and stayed on the tail of our plane. They were huge bright orange lights. They stayed there for two minutes. On my tail all the time. They were under perfect control. Then they turned away from us, and the fire seemed to go out.[10]

The Foo Fighters were not only witnessed by air crews. Hough and Randles cite a report from a former prisoner of war at the Heydebreck camp in Upper Silesia, Poland.

> At 3 p.m. on 22 January 1945 a number of men were being paraded by the Germans before being marched

away to evade the liberating Russian Army. A bomber appeared overhead, flying at about 18,000 feet, and the men gazed in horror at what seemed to be fire pouring from its rear end. Then they thought it might be a flare caught up in the slipstream of the aircraft. Finally, they realised it was neither of these things: the object was a silvery ball hugging the bomber, which was desperately trying to evade it. The foo fighter was still right on the tail of the aircraft as both passed into the distance.[11]

On 1 January 1945, Howard W. Blakeslee, science editor of the Associated Press, claimed that the mysterious Foo Fighters were nothing more than St Elmo's Fire, spontaneous lights produced by an electrostatic discharge on the fuselages of the Allied aircraft. According to Blakeslee, this explanation also accounted for the fact that the Foo Fighters did not show up on radar. The pilots who actually encountered the objects were unimpressed with Blakeslee's solution: most of them had been flying for a number of years, and knew St Elmo's Fire when they saw it. The Foo Fighters were something entirely different: the light they produced went on and off at intervals that seemed to be related to their speed; their shape was often clearly discernible as either discoid or spherical; and they were frequently reported as spinning rapidly on their vertical axis.[12] No Allied aircraft were ever brought down by Foo Fighters (which seemed more content to pace them and interfere with their radar), and so it was considered likely that the objects were dangerous German secret weapons, perhaps a radical development of V-weapon technology. The V-1s were already causing carnage in London, and it was known that German scientists were desperately trying to develop a ballistic missile that could hit America.

According to Vesco and Childress, several Foo Fighter stories were leaked in December 1944 to the *American Legion Magazine*, which then published the personal opinions of several US Intelligence officers that the Foo Fighters were radio-controlled radar-jamming devices sent up by the Germans.[13] Vesco and Childress go on to cite the testimony of another (unnamed) B-17 pilot who decided to intercept a Foo Fighter and succeeded in getting within a few hundred yards of the shining sphere. He reported hearing 'a strange sound, like the "backwash of invisible planes" '.[14] The last reported encounter with Foo Fighters occurred in early May 1945, near the eastern edge of the Pfalzerwald. A pilot, once again from the 415th Squadron, saw five orange balls of light flying in a 'V' formation in the distance.[15]

Ghost Rockets Over Scandinavia

In the two years between the end of the Second World War and the Kenneth Arnold sighting, strange unidentified aerial objects invaded the skies over Finland, Norway, Sweden and Denmark (and were later reported as far afield as Morocco and India). Nicknamed 'Ghost Rockets' because of their long, thin profile and occasional fiery exhaust, these objects were reported to perform astonishing manoeuvres such as diving and climbing rapidly at enormous speeds.[16]

The British UFO investigator Timothy Good cites the following confidential Department of State telegram from the American Embassy in Stockholm, dated 11 July 1946:

> For some weeks there have been numerous reports of strange rocket-like missiles being seen in Swedish and Finnish skies. During past few days reports of such objects being seen have greatly increased. Member of Legation saw one Tuesday afternoon. One landed on beach near Stockholm same afternoon without causing any damage and according to press fragments are now being studied by military authorities. Local scientist on first inspection stated it contained organic substance resembling carbide. Defense staff last night issued communiqué listing various places where missiles had been observed and urging public report all mysterious sound and light phenomena. Press this afternoon announces one such missile fell in Stockholm suburb 2:30 this afternoon. Missile observed by member

Legation made no sound and seemed to be falling rapidly to earth when observed. No sound of explosion followed however.

Military Attaché is investigating through Swedish channels and has been promised results Swedish observations. Swedes profess ignorance as to origin, character or purpose of missiles but state definitely they are not launched by Swedes. Eyewitness reports state missiles came in from southerly direction proceeding to northwest. Six units Atlantic Fleet under Admiral Hewitt arrived Stockholm this morning. If missiles are of Soviet origin as generally believed (some reports say they are launched from Estonia), purpose might be political to intimidate Swedes in connection with Soviet pressure on Sweden being built up in connection with current loan negotiations or to offset supposed increase in our military pressure on Sweden resulting from the naval visit and recent Bikini [atomic] tests or both.[17]

The suspicion voiced in this telegram that the Soviets might be responsible for the Ghost Rocket sightings was natural enough, given that the Cold War was then just getting under way. Both the Americans and Russians, of course, captured German weapons technology at the end of the war, and it was assumed by many in authority that the Russians were experimenting with V-1 and V-2 rocket designs. (Actually, a German V-2 rocket had already crashed in Sweden in the summer of 1944.) The fact that both the United States and the Soviet Union carried out extensive experiments with captured Nazi technology will gain yet more significance as we examine the claims of the Nazi-UFO proponents.

A number of British scientists were sent to Sweden to examine the Ghost Rocket reports, among them Professor R. V. Jones, the then Director of Intelligence of Britain's Air Staff and scientific advisor to Section IV of MI6. In *Most Secret War*, his account of his involvement with British Scientific Intelligence between 1939 and 1949, Professor Jones writes of the fears that the rockets were Russian:

The general interpretation ... was that [the Ghost Rockets] were long-range flying bombs being flown by the Russians over Sweden as an act of intimidation. This interpretation was accepted by officers in our own Air Technical Intelligence, who worked out the perform-ance of the bombs from the reported sightings in one of the incidents, where the object appeared to have dashed about at random over the whole of southern Sweden at speeds up to 2,000 mph. What the officers concerned failed to notice was that every observer, wherever he was, reported the object as well to the east. By far the most likely explanation was that it was a meteor, perhaps as far east as Finland, and the fantastic speeds that were reported were merely due to the fact that all observers had seen it more or less simultaneously, but that they had varying errors in their watches, so that any attempt to draw a track by linking up observations in a time sequence was unsound.[18]

Professor Jones considered it extremely unlikely that the Ghost Rockets could be Russian missiles based on German V-2 designs: he stated that the rockets seen over Scandinavia had more than twice the range of the V-2, an increase in performance that was too great given the short time since the capture of the German designs.

For myself, I simply asked two questions. First, what conceivable purpose could it serve the Russians, if they indeed had a controllable flying bomb, to fly it in great numbers over Sweden, without doing any more harm than to alert the West to the fact that they had such an impressive weapon? My second question followed from the first: how had the Russians succeeded in making a flying bomb of such fantastic reliability? The Germans had achieved no better than 90 per cent reliability in their flying bomb trials of 1944, at very much shorter range. Even if the Russians had achieved a reliability as high as 99 per cent over their much longer ranges, this still meant that one per cent of all sorties should have resulted in a bomb crashing on Swedish territory. Since there had been allegedly hundreds of sorties, there ought to be at least several crashed bombs already in Sweden, and yet nobody had ever picked up a fragment. I therefore said that I would not accept the theory that the apparitions were flying bombs from Russia until someone brought a piece into my office.[19]

Professor Jones goes on to relate an amusing incident that followed his challenge. When a substance that had allegedly fallen from a Ghost Rocket was collected and sent, via the Swedish General Staff and the British Air Staff, to the Royal Aircraft Establishment (RAE) at Farnborough, the scientists who analysed the fragments claimed that over 98 per cent of their mass consisted of an unknown element. Jones had already seen the samples, and had quickly concluded that they were lumps of coke, 'four or five irregularly shaped solid lumps, none of which looked as if it had ever been associated with a mechanical device'.[20] When he telephoned the head of chemistry at the RAE, enquiring whether they had thought to test for carbon, the chemist literally gasped. 'No one had stopped to look at the material, in an effort to get the analysis made quickly, and they had failed to test for carbon. The other lumps had similarly innocent explanations.'[21]

Nevertheless, some Ghost Rocket sightings remained puzzling. One of the objects was photographed near Stockholm by a Swede named Erik Reuterswaerd. When the Swedish authorities examined the photograph, they concluded that the object's trail was not issuing from its rear but was actually *enveloping* it. The London *Daily Telegraph*, which published the photograph on 6 September 1946, opined that a new method of propulsion was being tested.[22]

For their part, the Swedish Government concluded in October 1946 that, of the 1,000 reports of Ghost Rockets they had received, 80 per cent could be attributed to 'celestial phenomena'; the remaining 20 per cent, they stated, could not be either natural phenomena or the products of imagination.[23]

Radical Aircraft Designs: Feuerball *and* Kugelblitz

The conventional view of history is that, while the Germans possessed some remarkable and deadly weapons such as the V-1, the V-2 and the jet-engined Messerschmitt ME-262 fighter, their technological innovations did not extend much further than that. Indeed, serious historians treat claims of fantastic advances in Nazi technology with the utmost disdain. (We have already quoted Professor Jones's assertion that the Nazi flying bomb trials of 1944 were only 90 per cent reliable.) Nevertheless, we must ask the question: are they right to do so? Having looked briefly at the mystery of the Foo Fighters, Ghost Rockets and UFOs, which many professional scientists admit (however reluctantly and anonymously) constitute a puzzle worthy of serious investigation, we must now examine the claims of some UFO researchers that the wonderful devices seen so frequently flitting through the skies are actually machines based on Nazi designs for ultra-high-performance disc-shaped craft, capable of travelling not only through our atmosphere but also in outer space. The reader who baulks at this idea may well be further outraged by the claims made by some that the Nazis themselves succeeded in building prototypes of these machines. However, since we are already deep within the Absolute Elsewhere, we must press on through that weird realm, bearing in mind Pauwels's and Bergier's perceptive assertion that 'the historian may be reasonable, but history is not'.

As we have already noted, Renato Vesco is a pioneer of the Nazi-UFO theory. A graduate of the University of Rome, he studied aeronautical engineering at the German Institute for Aerial Development and during the war was sent to work at Fiat's underground installation at Lake Garda in northern Italy. In the 1960s, Vesco investigated UFO sightings for the Italian Air Ministry.[24] In 1971, he published the seminal work on the theory of man-made flying saucers; entitled *Intercettateli Senza Sparare* (roughly translated as 'Intercept Without Firing'), the book examines in great detail the possible technology behind the UFOs and reaches the astonishing and highly controversial conclusion that UFO technology (seen in terms of the perceived flight characteristics of the objects) is well within the capabilities of human science – and was so even during the Second World War. Indeed, Vesco is quite certain that the origin of the UFOs still seen today by witnesses all over the world can be placed firmly in Nazi Germany in the early 1940s. In addition, the technological principles behind these craft were, he believes, divided between the United States and the Soviet Union at the end of the war, with both superpowers going on to develop and refine the designs for their own ends.

According to Vesco, Luftwaffe scientists in Oberammergau, Bavaria conducted extensive research into an electrical device capable of interfering with an aircraft engine up to a distance of about 100 feet. Through the generation of intense electromagnetic fields, this device could short-circuit the target aircraft's ignition system, causing total loss of power. This short range, however, was considered impractical for a successful weapon, so they attempted to increase it to 300 feet. These plans were still only on the drawing board by the end of the war, so the weapon was never put into production. Nevertheless, these researches yielded a by-product that was put to use by Albert Speer and the SS Technical General Staff. They produced a device capable of 'proximity radio interference' on the delicate radar systems of American night-fighters.[25]

> Thus a highly original flying machine was born; it was circular and armored, more or less resembling the shell of a tortoise, and was powered by a special turbojet engine, also flat and circular, whose principles of operation recalled the well-known aeolipile of Hero, which generated a great halo of luminous flames. Hence it was named *Feuerball* (Fireball). It was unarmed and pilotless. Radio-controlled at the moment of take-off, it then automatically followed enemy aircraft, attracted by their exhaust flames, and approached close enough without collision to wreck their radar gear.[26]

The fiery halo around the craft's perimeter was generated by a combination of the rich fuel mixture and chemical additives causing the ionisation of the atmosphere around the *Feuerball*. As it approached the target aircraft, this ionisation would produce powerful electrostatic and electromagnetic fields that would interfere with its H2S radar. 'Since a metal arc carrying an oscillating current of the proper frequency – equal, that is, to the frequency used by the radar station – can cancel the blips (return signals from the target), the *Feuerball* was almost undetectable by the most powerful American radar of the time, despite its night-time visibility.'[27]

Vesco goes on to state that this night-time visibility had an additional advantage for the *Feuerball*: in the absence of daylight, the halo produced by the engine gave the impression of an enormous size, which had the effect of unnerving Allied pilots even more. As the *Feuerballe* approached, the pilots refrained from firing on them for fear of being caught in a gigantic explosion.[28] In fact, the devices did carry an explosive charge that would destroy them in the event of capture, in addition to an ingenious feature that would ensure a quick escape in the event of an attack by Allied aircraft. Underneath its armoured outer shell, each *Feuerball* contained a thin sheet of electrically insulated aluminium. Should a bullet pierce the armour, contact would be made between it and the aluminium sheet, thus closing a circuit, activating a vertical maximum acceleration device and taking the craft out of weapons range in a matter of seconds.[29]

The *Feuerballe* were constructed at the Henschel-Rax aeronautical establishment at Wiener Neustadt. According to one (unnamed) witness who saw them being test-flown, in daylight the craft looked like shining discs spinning on their vertical axes, and at night like huge burning globes. Hermann Goering inspected the progress of the *Feuerball* project on a number of occasions, hoping that the mechanical principles could be applied to a much larger offensive saucer-shaped aircraft. His hopes were to be quickly realised.

Vesco calls the *Kugelblitz* (Ball Lightning) automatic fighter 'the second authentic antecedent [after the *Feuerball*] of the present-day flying saucers', and the first example of the 'jet-lift' aircraft.[30] In 1952, a former Luftwaffe engineer named Rudolph Schriever gave a series of interviews to the West German press in which he claimed to have designed an aircraft strikingly similar to Vesco's *Kugelblitz*. Schriever had been an engineer and test pilot for the Heinkel factory in Eger. In 1941, he began to toy with the idea of an aircraft that could take off vertically, thus eliminating the need for runways, which were vulnerable to enemy bombing.

By June the following year, he had built and test-flown a working model of his design, and work immediately began on a full-size fifteen-foot version. In mid-1944, Schriever was transferred to the BMW plant near Prague, Czechoslovakia, where he was joined by an engineer from the rocket site at Peenemünde named Walter Miethe, another engineer named Klaus Habermohl and an Italian physicist from the aero-nautical complex at Riva del Garda, Dr Giuseppe Belluzzo. Together, they built an even larger, piloted version of the disc, featuring a domed pilot's cabin sitting at the centre of a circular set of multiple wings driven by a turbine engine mounted on the disc's vertical axis.

The German disc programme went under the title 'Project Saucer' (which W. A. Harbinson also took as the title for his excellent five-novel series inspired by the Nazi-UFO theory). According to the military historian Major Rudolph Lusar, Schriever's disc consisted of 'a wide-surface ring which rotated around a fixed, cupola-shaped cockpit'. The ring contained 'adjustable wing-discs which could be brought into appropriate position for the take-off or horizontal flight'.[31] The Model 3 flying disc had a diameter of 138 feet and a height of 105 feet.

According to Schriever, the finished disc was ready for test-flying early in 1944, but was destroyed by its builders to prevent it from falling into the hands of the advancing Allies. Schriever and his colleagues fled as the BMW plant was taken by Czechoslovakian patriots. In spite of Schriever's claim, Renato Vesco states that a highly advanced supersonic disc-shaped aircraft called the *Kugelblitz* was indeed test-flown near the Nordhausen underground rocket complex in February 1945.[32] Also known as the V-7, this machine was said to have climbed to a height of 37,600 feet in just three minutes, and reached a speed of 1,218 mph. This craft and the technicians who built it were apparently seized by the Russians and taken to Siberia, where the disc project continued under Soviet control.

While Vesco concedes that the hard evidence for a German flying-disc programme is 'very tenuous', he notes that 'the senior official of a 1945 British technical mission revealed that he had discovered German plans for "entirely new and deadly developments in air warfare"'. Vesco continues:

These plans must obviously have gone beyond normal jet aircraft designs, as both sides already had jet-powered aircraft in production and operational service by the end of the war. Moreover, before Rudolf Schriever died some fifteen years after the war he had become convinced that the large numbers of post-war UFO sightings were evidence that his designs had been built and developed.[33]

On 2 May 1980, another man claimed to the German press that he had worked on Project Saucer. Heinrich Fleißner, then 76 years old, told *Neue Presse* magazine that he had been a technical consultant on a jet-propelled, disc-shaped aircraft that had been built at Peenemünde from parts manufactured in a number of other locations. Fleißner also claimed that Goering had been the patron of the project and planned to use the disc as a courier plane, but that the Wehrmacht had destroyed most of the plans in the face of the Allied advance.[34] Nevertheless, some material did reach both America and Russia. According to Harbinson, 'The notes and drawings for Fleißner's flying saucer, first registered in West Germany on 27 March 1954, were assigned to Trans-Oceanic, Los Angeles, California on 28 March the following year and registered with the United States Patent Office on 7 June 1960.'[35]

According to Vesco, the Austrian inventor Viktor Schauberger, after being kidnapped by the Nazis, designed a number of disc-shaped aircraft for the Third Reich between 1938 and 1945. The saucers were powered by what Schauberger called 'liquid vortex propulsion': 'If water or air is rotated into a twisting form of oscillation known as "colloidal",' he said, 'a build-up of energy results, which, with immense power, can cause levitation.'[36] Whether this bizarre form of propulsion is workable is, of course, open to debate. Once again, however, the Americans seem to have taken many of Schauberger's documents at the end of the war, with the Russians taking what was left and blowing up his apartment when they had finished. Schauberger supposedly went to America in the 1950s to work on a top secret project in Texas for the US Government, although this unspecified project was apparently not particularly successful. Schauberger died in 1958, reportedly saying on his deathbed: 'They took everything from me. Everything. I don't even own myself.'[37]

There is no doubt that radical aeroform designs were being tested at this time. For example, the Messerschmitt 163A was powered by a liquid-fuel Walter rocket, and was given its first powered flight in August 1941. It achieved speeds of over 600 mph, nearly twice as fast as the average speed of a fighter aircraft at that time. A second version, the Me 163B, was built with a more powerful motor. The design was not perfected, however, until mid-1944, when approximately 370 were built and deployed throughout Germany in a last-ditch attempt to thwart the Allied forces. The RAF and USAAF air crews who encountered them commented in their reports on how fast and dangerous these craft were: on many occasions, the Me 163s were so fast that the Allied air gunners had no chance to deal with them. However, the Me 163 could only remain in a combat situation for 25 minutes, for most of which time it was unpowered, and their relatively small number prevented them from having much success against the Allied advance.[38]

Hans Kammler

If the Germans did succeed in producing a piloted flying disc, what became of it? As several researchers have noted, the answer may lie with SS Obergruppenführer Dr Hans Kammler, who towards the end of the war had access to all areas of secret air-armaments projects. Kammler worked on the V-2 rocket project, along with Wernher von Braun (who would later head NASA's Apollo Moon programme) and Luftwaffe Major General Walter Dornberger (who would later become vice-president of the Bell Aircraft Company in the United States).[39]

Heinrich Himmler planned to separate the SS from Nazi Party and state control through the establishment of a number of business and industrial fronts, making it independent of the state budget. Hitler approved this proposal early in 1944. (As Jim Marrs notes, this strategy would subsequently be copied by the CIA in America.[40])

By the end of the war, Hans Kammler had decided to use V-2 rocket technology and scientists as bargaining chips with the Allies. On 2 April 1945, 500 technicians and engineers were placed on a train along with 100 SS troops and sent to a secret Alpine location in Bavaria. Two days later, von Braun requested permission from Kammler to resume rocket research, to which Kammler replied that he was about to disappear for an indefinite length of time. This was the last anyone saw of Hans Kammler.[41] In view of the undoubted advantage he held when it came to negotiating for his life with the Allies, Kammler's disappearance is something of a puzzle, until we pause to consider the possibility that he possessed plans for a technology even more advanced than the V-2. 'Did the Reich, or an extension of it, have the capability to produce a UFO or the clout to deal from a position of strength with one of the Allied nations?'[42] Although it is assumed that Kammler committed suicide when about to be apprehended by the Czech resistance in Prague, there is no proof of this. What really happened to Kammler? In the final chapter, we will examine the theory that he, along with many other high-ranking Nazis, survived the end of the war and escaped to an unlikely location.

The Avrocar

The opinion of orthodox history is that, while many highly advanced weapons designs were on the drawing board, with some actually being put into limited production in the final months of the war, nothing with the design or performance characteristics of flying saucers was ever built in Nazi Germany. And yet, in 1953, only eight years after the end of the war, the Canadian *Toronto Star* announced that a flying saucer was being developed by the A. V. Roe company (AVRO-Canada) at its facilities near Malton, Ontario. According to the report, apparently leaked by a well-informed source within the company, the machine would have a top speed of 1,500 mph.

This understandably provoked a sudden and intense interest in the subject from other members of the press, who asked for clarification from the Canadian Government. A statement was released, declaring: 'The Defense authorities are examining all ideas, even revolutionary ones, that have been suggested for the development of new types of supersonic aircraft, also including flying discs. This, however, is still in the beginning phase of research and it will be a number of months before we are able to reach anything positive and seven or more years before we come to actual production.'[43]

On 16 February 1953, C. D. Howe, the Minister of Defense Production, told the Canadian House of Commons that the government was studying new fighter-aircraft concepts 'adding weight to reports that AVRO is even now working on a mock-up model of a "flying saucer" capable of flying 1500 miles per hour and climbing straight up in the air'.[44] Less than two weeks later, on 27 February, the AVRO President, Crawford Gordon, Jr., wrote in the company's journal: 'One of our projects can be said to be quite revolutionary in concept and appearance. The prototype being built is so revolutionary that when it flies all other types of supersonic aircraft will become obsolescent. This is all that AVRO-Canada are going to say about this project.'[45]

This statement was followed by two months of silence, after which press interest was fired to an even greater degree by another revelation in the *Toronto Star* of 21 April:

Field Marshal Montgomery . . . became one of a handful of people ever to see AVRO's mock-up of a 'flying saucer,' reputed to be capable of flying 1500 miles an hour. A guide who accompanied Montgomery quoted him as describing it as 'fantastic.' ... Security precautions surrounding this super-secret are so tight that two of Montgomery's escorts from Scotland Yard were barred from the forbidden, screened-off area of the AVRO plant.[46]

On 24 April, the *Toronto Star* added that the flying disc was constructed of metal, wood and plastics, and referred to it as a gyroscopic fighter, with a revolving gas turbine engine. Little more was written in the Canadian press until 1 November, when a brief report appeared stating: 'A mock-up of the Canadian flying saucer, the highly secret aircraft in whose existence few believe, was yesterday shown to a group of twenty-five American experts, including military officers and scientists.'[47] This $200 million-dollar prototype was also known as the AVRO Omega, probably because its shape was more like the Greek letter than a perfect circle.

The press claimed that the Canadian Government planned to deploy squadrons of flying saucers for the defence of the far north of the country, their VTOL (vertical take-off and landing) capabilities making them ideal for forested and snow-covered terrain. Once again, however, there followed a period of official and press silence on the matter, broken only by the revelation that the project's principal designer was the aeronautical engineer J. C. M. Frost, and persistent rumours that the US military had become involved. Vesco quotes an unnamed press source, who stated enthusiastically:

This is a ship that will be able to take off vertically, to hover in mid-air and to move at a speed of about 1850 mph. That is, it would be capable of performing all the maneuvers that flying discs are said to be capable of. This astonishing craft is the brain child of the English aeronautical engineer John Frost, who worked for the large de Havilland factory in England during the war and who later went on to A. V. Roe, in Malton, Canada. The aircraft that will be built for the U.S. Air Force is not, however, the first of this type that Frost has designed. Two years ago he had designed and submitted to American experts an aircraft which was called the Flying Manta because of its behavior on take-off. It more or less resembled the present disc, but it could not take off vertically. In addition, its top speed did not exceed 1430 mph. The Manta had interested the American General Staff, but in view of these operating deficiencies, it was decided not to build it.[48]

These high hopes for US-Canadian flying discs were dashed when, on 3 December 1954, the Canadian Defense Ministry suddenly announced that the project was to be abandoned on the grounds that the technology required to make it work was too expensive and speculative.

Nearly a year later, however, on 25 October 1955, US Air Force Secretary Donald Quarles made an intriguing statement through the Department of Defense press office.

We are now entering a period of aviation technology in which aircraft of unusual configuration and flight characteristics will begin to appear ... The Air Force will fly the first jet-powered vertical-rising airplane in a matter of days. We have another project under contract with AVRO Ltd., of Canada, which could result in disc-shaped aircraft somewhat similar to the popular concept of a flying saucer ... While some of these may take novel forms, such as the AVRO project, they are direct-line descendants of conventional aircraft and should not be regarded as supra-natural or mysterious ... Vertical-rising aircraft capable of transition to supersonic horizontal flight will be a new phenomenon in our skies, and under certain conditions could give the illusion of the so-called flying saucer. The Department of Defense will make every effort within the bounds of security to keep the public informed of these developments so they can be recognized for what they are ... I think we must recognize that other countries also have the capability of developing vertical-rising aircraft, perhaps of unconventional shapes. However, we are satisfied at this time that none of the sightings of so-called 'flying saucers' reported in this country were in fact aircraft of foreign origin.[49]

Quarles's surprising statement notwithstanding, the AVRO company was in fact going through something of a bad patch following the cancellation by the Canadian Government of the contract for the CF-105 Arrow heavy bomber, on the pretext of the diminished air threat from Russia which had only a limited number of intercontinental bombers. This decision resulted in 10,000 people being laid off, most of them specialists working on the saucer project, renamed the AVRO-Car.

It was not until August 1960 that American authorities decided to allow the press to see the prototype of the AVRO-Car. Its performance was less than impressive: it managed to do little more than hover a few feet above the ground, prompting an official statement that 'even for this type of VTOL plane . . . the principal problem is low-speed stability. Tests with a full-scale model have been made at the large forty-by-eighty-foot wind tunnel at the Ames Research Center, belonging to NASA, but they were not completely successful. It became clear, however, that the various problems inherent in a circular aircraft of this type are not insurmountable.'[50]

Just over a year later, it was announced that the US Department of Defense would be withdrawing from the AVRO-Car project, on the grounds that it was unlikely that the design could ever be made to work successfully.

The lamentable story of the AVRO-Car (and its illustration of the problems besetting disc-shaped aircraft) has done nothing to dissuade Nazi-UFO proponents from maintaining that their basic thesis is correct. However, British ufologist Timothy Good quotes a CIA memorandum from W. E. Lexow, Chief of the Applied Science Division, Office of Scientific Intelligence, dated 19 October 1955, which may lend weight to this idea. According to the memorandum, John Frost, the designer of the AVRO-Car, 'is reported to have obtained his original idea for the flying machine from a group of Germans just after World War II. The Soviets may also have obtained information from this German group'.[51]

The Problem of the UFO Occupants

Any theory of the origin of UFOs must, of course, take into account all the available evidence, and this includes reported encounters with and descriptions of UFO occupants. Having looked at the idea that UFOs are man-made aircraft inspired by designs developed by Nazi scientists in the Second World War, we now find ourselves confronting material that would, at first sight, be sufficient to make the Nazi-UFO theory completely untenable. For as soon as the UFO lands and opens its hatches, we meet a variety of creatures that are anything but human. (To be sure, *some* UFO occupants are described as being completely human-looking but they seem to be very much in the minority.) This has naturally led the majority of UFO researchers and investigators to conclude that UFOs are extraterrestrial devices. Before dealing with this problem, let us illustrate it by examining briefly some of these alleged contacts with UFO occupants.

Over the decades since the modern era of ufology began with the Arnold sighting in 1947, people all over the world have claimed to have encountered an astonishing variety of creatures linked with UFOs on the ground. In the 1950s and 1960s these people were known as 'contactees' and, according to their testimony, humanity had nothing whatsoever to fear from the ufonauts. They were almost invariably described as being tall and strikingly attractive, with long, sandy-coloured hair and blue eyes, a description which resulted in their being classified as 'Nordic' aliens. (In the present context, this description has obvious and sinister connotations but, as we shall see, is almost certainly coincidental.)

The most famous of the 1950s contactees was George Adamski who, on 20 November 1952, encountered a man claiming to come from Venus. Adamski, a self-styled philosopher and mystic, was running a hamburger stand a few miles from the Mount Palomar Observatory in California when he had his encounter. He was having lunch with several friends near Desert Center when they allegedly saw a gigantic cigar-shaped object in the sky. Telling his friends to remain behind, Adamski drove into the desert, where he witnessed the landing of a disc-shaped 'scout craft'. When the ship's single occupant appeared, Adamski was able to communicate with him through a combination of hand signals and telepathy and learned that the Venusians (together with other intelligent races throughout the Solar System) were deeply concerned at humanity's misuse of nuclear energy (a theme that would be repeated again and again by the contactees).

In common with the other contactees, Adamski's claims suffered from egregious scientific inaccuracies, not least of which was the utter inability of all the other planets in the Solar System to support intelligent humanoid life. In Adamski's case, this difficulty was somewhat compounded by a comment he made to two followers regarding Prohibition. During this period, he had secured a special licence from the government to make wine for religious purposes (he had founded a monastery in Laguna Beach), with the result that he claimed to have made 'enough wine for all of Southern California'. If it had not been for the repeal of Prohibition, he told his friends, 'I wouldn't have had to get into this saucer crap'.[52]

The contactee claims of the 1950s are rightly regarded as extremely dubious by most ufologists; however, in the decades since there have been a number of contact claims that demand more serious attention. Before proceeding, it is necessary for us to look briefly at some of the most impressive reports, since they form the backdrop to an increasingly popular conspiracy theory regarding Nazi activities in the post-war period.

When we examine reports of encounters with UFO occupants (particularly since the early 1960s), we see that the defining characteristic reveals itself to be what has come to be known as 'abduction', in which witnesses are taken from their normal environment against their will and are forced to interact in various ways with apparently non-human entities.

One of the most famous abduction cases occurred on 11 October 1973 on the shores of the Pascagoula River in Mississippi, USA. Charlie Hickson, 45, and Calvin Parker, 18, were fishing in the river when they witnessed the approach of a UFO. The following day, the United Press International news service carried the following report:

PASCAGOULA, Miss. Two shipyard workers who claimed they were hauled aboard a UFO and examined by silver-skinned creatures with big eyes and pointed ears were checked today at a military hospital and found to be free of radiation.

. . . Jackson County chief deputy Barney Mathis said the men told him they were fishing from an old pier on the west bank of the Pascagoula River about 7 p.m. Thursday when they noticed a strange craft about two miles away emitting a bluish haze.

They said it moved closer and then appeared to hover about three or four feet above the water, then 'three whatever-they-weres came out, either floating or walking, and carried us into the ship,' officers quoted Hickson as saying.

'The things had big eyes. They kept us about twenty minutes, photographed us, and then took us back to the pier. The only sound they made was a buzzing-humming sound. They left in a flash.'

'These are reliable people,' Sheriff Diamond said. 'They had no reason to say this if it had not been true. I know something did happen to them.'

The sheriff said the 'spacecraft' was described as fish-shaped, about ten feet long with an eight-foot ceiling. The occupants were said to have pale silvery skin, no hair, long pointed ears and noses, with an opening for a mouth and hands 'like crab claws.'

Inside the UFO, the two men were placed on a table and examined with a device that resembled a huge eye. They were later interviewed by Dr J. Allen Hynek, the astronomer whose work as a consultant for the US Air Force's UFO investigation project, *Blue Book*, turned him from sceptic to cautious advocate of UFO reality. Hynek concluded that Hickson and Parker were in a state of genuine fright. Dr James A. Harder, a consultant for the Aerial Phenomena Research Organization (APRO) who also investigated the case, described the UFO occupants as 'automata', or 'advanced robots', judging from the witnesses' descriptions.

Many people who are sceptical of UFO and alien abductions state, quite reasonably, that an advanced spacefaring civilisation would not need to conduct the highly intrusive and traumatic experiments on human beings that their representatives are reported to conduct. The repeated taking of samples of blood, flesh, sperm and ova from unwilling subjects implies a curiously primitive medical technology for beings allegedly capable of building interstellar spacecraft. However, there is an intriguing correlation between the atrocities committed by 'aliens' on their human victims and those committed by Nazi 'doctors' (I use the term loosely) in the concentration camps during the Second World War. As we shall see later in this chapter, proponents of the Nazi-UFO Theory, such as W. A. Harbinson, have suggested that this may be due to an ongoing (and for the moment highly secret) Nazi plot to create a master-race from the raw material of humanity in its present form.

One of the most impressive and carefully investigated abduction cases occurred on 26 August 1976. Four art students, Charlie Foltz, Chuck Rak and brothers Jack and Jim Weiner were on a camping trip on the Allagash River in Maine, USA. While fishing in a boat on East Lake, they watched the approach of a large spherical light that frightened them considerably. The next thing they knew, they were standing on the shore of the lake, watching the object shoot up into the sky. There was nothing left of their blazing camp fire but a few glowing embers, implying that they had been away for several hours although they only remembered being on the lake for about twenty minutes.

Several years later, the case came to the attention of the respected UFO researcher Raymond E. Fowler, who investigated on behalf of the Mutual UFO Network (MUFON), the largest civilian UFO organisation in the world. Fowler arranged for the four witnesses to undergo hypnotic regression to recover their lost memories of the evening. Each of the men (who had promised not to discuss with each other their individual hypnosis sessions) recalled being taken into the UFO through a beam of light. Once inside, they encountered several humanoid entities who forced them (apparently through some form of mind control) to undress and sit in a mist-filled room. Their bodies were examined and probed with various instruments, and samples of saliva, blood, skin, sperm, urine and faeces were taken. When the examination had been completed, the men were forced to walk through a circular doorway, whereupon they found themselves floating back down to their boat through the light beam.

Fowler later discovered that Jack Weiner had had an 'anomalous lump' surgically removed several years earlier. The pathologist who examined it had been somewhat mystified and had sent it on for analysis to the Center for Disease Control in Atlanta, Georgia. At Fowler's request, Jack Weiner asked for his medical records and discovered that the lump had been sent to the Armed Forces Institute of Pathology (AFIP) in Washington, D.C., instead of the Center for Disease Control. When Fowler telephoned the AFIP for an explanation, he was told by the public information officer that the AFIP occasionally assisted civilian doctors. 'When Jack asked why the lump was sent to the AFIP rather than the Center for Disease Control, he was told by his surgeon's secretary that it was less costly even though Jack was covered by insurance!'[53]

The Pascagoula and Allagash encounters display many of the hallmarks of the typical UFO abduction, the principal elements of which can be listed as follows: (1) the initial appearance of the entities and the taking of the percipient; (2) medical probing with various instruments; (3) machine examinations and mental testing; (4) sexual activity, in which the percipient is sometimes forced to 'mate' with other humans or even with the entities themselves; and (5) the returning of the percipient to his or her normal environment.[54] Although an extremely wide variety of 'alien' types has been encountered by people all over the world, one type in particular has become more and more commonly reported (particularly in the United States). The so-called 'Grey' is now regarded as the quintessential alien being and is one of the most immediately recognisable images in today's world.

In the unlikely event that the reader is unfamiliar with this image, we can briefly describe the Greys' physical characteristics as follows: they are usually described as approximately four feet tall (although some are as tall as eight feet), with extremely large craniums and enormous jet-black, almond-shaped eyes. They have no nose or ears to speak of, merely small holes where these should be; likewise, their mouths are usually described as no more than lipless slits. The torso and limbs are described as being very thin, almost sticklike, and more than one abductee has reported the impression that they seem to be made of an undifferentiated material, with no bone or muscular structure. Their hands are long and thin, sometimes with three fingers, sometimes with four. In addition, the Greys are frequently reported to be rather uncaring in their attitude towards humans, treating us much as we treat laboratory animals. Indeed, they have been described by some as militaristic and by others as hivelike in their demeanour, as if they had no individual consciousness of their own but were carrying out commands from some higher source.

It is clear that any claims of a Nazi origin of modern UFO encounters must take account of the bizarre creatures associated with the discs. This problem might seem insurmountable in view of the fact that, while we may not expect the UFO pilots to be strutting around in black leather trench coats and jackboots, they would surely nevertheless be recognisable as human beings. However, the research undertaken by W. A. Harbinson may offer a way around this apparent impasse, as well as providing us with some extremely unsettling food for thought.

Nazi Cyborgs?

Harbinson's thesis, that UFO occupants may well be cyborgs – biomedically engineered amalgamations of human and machine – is supported to a certain extent by medical research conducted since the 1960s. Although this research was at the time highly secret, the gruesome details have since come to light in the form of books and articles that describe not only the nature of the experiments conducted but also the frightening attitude of some members of the medical profession. According to David Fishlock: 'Even today there are people who believe that convicts, especially the criminal lunatic, and even conscientious objectors, should be compelled to lend themselves to science.'[55]

Referring to *The People Shapers* (1978) by Vance Packard, Harbinson reminds us of the direction in which medical research was heading more than 30 years ago.

[I]n the Cleveland Clinic's Department of Artificial Organs, not only medical specialists, but 'mechanical, electrical, chemical, and biomedical engineers, as well as biochemists and polymer chemists', were, in their busy operating theatres, enthusiastically engaged in 'surgery connected to the development of artificial substitutes for . . . vital organs such as the liver, lungs, pancreas, and kidneys'. Conveniently within walking distance of the Cleveland Clinic's Department of Artificial Organs are the Neurosurgical Research Laboratories of the Cleveland Metropolitan General Hospital, where great interest was being expressed, as far back as 1967, in the possibility of transferring the entire head of one human being to another. Switching human *brains* from one head to another would be complicated and costly, but, as Packard explains: 'By simply switching heads, on the other hand, only a few connections need to be severed and then re-established in the neck of the recipient body.'[56]

This procedure was successfully carried out on monkeys at the Cleveland Clinic, with each head apparently retaining its original mental characteristics when attached to its new body. In other words, if a monkey had been aggressive before the operation, it would remain so when its head was transplanted to another body. The eyes of the monkeys followed people as they walked past, implying that the heads retained some level of awareness. The unfortunate subjects of these procedures only lived for about one week.

Of course, the main problem in a procedure of this kind would be the regeneration of the severed spinal cord so that the brain could send nerve impulses to its new body; and yet even this feat seems not to be outside the bounds of possibility. In June 1976, a Soviet scientist named Levon A. Matinian 'reported from the fourth biennial conference on Regeneration of the Central Nervous System that he had succeeded in regrowing the spinal cords of rats'.[57] Harbinson suggests, almost certainly with some justification, that this area of research must have been continued 'behind closed doors' at military and scientific establishments since then. It is surely reasonable to suppose that, if this is the case, scientists have progressed well beyond the level of rats.

One can be forgiven for wondering what conceivable use such barbaric experiments could possibly have for humanity. While it is mercifully unlikely that head transplants will ever be in vogue, such research undoubtedly holds much potential for the enhancement of human beings who will eventually conduct routine work in hostile environments, such as the ocean floor and outer space. Fusion of a sort between human and machine has already been achieved, in the form of the so-called Cybernetic Anthropomorphous Machine System (CAMS), 'slave' machinery that mimics the movement of its human operators. According to Harbinson:

> In an aerospace conference given in Boston in 1966, engineer William E. Bradley, who developed the idea of cable-less man-machine manipulator systems for the US Defense Department's Institute for Defense Analysis, stated his belief that man and machine would eventually be linked in such a way that by performing the manoeuvres himself, the man would cause them to take place, through the machine, at a distance of thousands of miles. This concept soon led to the weapon-aiming system devised by the Philco Corpor-

ation for the US Air Force, in which the pilot's helmet is coupled with a servo-system that enables him to aim and fire his weapons automatically by merely swivelling his head until a camera located in his helmet shows the target.[58]

In addition, as early as 1967 US Air Force scientists had succeeded in transmitting thought impulses to a computer using a variation on Morse code composed of long and short bursts of alpha waves[59] (alpha waves are produced by the brain when it is at rest). This technology has developed to the point where today we have the potential for amputees to control their prosthetic limbs by means of nerve impulses directly from the brain.

In the field of organ transplantation, we have seen astonishing progress over the last 30 years and it is surely not rash to suggest that we will soon see artificial hearts and other organs routinely replacing those damaged through illness or accident. Likewise, in spite of concerns regarding the ethical implications of human cloning, we may also see the day when human organs are produced in the laboratory, ready for transplanting when the need arises. In view of the fact that research conducted under the aegis of national security is between ten and twenty years ahead of what is made public at any particular time (work on the Stealth fighter began in the mid-1970s, although the public were not made aware of its existence until the late 1980s), it is possible – perhaps likely – that advances in the field of medical and bioengineering research have already extended into the realm of what the public would consider science fiction.

Harbinson believes that what the public knows is merely the tip of the iceberg, and reminds us that 'the US Navy, Air Force, Army and government agencies such as NASA – all with top-secret research establishments in the White Sands Proving Ground and similar areas – have a particular need for advanced man-machine manipulations or cyborgs'.[60] He adds that the creatures seen in and around landed UFOs could be such cyborgs: human beings radically augmented by sophisticated mechanical prosthetics.

Theoretically, the lungs of such creatures would be partially collapsed and the blood in them artificially cooled. The cyborgs' respiration and other bodily functions would then be controlled cybernetically with artificial lungs and sensors which maintain constant temperature, metabolism and pressure, irrespective of external environmental fluctuations – thus, even if not protected by an antigravity (or gravitic) propulsion system, they would not be affected by the extraordinary accelerations and direction changes of their craft. The cyborgs would have no independent will, but could be remote-controlled, both physically and mentally, even across great distances, by computer-linked brain implants. Since this operation would render the mouth and nose superfluous, these would be sealed . . . and completely non-functioning.[61]

If we remember the basic description of the Greys noted earlier, with their slit-like and apparently useless mouths, vestigial noses and thin torsos, we can begin to see a frightening correspondence with the theoretical human-built cyborg, a nightmarish combination of genetically engineered human and highly sophisticated machine. To a startled, disorientated and terrified UFO witness, such a creature would surely look like nothing on earth . . . would look, in fact, like an extraterrestrial alien.

Interestingly, many people claiming to have encountered UFO crews mention the presence of normal-looking humans alongside the bizarre entities. Some ufologists suggest that these human types are the Nordic aliens mentioned earlier, working alongside the Greys and perhaps forming part of some interplanetary federation; other, more conspiracy-minded researchers believe that the human types are just that: human beings who are in league with a hostile alien occupation force. There is, however, another possibility, based on the information we have just considered. It is conceivable that the humans seen on board UFOs are actually the controllers of the Greys/cyborgs. It is also conceivable that these humans are members of an ultra-secret group, existing completely independently of any nation on Earth, and perhaps hostile to all nations and all other humans.

Conceivable, yes – but true?

These suggestions, of course, raise a number of serious and difficult questions. If the controllers of the UFOs and their not-quite-human crew members really are from Earth, who are they? If they place their allegiance with no known nation, with whom *does* their allegiance lie? Why do they abduct what is apparently an enormous number of ordinary humans, some of whom are never returned? Such an organisation or society could not operate without a well-supplied, protected and highly secret home base. Where is it?

In the final chapter of our survey, we will examine some of the theories that have been put forward to account for the origin and activities of this sinister group of humans. But first, we can attempt to answer one of the questions we have just posed. The answer, if true, is terrifying, and leads us inevitably to the final stage of our journey through the Absolute Elsewhere.

Telemetric Mind Control

What is the secret of so-called UFO abductions? Are hostile alien beings responsible, or is the solution to the mystery to be found right here on Earth? For a possible answer to these questions, we must look at the history of a subject that most people would assume lies firmly within the boundaries of science fiction and that has no place in the world of everyday experience. The subject is the control of the human mind from a distance and, as we shall now see, it is frighteningly practicable.

According to the US Air Force Scientific Advisory Board in its 1996 study of weapons technology, *New World Vistas: Air and Space Power for the 21st Century*, it is possible to achieve the coupling of human and machine through what is known as Biological Process Control. 'One can envision the development of electromagnetic energy sources, the output of which can be pulsed, shaped, and focused, that can couple with the human body in a fashion that will allow one to prevent voluntary muscular movements, control emotions (and thus actions), produce sleep, transmit suggestions, interfere with both short-term and long-term memory, produce an experience set, and delete an experience set.' Researcher David Guyatt informs us that 'experience set' is jargon for one's life's memories: this technology is quite literally capable of deleting one's memories and replacing them with an entirely new set.[62]

Those who believe that such technology must still be decades away from perfection may be surprised to learn that Dr Jose Delgado, a neurophysiologist at the Yale University School of Medicine, has been experimenting with Electronic Stimulation of the Brain (ESB) since the late 1940s. Perhaps his most impressive experiment was conducted in 1964, with the financial backing of the US Office of Naval Research. An electronic probe was implanted in the brain of a bull and a small radio receiver strapped to its head. The animal was then placed in a bullring, along with Dr Delgado who was equipped with a remote-control handset. As the bull charged him, Delgado flipped a switch on the handset and the one-ton animal stopped dead in front of him, clearly in a state of confusion. This process was repeated several times. Guyatt writes: 'Speaking two years later, in 1966, Delgado stated that his experiments "support the distasteful conclusion that motion, emotion, and behaviour can be directed by electrical [means] and that humans can be controlled like robots by push buttons".'[63] According to Delgado, this would eventually result in a 'psycho-civilised' society, whose citizens' brains would be computer-controlled through the use of implanted 'stimoceivers'. Guyatt informs us that in 1974 neurophysiologist Lawrence Pinneo of the Stanford Research Institute (SRI) developed a computer system capable of reading a person's mind by correlating brain waves on an electroencephalograph (EEG) with specific commands.[64]

Eighteen years earlier, in 1956, at the National Electronics Conference in Chicago, Curtiss Shafer, an electrical engineer for the Norden-Ketay Corporation, had stated that 'The ultimate achievement of biocontrol may be man himself'. He continued: 'The controlled subjects would never be permitted to think as individuals. A few months after birth, a surgeon would equip each child with a socket mounted under the scalp and electrodes reaching selected areas of brain tissue'. The subject's 'sensory perceptions and muscular activity could be either modified or completely controlled by bioelectric signals radiating from state-controlled transmitters'.[65]

Among the horrors perpetrated at Auschwitz and Dachau concentration camps were frequently fatal experiments in mind control, conducted mainly with hypnosis and narco-hypnosis, using drugs such as mescaline and various barbiturates. After the war, many Nazi scientists, doctors, engineers and intelligence personnel were secretly taken to the United States in the operation known as Project PAPERCLIP. Thirty-four Nazi scientists were sent to Randolph Air Force Base in San Antonio, Texas to continue their narco-hypnosis experiments on non-volunteer subjects, including prisoners, mental patients and members of ethnic minorities.[66] The results of the narco-hypnosis experiments suggested that the technique was unreliable (the main intention being to produce a programmable assassin), and greater emphasis was placed on electronic technology to erase a person's personality (a process known as 'depatterning') and replace it with a new personality devised by the experimenter (a technique called 'psychic driving').[67]

As might be expected, the CIA has always been extremely interested in the concept of mind control. One of their experimental facilities was contained within the Allen Memorial Institute, the psychiatric division of McGill University in Montreal, Canada, directed by Dr Ewen Cameron MD on a grant from the Rockefeller and Gerschickter Foundations. Cameron established a Radio Telemetry Laboratory in which experiments were conducted on non-volunteer subjects. Mind control researcher Alex Constantine provides us with a glimpse of the nature of these experiments, which included depatterning and psychic driving.

The psychotronic heart of the laboratory was the Grid Room, with its verticed, *Amazing Tales* interior. The subject was strapped into a chair involuntarily, by force, his head bristling with electrodes and transducers. Any resistance was met with a paralyzing dose of curare. The subject's brain waves were beamed to a nearby reception room crammed with voice analyzers, a wire recorder and radio receivers cobbled together by [Cameron's assistant] Rubenstein. The systematic anni-hilation, or 'depatterning' of a subject's mind and memory, was accomplished with overdoses of LSD, barbiturate sleep for 65 days at a stretch and ECT shocks at 75 times the recommended dosage. Psychic driving, the repetition of a recorded message for 16 hours a day, programmed the empty mind.[68]

The CIA has, over the years, established a number of secret projects to study and experiment with methods of mind control, using drugs and various forms of electromag-netic (EM) radiation. The notorious MKULTRA behaviour-control programme is merely the best-known of these projects. The others include: Project CHATTER, a US Navy programme aimed at the elimination of free will in subjects through the use of drugs and psychology; Project BLUEBIRD, a CIA/Office of Scientific Intelligence programme to develop behavioural drugs for use in 'unconventional warfare'; and Project PANDORA, which was established as a result of the Soviet bombardment of the US embassy in Moscow with low-intensity microwaves during the 1960s and 1970s.[69] PANDORA was set up to study the health effects of microwave radiation and experimented with the induction of hallucinations and heart seizures. According to Richard Cesaro, the director of the Defense Advanced Research Projects Agency (DARPA), the initial goal of PANDORA was to 'discover whether a carefully controlled microwave signal could control the mind'.[70]

According to Constantine, CIA researchers conducted further experiments with radio waves, which resulted in their subjects experiencing various emotions, sensations and visions. At the University of California at Los Angeles (UCLA), 'Dr Ross Adey (who worked closely with émigré Nazi technicians after WW II) rigged the brains of lab animals to transmit to a radio receiver, which shot signals back to a device that sparked any behaviour desired by the re-searcher'.[71]

The use of electronic 'stimoceivers' inside the brains of subjects to control thought and behaviour is paralleled by one of the most disturbing aspects of UFO abduction: the so-called 'alien implants' which, it is claimed, are inserted into the bodies of abductees for unknown purposes. Alien implants first came to widespread public attention with the publication of *Communion* (1987) by Whitley Strieber and *Missing Time* (1981) by Budd Hopkins. One of the defining characteristics of alien abduction is the introduction into the abductee's body of one or more small devices, frequently through the top of the nasal cavity and into the brain but also beneath the skin of arms, hands and legs. Some researchers speculate that the mysterious, so-called 'unknown bright objects' that occa-sionally show up on X-rays and CAT scans of the head are actually alien implants.

In the last few years, intensive efforts have been made by researchers and investigators to retrieve these objects from the body for scientific study. They have met with a good deal of success, with many alleged 'implants' having been surgically removed. The results of analysis, however, have been inconclusive, with no absolute proof of an extraterres-trial origin forthcoming to date. Indeed, the objects (which are typically two or three millimetres in length) have been shown to be composed of earthly materials such as carbon, silicon, oxygen and other trace elements. (Supporters of an extraterrestrial origin for implants state, quite reasonably, that these substances are common throughout the Universe and that this should not be taken as proof of their earthly origin. Nevertheless, one would expect a genuine alien artefact, even if constructed of materials found on Earth, to show utterly unusual combinations or methods of construction.)

While the exact purpose of the implants is unknown, it has been suggested by various researchers that they may be tracking devices, by which the 'aliens' can keep tabs on humans they wish to abduct (in much the same way as zoologists tag animals in the wild). Alternatively, they may function as monitors of metabolism and other physical processes within the body. Some investigators, fearful of a possible alien invasion of our planet, suggest that the implants are mind-control devices that will be activated if and when the aliens finally come out into the open, thus turning what may be millions of humans into a gigantic army of alien-controlled robots.

Although these ideas might seem rather paranoid and far-fetched, the last one raises the intriguing and extremely unsettling possibility that what are assumed by many to be *alien* implants are actually *human* implants – electromagnetic microwave devices giving the controllers direct access to the minds of the abductees. Naturally, in this scenario, the abductions themselves have nothing to do with alien activity: as the French-American ufologist Jacques Vallée has noted,[72] many apparent 'alien abductions' give every indication of being carefully engineered hoaxes – hoaxes, moreover, not perpetrated by the witnesses themselves but rather by a human agency with access to high technology and vast resources.

To illustrate this possibility, let us look at the case of an unfortunate man named Leonard Kille. A talented and successful electronics engineer, Kille was the co-inventor of the Land camera (named after Edwin Land of the Polaroid Corporation, who founded the Scientific Engineering Institute [SEI] on behalf of the CIA).[73] Alex Constantine writes: 'At South Vietnam's Bien Hoa Hospital ... an SEI team buried electrodes in the skulls of Vietcong POWs and attempted to spur them into violence by remote control. Upon completion of the experiments, the POWs were shot and cremated by a company of "America's best," the Green Berets.'[74]

In 1966, Kille suspected his wife of having an affair with a lodger. He did not believe her denials, and a psychiatrist interpreted his resultant anger as a 'personality pattern disturbance'. He was referred to CIA psychiatrists for neurological tests. They concluded that Kille was a paranoid and a mild psychomotor epileptic. Kille was admitted to the

Massachusetts General Hospital and his wife threatened to divorce him if he did not submit to brain surgery. In fact, his wife *had* been conducting an affair with their lodger, and did divorce Kille after his surgery.[75]

The surgery conducted on Leonard Kille consisted of four electrical strands, each containing twenty electrodes, being implanted in his brain. The insertion of these stimoceivers totally disabled Kille and left him terrified that he would be operated on again. According to Constantine, 'in 1971 an attendant found him with a wastebasket on his head to "stop the microwaves" '.[76] When he was transferred to Boston's VA Hospital, his doctors were not informed that he had been implanted with electrode strands and therefore assumed that his claims were those of a delusional paranoiac. Kille's moods were controlled with electronic stimulation. 'The "haunting fear" left by Kille's ordeal, a psychiatrist wrote in the *New England Journal of Medicine*, is that "men may become slaves, perhaps, to an authoritarian state".'[77]

Constantine believes that UFO activity is conducted by human intelligence agencies:

> UFOs are strictly terrestrial, as one UFO abductee recognized. She phoned Julianne McKinney at the [Electronic] Surveillance Project in Washington to report her abduction, aware that it was government-directed. 'Her house is being shot at,' McKinney says, 'and they are harassing her viciously, the target of massive microwave assault.' The abuse of psychoactive technology is escalating, unbeknownst to the American public. Recurrent hypno-programmed stalkers, ritual and 'alien' outrages and psychotronic forms of political persecution are on the upswing at the hands of the DIA [Defense Intelligence Agency], CIA, FBI, NSA [National Security Agency] and other covert branches of government. Hired guns in media, law enforcement and psychiatry protect them by discrediting the victims. In effect, an ambitious but meticulously concealed, undeclared *war* on American private citizens is in progress – a psywar.[78] [Original emphasis.]

More and more people in America are coming forward with complaints of psychotronic harassment. One of their greatest champions was Julianne McKinney (mentioned above), a CIA-trained military officer who decided to do something to help the victims and used her retirement bonus to finance the Electronic Surveillance Project (ESP), based in the offices of the Association of National Security Alumni in Washington, D.C. The running of the organisation eventually drained all her savings, and in late 1995 McKinney left Washington. She has not been seen since, although she is rumoured to be still alive.[79]

Microwave harassment and mind control experiments are not confined to the United States. Following a routine operation in a Stockholm hospital, Swede Robert Naeslund discovered that he had been implanted with a radio-hypnotic intracerebral control device and had become the target of directed microwave radiation. He subsequently claimed that he was unable to receive corrective treatment from any doctor in Sweden due to interference from SAPO, the Swedish security service. Naeslund travelled to Indonesia and succeeded in finding a surgeon willing to remove the implants; however, the operation was allegedly halted midway by the CIA. Although he has made numerous attempts to focus public awareness on his plight and that of others in his position, this has merely resulted in more electromagnetic harassment.[80]

In the United Kingdom, it has been claimed that the women who began protesting against the stationing of tactical nuclear weapons at the Greenham USAF base on Greenham Common in 1981 were also the victims of electromagnetic harassment. 'Protestors complained of severe headaches, temporary paralysis, nausea, palpitations and other classic symptoms of microwave poisoning. Tests revealed microwave radiation up to 100 times greater than background readings taken around the base.'[81]

In addition, targeted electromagnetic radiation has been implicated in the deaths of 25 British scientists who were working on secret electronic warfare projects for NATO, including the Strategic Defence Initiative ('Star Wars') in the mid-1980s. According to Alex Constantine:

A pattern to the killings in Great Britain begins with the fact that seven of the scientists worked for Marconi, a subsidiary of General Electric. At the time, Marconi was under investigation for bribing and defrauding ministers of government. But Britain's MoD found 'no evidence' linking the deaths. Blame for the sudden outbreak of suicides among Marconi engineers was laid on stress. (Another unlikely explanation was given for the 'hum' in Bristol, home of Marconi, a low-frequency noise . . . blamed on 'frogs'.) Jonathan Walsh, a digital communications specialist at Marconi, was assigned to the secretive Martlesham Heath Research Laboratory under a General Electric contract. (GE has long led the field in the development of anti-personnel electronic weapons, an interest that gestated with participation in Project Comet, the Pentagon-based research program to explore the psychological effects of frequencies on the electromagnetic spectrum.) Walsh dropped from his hotel window in November 1985.[82]

It has been suggested that these scientists, one of whom killed himself by chewing on live electrical wires, were driven to their deaths through electromagnetic mind control.

Alex Constantine and other mind control researchers firmly believe that American and European intelligence services are to blame not only for barbaric mind control experiments but also for staging UFO sightings and 'alien' encounters as a cover for their activities. As we have seen, there is much evidence to support these assertions. However, we have also noted that there is evidence to suggest that modern UFOs are based on highly secret designs that were drawn up by Nazi engineers towards the end of the Second World War. Taken together, these claims have led some UFO researchers and conspiracy theorists to turn their backs on the concept of alien visitation and to suggest that innocent people throughout the world are being victimised and abused by a sinister, ultra-secret society – a society having little or nothing to do with the United States, Russia or any other country.

The outrageous suggestion put forward by these re-searchers is that this society is actually composed of Nazis who escaped from the ruins of Germany at the end of the Second World War, and who are continuing their pursuit of world domination from the icy fastness of Antarctica.

9 Invisible Eagle

Rumours of Nazi Survival to the Present

T HERE ARE, OF COURSE, A NUMBER OF PROBLEMS posed by the idea that the pattern of world events is being controlled by a secret colony of Nazis operating out of an impregnable fortress somewhere in Antarctica. The claims made by conspiracy theorists about ongoing Nazi activity in the present day sound at best like lurid and rather distasteful science fiction, at worst like the ravings of seriously unbalanced minds. Among the questions one feels obliged to ask are: how would such an operation be financed? How could such an elaborate colony remain hidden for the last 55 years? For that matter, how could it have been built in the first place? And what could be its ultimate aim? Given the enormous power and fantastic technology attributed to it by conspiratologists, what are its (doubtless nefarious) plans for the rest of humanity? In this final chapter, we will look at some of the claims concerning Antarctica's hidden residents, and at the evidence for the reality of this ultimate conspiracy.

Operation Eagle Flight

As we have just noted, one of the most important questions raised by the Nazis-in-Antarctica theory involves finance: how could a large, permanent base be constructed and maintained for more than half a century on the most inhospitable continent in the world? For an answer to this question, we must return to the closing months of the Second World War when it was becoming clear to Nazi officials that their 'Thousand-Year Reich' faced imminent destruction.

In August 1944, while an amphetamine-fuelled Adolf Hitler was venting his contempt for the German people whose incipient defeat had betrayed his vision ('If the German people was to be conquered in the struggle,' he said, 'then it had been too weak to face the test of history, and was fit only for destruction'[1]), his deputy, Reichsleiter Martin Bormann, was at the Hotel Maison Rouge in Strasbourg planning the continuation of Nazi power and ideology. Addressing the meeting of Nazi Party officials and German business leaders, Bormann stated: 'German industry must realize that the war cannot now be won, and must take steps to prepare for a postwar commercial campaign which will in time ensure the economic resurgence of Germany.'[2]

These steps were implemented under the code name *Aktion Adlerflug* (Operation Eagle Flight) and resulted in the 'massive flight of money, gold, stocks, bonds, patents, copyrights, and even technical specialists from Germany'.[3] Along with the central Deutsche Bank and the chemical cartel I. G. Farben, one of the largest industrial organisations in Europe, Bormann succeeded in establishing 750 front corporations in Portugal, Spain, Sweden, Switzerland, Turkey and Argentina. Of course, Bormann would have been unable to achieve this without substantial help from both within and outside Germany. This came in the form of connections with banks and businesses dating back to before the war,[4] indeed to the financing of the Nazi Party itself following the elections of 1933. On 20 February of that year, 25 of the most prominent industrialists in Germany were invited by Hermann Goering to a meeting with Adolf Hitler, who stated: 'An impossible situation is created when one section of a people favors private property while another denies it. A struggle of that sort tears a people apart and the fight continues until one section emerges victorious . . . It is not by accident that one man produces more than another; the concept of private property is rooted in this fact . . . Human beings are anything but equal. As far as the economy is concerned, I have but one desire, namely, that it may enter upon a peaceful future ... There will, however, not be a domestic peace unless Marxism has been exterminated.'[5]

Another of these connections was with the American International Telephone & Telegraph Corporation (ITT), which continued to trade with Nazi Germany after America's entry into the war, selling communications and military equipment such as artillery fuses. Journalist Jim Marrs states that ITT's German chairman, Gerhardt Westrick, was 'a close associate of John Foster Dulles, who would become US secretary of state under President Dwight Eisenhower, and partner to Dr Heinrich Albert, head of the Ford Motor Co. in Germany until 1945'. He adds: 'Two ITT directors were German banker Baron Kurt von Schroder and Walter Schellenberg, head of counter-intelligence for the Nazi Gestapo.'[6]

According to former *New York Times* writer Charles Higham, Standard Oil of New Jersey (ESSO) secretly sold gasoline to Germany and fascist Spain. 'The shipments to Spain indirectly assisted the Axis through Spanish transferences to Hamburg.'[7] By changing the country of registration for Standard's tanker fleet to Panama, company spokesmen could claim that the oil was coming not from the United States but the Caribbean.[8]

There were also numerous banking connections, one of which was the partnership established in 1936 between the J. Henry Schroder Bank of New York and several Rockefeller family members to form Schroder, Rockefeller and Company, Investment Bankers that provided economic support to the Rome-Berlin Axis. 'The partners in Schroder, Rockefeller and Company included Avery Rockefeller, nephew of John D., Baron Bruno von Schroder in London, and Kurt von Schroder [of the Bank of International Settlements] and the Gestapo in Cologne ... Standard Oil's Paris representatives were directors of the Banque de Paris et de Pays-Bas, which had intricate connections to the Nazis and to Chase [National Bank].'[9]

According to investigator Paul Manning, Hermann Schmitz, head of I. G. Farben, was president of Chase

National Bank for seven years prior to the war, and later held as much stock in Standard Oil as did the Rockefellers. He held other shares in General Motors 'and other US blue chip industrial stocks, and the 700 secret companies controlled in his time by I. G. [Farben], as well as shares in the 750 corporations he helped Bormann establish during the last years of World War II'. Manning continues: 'The Bormann organization in South America utilizes the voting power of the Schmitz trust along with their own assets to guide the multinationals they control, as they keep steady the economic course of the Fatherland. The Bormann organization is not merely a group of ex-Nazis. It is a great economic power whose interests today supersede their ideology.'[10]

The financial relationship between the Nazis and the Swiss banks has been well documented. Through processes of investment and money laundering, approximately 15 billion *Reichsmarks* was moved through Switzerland, equivalent to three per cent of America's gross domestic product (GDP) in 1944. 'To put this into today's terms, three percent of America's GDP is $200 billion, which is more than the entire GDP of Switzerland. Allow for interest, compounded over 50 years, and the value of the Nazi cache that went through Switzerland moves into the region of a trillion dollars.'[11]

Over the years there has been considerable speculation on the fate of Martin Bormann, Hitler's deputy and the second most powerful man in the Third Reich. One of the main characteristics of the Nazi survival theory is, perhaps unsurprisingly, the idea that the Nazi leaders themselves managed to escape from Berlin during the Allies' final assault. Since Bormann played such a large part in planning the continuation of Nazi financial interests and power after the war, it is worth pausing briefly to note the findings of the internationally esteemed historian Hugh Trevor-Roper who, as a wartime intelligence officer, was charged with the task of establishing the ultimate fate of Hitler and his inner circle. According to Trevor-Roper:

In 1945 the evidence [on Bormann's fate] was conflicting and uncertain. Several witnesses maintained that Bormann had been killed in a tank which exploded when hit by a *Panzerfaust* [bazooka] on the Weidendammer Bridge during the attempted breakthrough on the night of 1–2 May. On the other hand, all these witnesses have admitted that the scene was one of great confusion and none of them claims to have seen Bormann's body ... Further, even in 1945 I had three witnesses who independently claimed to have accompanied Bormann in his attempted escape. One of these witnesses, Artur Axmann, claimed afterwards to have seen him dead. Whether we believe Axmann or not is entirely a matter of choice, for his word is unsupported by any other testimony. In his favour it can be said that his evidence on all other points has been vindicated. On the other hand, if he wished to protect Bormann against further search, his natural course would be to give false evidence of his death. This being so I came in 1945, to the only permissible conclusion, *viz*: that Bormann had certainly survived the tank explosion but had possibly, though by no means certainly, been killed later that night. Such was the balance of evidence in 1945.[12]

Trevor-Roper adds that by 1956 the situation remained unchanged by new evidence. In 1953, a former SS major, Joachim Tibertius, made a statement to a Swiss newspaper, *Der Bund*, in which he claimed to have seen Bormann after the tank explosion, at the Hotel Atlas. According to Tibertius: 'He had by then changed into civilian clothes. We pushed on together towards the Schiffbauerdamm and the Albrechtstrasse. Then I finally lost sight of him. But he had as good a chance to escape as I had.'[13]

The absence of concrete evidence for Bormann's death in 1945 spawned a number of claims of his survival, including one that placed him in Bolivia. Another claim came from Reinhardt Gehlen, who had been an *Abwehr* officer during the war and had subsequently become head of the new West German intelligence service, the *Bundesnachrichtendienst*, 'thanks to his useful experience ... and the beginning of the Cold War'.[14] In 1971, Gehlen stated in his memoirs that during the war he had come to the conclusion that Bormann was actually a Soviet spy. Following the war, 'Bormann had sought and found protection in Moscow, where he had occasionally been seen by reliable witnesses and had recently died'.[15]

However, as Trevor-Roper informs us, Gehlen's claims were refuted in 1972 'when two human skeletons, which had been dug up in waste ground near the Lehrter Station in West Berlin – i.e. not far from the place where Axmann claimed to have seen the bodies – were forensically examined and identified as those of Bormann and his companion in flight, Dr [Ludwig] Stumpfegger', Hitler's surgeon.[16]

Although it has been established since 1972 that Bormann's attempt to escape from the ruins of the Third Reich ended in death, it is equally certain that his brainchild, Operation Eagle Flight, met with considerably greater success. According to conspiracy researcher Jim Keith, the Research and Analysis branch of the Office of Strategic Services (OSS), the forerunner of the CIA, stated in 1945 that 'Nazi Party members, German industrialists and the German military, realizing their victory can no longer be attained, are now developing postwar commercial projects, endeavoring to renew and cement friendships in foreign commercial circles and planning for renewals of pre-war cartel agreements'.[17] Keith goes on to quote the minutes of the secret meeting between Bormann and a group of German industrialists, mentioned earlier: 'The [Nazi] Party is ready to supply large amounts of money to those industrialists who contribute to the post-war organization abroad. In return, the Party demands all financial reserves which have already been transferred abroad or may be later transferred, so that after the defeat a strong new Reich can be built.'[18]

Project PAPERCLIP

Those who subscribe to the idea of Nazi survival in the post-war period cite another documented historical fact in support of their theories. After the end of the war, both the

Americans and the Russians began to search throughout occupied Germany for technical, intelligence, military and other scientific information. In September 1946, President Harry Truman authorised Project PAPERCLIP, a programme to bring selected German scientists to America. Aside from expertise in their fields, the main requisite for their acceptance for residence in the United States was proof that they had not been active members of the Nazi Party, and had not displayed any allegiance to Hitler.

Background investigations of various German scientists were conducted by the Joint Intelligence Objectives Agency (JIOA), which found them all to have been enthusiastic Nazis. Nevertheless, it was decided that to send them back to Germany would probably result in their expertise being exploited by the Soviets and would thus constitute a greater threat to US security than any Nazi sympathies they might have had. Among these scientists was, of course, Wernher von Braun, who had been technical director of the Peenemünde rocket research centre, home of the dreaded V-2 missile that had caused such carnage in London and elsewhere. According to conspiratologists, OSS Director Allen Dulles ordered the scientists' dossiers to be cleansed of Nazi references, with the result that by 1955 more than 760 German scientists had been granted US citizenship. This was done without the knowledge of President Truman.

One of those who benefited from Project PAPERCLIP was the *Abwehr* officer Reinhardt Gehlen, whose insurance policy of microfilming a vast number of documents concerning Soviet intelligence came to the attention of Dulles. Gehlen and Dulles formulated an arrangement by which the Nazi and American intelligence apparatus would be combined, ostensibly on the basis of a common interest in a defence against communism. However, far from being committed exclusively to the protection of the United States and Western Europe, Gehlen's organisation was committed exclusively to the security of the ODESSA (Organisation of Veterans of the SS) and other 'rat lines' that had been set up to aid the escape of more than 5,000 Nazis – and to set up Nazi colonies throughout the world.

Jim Keith writes:

Once the Gehlen Org[anisation] was in place, with an estimated 4,000 intelligence specialists in Germany and more than 4,000 undercover operatives in the Soviet bloc, the perceived threat to the United States by the Soviets was aggravated by Nazi intelligence, and the Cold War was inevitable. Gehlen and his cronies seemingly never admitted that Germany had lost the war and simply persisted with Nazi objectives, using different means to destroy the USSR, namely collaboration with the United States and the OSS/CIA. The Nazis may have, in addition, foreseen the devastating results of a Cold War between the US and the USSR. The Cold War provided a financial burden which has destroyed Russia and left the United States as the world's biggest debtor nation . . .[19]

With secret control of hundreds of billions of dollars in financial and industrial assets, not to mention access to the intelligence agencies of the post-war superpowers and with hidden colonies throughout the world, this 'Nazi International' was in a position to reverse the failure of the Third Reich and finally achieve global domination. According to conspiratologists, the main headquarters of the Nazi International was – and is – in Antarctica.

The Mysterious Voyage of Captain Schaeffer

On 25 April 1945, the German submarine U-977 embarked on one of the most remarkable voyages of the Second World War. Commanded by Captain Hans Schaeffer, the submarine left Kiel Harbour in the Baltic, stopped briefly for fuel at Christiansand South the following day, and arrived at Mar del Plata, Argentina nearly four months later, on 17 August.[20] In his subsequent interrogation by the Allies, Schaeffer stated that he had heard over the radio that the war had ended several days after leaving Christiansand South, and had decided to make for Argentina rather than staying in Europe. He offered his crew the option of being put off the submarine on the Norwegian coast or continuing on with him.

Some of Schaeffer's crew opted to return to Germany, so the U-977 remained hidden in Norwegian waters until 10 May, when the departing crew members were put ashore near Bergen. Schaeffer and the rest of his crew 'then embarked upon what surely must have been one of the most remarkable naval feats of the war: a journey through the North Sea and English Channel, past Gibraltar and along the coast of Africa, to finally surface, all of sixty-six days later, in the middle of the South Atlantic Ocean'.[21] Over the next month, the U-977 evaded capture by diving, surfacing, and erecting imitation sails and funnel to make it look like a cargo steamer from a distance.[22]

On 17 August 1945, the U-977 put into Mar del Plata, in spite of Schaeffer having heard over the radio that the crew of another fleeing German submarine, the U-530, had been apprehended on the River Plate and handed over to the United States. During his initial interrogation by the Argentine authorities, Schaeffer was asked if he had carried anyone of 'political importance' on the voyage, to which he replied that he had not. Harbinson informs us that several weeks later Schaeffer was again interrogated, this time by a special Anglo-American commission composed of high-ranking officers. It seems that this commission wanted to explore the possibility that the U-977 had transported Hitler and Martin Bormann first to Argentina and then on to a secret Nazi base in Antarctica.[23]

The English and Americans apparently considered this to be a realistic possibility, for they subsequently flew both Schaeffer and Otto Wehrmut, the commander of the U-530, to Washington, D.C., where the interrogations continued for several more months. It is not clear what happened to Wehrmut at this point, but Schaeffer was taken to Antwerp, Belgium, where he was interrogated yet again. The U-977 itself was thoroughly searched and then taken to the United States where it was destroyed under orders from the US War Department. Schaeffer was then sent back to Germany, but decided to leave his country and return to Argentina.[24]

The testimony of Captain Schaeffer served as an early inspiration for the idea that high-ranking Nazis had escaped the destruction of the Third Reich and were continuing with their plans for world domination in one or more secret locations. Schaeffer's voyage suggested to some that the ultimate destination for escaping Nazis was Antarctica, via Argentina. The German Navy Admiral Karl Doenitz is reported to have stated in 1943: 'The German submarine fleet is proud of having built for the Führer in another part of the world a Shangri-la on land, an impregnable fortress.'[25]

Where was this 'impregnable fortress' – if it existed? It is a matter of historical fact that Nazi Germany maintained an intense interest in the Antarctic continent throughout the war. As we shall now see, that beautiful, mysterious and hostile place also holds a prominent position in the thoughts of those who subscribe to the Nazi-survival theory.

Operation Highjump

Between 1946 and 1947, Rear Admiral Richard E. Byrd contributed to the US Navy Antarctic Developments Project, also known as Operation Highjump (see page 179). This operation was ostensibly an exercise in polar combat, survival and exploration; however, conspiracy theorists have suggested another, far more sinister purpose. Operation Highjump began approximately one year after the arrival of the U-977 at Mar del Plata, Argentina. The vast resources placed at Byrd's disposal have suggested to many that the operation was intended as an actual assault force – but an assault against what, or whom?

The British author W. A. Harbinson has perhaps done more than any other writer to popularise the idea that the Nazis had developed extremely advanced aircraft designs by the end of the Second World War. In his novel sequence *Projekt Saucer* and his non-fiction study *Projekt UFO*, he also offers evidence of a secret flying-disc base in Antarctica. In his novel *Genesis* (1980) Harbinson includes a lengthy afterword, which was later reprinted as the introduction to

Man-Made UFOs 1944-1994: 50 Years of Suppression (1994) by Renato Vesco and David Hatcher Childress and which describes how, in May 1978, a single-issue tabloid paper called *Brisant* was being given away at Stand 111, in a scientific exhibition in the Hannover Messe Hall. This paper contained two articles: one on the scientific future of Antarctica, and the other on flying-disc technology at the end of the war (see Chapter Eight).

In its article on Antarctica, *Brisant* asked why the Operation Highjump assault force docked near the German-claimed region of *Neu Schwabenland* on 27 January 1947, why it then divided into three separate task forces and, most importantly, why there had been so many foreign press reports that the operation had been a disaster. Harbinson writes:

> That expedition became something of a mystery. Subsequent official reports stated that it had been an enormous success, revealing more about the Antarctic than had ever been known before. However, other, mainly foreign reports suggested that such in fact had not been the case: that many of Byrd's men were lost during the first day, that at least four of his airplanes inexplicably disappeared, and that while the expedition had gone provisioned for six to eight months, the men actually returned to America in February 1947, after only a few weeks. According to *Brisant*, Admiral Byrd later told a reporter (I could find no verification on this) that it was 'necessary for the USA to take defensive actions against enemy air fighters which come from the polar regions' and that in the case of a new war the USA would be 'attacked by fighters that are able to fly from one pole to the other with incredible speed.' Also, according to *Brisant*, shortly after his return from the Antarctic, Admiral Byrd was ordered to undergo a secret cross-examination – and the United States withdrew from the Antarctic for almost a decade.[26]

The article carried a serious and startling implication: that Operation Highjump had been a military invasion force disguised as a training and exploratory group, that it had intended to deal with a secret colony of Nazi survivors in an elaborate underground facility that had been constructed during the Second World War, and that this invasion force had met its match in the form of a squadron of Nazi-built flying discs based at the colony. The reason for the United States' temporary withdrawal from Antarctica was, allegedly, to allow itself time to develop its own flying discs, based upon designs captured at the end of the war.[27]

Nazi UFO Bases in Antarctica?

Most reasonable people would dismiss as fantastic nonsense the idea that many Nazis fled the ruins of the Third Reich and took up residence in a secret Antarctic colony, armed with a squadron of flying discs with which to protect themselves. However, the paranoid conspiracy theories that have proliferated in the second half of the twentieth century are based not so much on reason but rather on elaborate extrapolations of puzzling but inconclusive evidence. In the present case, this evidence centres on the undeniable interest the Third Reich maintained in Antarctica throughout the war: German ships and U-boats constantly patrolled the South Atlantic between South Africa and the region of Antarctica containing *Neu Schwabenland*, and it is certainly possible that many of these voyages could have included shipments of personnel and supplies for the construction of heavily fortified facilities. When we add to this the testimony of the captain of the U-977, Hans Schaeffer (which admittedly may well be false), the claims of the neo-Nazi publication *Brisant* that such trips included the transfer of flying-disc research teams and disc components, and the rumours regarding the disastrous failure of Byrd's Operation Highjump, we have the ingredients of a powerful and enduring modern myth, in which the evils of Nazism did not meet destruction at the hands of the victorious Allies in 1945 but continue to exert a terrible influence over human affairs to this day.

Indeed, it is somewhat ironic that the political system that identified the Jews as its scapegoat and moved with such barbarism against them should now be chosen by many conspiracy theorists as the scapegoat responsible for the machinations of a putative 'New World Order'. It is quite possible that the concept of Nazi survival itself has survived to the present day because of the very extremity of the crimes perpetrated by the Third Reich. While it may be argued that our continuing interest in Nazi Germany constitutes an unhealthy fascination with the suffering and terror of an ultimate inhumanity, there is also a case for saying that this interest is born of a deep and despairing bafflement (see the Introduction). I believe it is not going too far to suggest that the elaborate conspiracy theory involving Nazi survival is born of a deeply ingrained suspicion that such wickedness could not have been completely defeated at the war's end; this suspicion may well have been reinforced by the fact that the *völkisch* and Pan-German forerunners of the Nazi Party were influenced by occult and mythological belief systems, combined with the more generalised occult revival occurring throughout Europe in the post-war years.

Of course, conspiracy theories cannot survive without conspiratologists to conceive and propagate them. We shall now, therefore, turn our attention to the means by which the theory of Nazi survival has been developed.

The Black Order

Throughout the post-war period, material has been added constantly to the sinister mythological system built around the idea that the Third Reich continues its activities in a hidden location. This cabal of surviving Nazis is sometimes referred to as the Fourth Reich but more often as the 'Black Order'. Those who contend that such a concept can have no place in a rational person's world view are underestimating the subtle power exerted by the strange concepts contained within the field of popular occultism. The British writer Joscelyn Godwin has produced a splendid, highly informative study of this field in his book *Arktos: The Polar Myth in Science, Symbolism, and Nazi Survival*, in which he maintains an admirably sceptical standpoint while acknowledging that the notions embodied in popular occultism must be treated with respect, if only for their powerful influence over the public mind. He also includes a pertinent quote from the German Pastor Ekkehard Hieronimus regarding popular beliefs:

> What is going on in the lower reaches of society is probably very much more potent and effective than what happens in intellectual circles. We think, of course, that it is the intellectuals – now in the broadest sense of the term, in which I include the scientists – who define our life. But lately the intellectuals have been rather like a film of oil on a great puddle of water: it shines mischievously and thinks that it is the whole thing, but it is only one molecule thick. I can see quite definite things coming towards us. The things going on in the so-called cultural underground, or the so-called subculture, are very strange.[28]

Godwin then wryly offers an example of a product of this 'subculture', a report from the 16 April 1991 issue of the London newspaper the *Sun*, that claims that the ruins of Atlantis have been discovered in the Arctic by a joint French-Soviet research expedition. The 'proof' is a photo-montage of some Doric columns rising from an icy landscape. While the vast majority of people seeing this would probably think it interesting but almost certainly spurious, the idea is nevertheless firmly embedded in their unconscious. As Godwin notes (and as we have discussed in earlier chapters), uncritical belief in the literal reality of certain occult concepts aided in no small degree the rise of National Socialism. 'One has to be thankful that our tabloids are not proclaiming Aryan supremacy or describing Jewish ritual murder; but one may well ask what collective attitudes are being formed by the currents in the "great puddle" of popular occultism.'[29]

It is one thing for a collective attitude to admit the possibility of visitation by alien spacecraft, or the existence of ghosts or relict hominids such as Bigfoot, the Yeti and so on;

it is quite another to admit of the undying – perhaps supernatural – power of an ideology that has already irreparably demeaned humanity and could quite conceivably wreak havoc once again.

'Götzen Gegen Thule'

In 1971, Wilhelm Landig published a strange novel entitled *Götzen gegen Thule* (*Godlets Against Thule*). In an echo of the nineteenth-century vogue for presenting fantasy as a 'true story', Landig subtitles his novel 'a fiction full of facts' and claims that it contains accurate information on the radical advances in aviation and weapons technology made in the years since the end of the war. *Götzen gegen Thule* is fundamentally an adventure story that follows the exploits of two German airmen, Recke and Reimer (which Godwin translates as 'Brave Warrior' and 'Poet' respectively[30]), who are sent to a secret German base in the far north of Canada towards the end of the Second World War. This base, known as Point 103, is a large underground facility possessing highly advanced technology and supplied by powerful allies in the United States. Its occupants constitute a force opposed to the Third Reich, which is seen as a Satanic force.

Point 103 is, in fact, solidly anti-racist, as evidenced by one scene in which a conference there is attended by 'a Tibetan lama, Japanese, Chinese, and American officers, Indians, a Black Ethiopian, Arabs, Persians, a Brazilian officer, a Venezuelan, a Siamese, and a full-blooded Mexican Indian'.[31] Travel to and from this remote and ultra-secret facility is by a highly advanced aircraft called the V7, which is shaped like a sphere with a rotating circular wing containing jet turbines. Interestingly enough, even the responsible and sceptical Godwin is willing to concede that this part of Landig's novel may well have a basis in fact (see Chapter Eight).

The two airmen are sent on a mission to Prague to prevent the disc-plane technology from falling into Allied hands; following the end of the war and the defeat of Nazi Germany, Point 103 declares itself independent and continues with its pursuit of Thulean ideals. These ideals are explained by another character, an ex-Waffen-SS officer named Gutmann ('Good man'). Godwin provides a summary of the Thulean philosophy:

> The light of Thule comes not from the East but from the North. Its tradition is 'Uranian,' being derived from Uranos, lord of the cosmic world order and of the primordial Paradise of the Aryan Race, situated at the North Pole. It was Uranos's usurping son Saturn who brought upon this originally happy and unified humanity the dubious gift of the egoic state. The temptations consequent upon this change in the human constitution lead to the loss of primeval unity and, eventually, the destruction of Saturn's realm, Atlantis. Thereupon the warm climate of the secret island of the Hyperboreans was suddenly replaced by bitter winter. The primordial races of the Arctic and of the Nordic Atlantis both lost their homes, and were forced to migrate southwards. Wherever they settled – in Europe, Persia, India, and elsewhere – they tried to remake their lost Paradise, and in their myths and legends cherished the memory of it.[32]

As Godwin notes, Uranos and Saturn seem to be personifications of events in remote antiquity; however, the Thulean religion included an unmanifested God beyond space and time, and a Son through whom the will of the Father operates and who is identified with the laws of nature. Landig himself identifies the legend of Thule (which in geographical terms is located close to Point 103) with that of the spiritual centre of the world, sometimes called Shambhala. The reader will recall Nicholas Roerich's encounter with a golden flying disc, described in Chapter Four, and how his guide stated that the UFO represented the beneficent influence of Rigden-Jyepo, the King of the World, who was watching over them. Through another character, a French collaborator named Bélisse ('from Bélisane, sun god of the Gauls'[33]), Landig describes in elaborate detail the nature of this phenomenon, which he calls 'Manisolas'. They are living, intelligent bio-mechanical entities with a complex life cycle that begins as a circle of light and continues through a metallic form before reaching the reproductive stage. Through a regenerative process, a new Manisola grows within the womb of the adult.

> The regenerated part is expelled by the remaining mother-nucleus as a new energetic circle of light, corresponding to a birthing technique. This new circle enters on the same seven developmental stages, while the expelling maternal element rolls itself into a ball, which then explodes. The metallic remains contain particles of copper. The optical impressions that eyewitnesses of these Manisolas have had up to now are basically quite uniform. In the daytime they display an extremely bright gold or silver luminescence, some-times with traces of rose-colored smoke which then often condense into grayish-white trails. At night the disks shine in glowing or glossy colors, showing on occasion long flames at the edges and red and blue sparks, which can grow so strong as to wreathe them in fire. Most remarkable is their power of reaction against pursuers, like that of a rational creature, far exceeding any possible electronic self-steering or radio control.[34]

Landig goes on to describe how, throughout the ages, all mythologies refer in one way or another to the Manisolas, which are seen as symbols of spiritual potency, unity and love. Although Point 103 is claimed to be a non-racist society, the Thuleans nevertheless consider Israel to be in eternal opposition to their ideals, and remember the time when their ancestors, the Nordic Atlanteans, were held in slavery by Semitic sorcerers.

Perhaps unsurprisingly, the Ark of the Covenant is brought into this bizarre occult adventure and is described as a kind of battery for astral energy to be used in magical operations. This energy is the fertilising 'force-field of the Aryans', which is stolen by Hebrew magicians and stored in the Ark for their own anti-Aryan purposes. The international conspiracy against the Aryans is further defined when the characters travel to Tibet and meet another German, Juncker ('Aristocrat'[35]), who tells them that the Asiatic peoples are waiting for a great warrior who will come from the subterranean realm of Agartha and lead them to domination of the world. We then learn of the nature of 'Shambala' and 'Agartha', which is another perversion of Buddhist teaching, similar to that suggested by Ravenscroft in *The Spear of Destiny* (see Chapter Five). The central point of *Götzen gegen Thule* is that the Third Reich arose with the assistance of the twin power centres of Agartha and Shambhala and was defeated when it succumbed to the materialistic attractions of Shambhala, thus destroying the balance between the two. We can look again to Godwin for a good translation of Landig's original:

> The source of material energies of the left hand, which have their seat in Shambala, is the upper-earth city of power and might, which is ruled by a great King of Fear. But it is the same seat of Shambala that a part of the western secret brotherhoods and lodges regards as their point of origin, from which come the promises and warnings of a Lord of the World. This Shambala is a searchlight of our will! Then there is the second source: Agartha, the inner, underworld realm of contemplation and its energies. There too is a Lord and King of the World, who promises his domination. At the proper moment, this center will lead good men against the evil ones; and it is firmly connected with Brahytma, that is, God. And that is the king to serve, the one who will set up our empire and rule over the others . . . [T]he men in [the Third] Reich . . . joined themselves with the energies of Shambala, of pure force, and in their secret way worked against the other men of [the] Reich . . . And behind these energies which manifest themselves in Shambala stands the Caucasian, Stalin-Dugaschvili! He knew everything, he knew the men of the circle in [the] Reich and he played his own cards

with them as if they were their own. Stalin-Dugaschvili had the support of the Lord of Fear and Power against [the] Reich![36]

In the final stages of the novel, the heroes leave Tibet but are captured in India by the British, who place them in a prisoner-of-war camp. When they finally return to Germany, it becomes clear that they will probably never rejoin Point 103, which 'seems to have forgotten them: they ruefully admit . . . that if it still exists, it has probably had to isolate itself completely from the world of today'.

All that remains to [the Thuleans] is to constitute a 'Fourth Reich in exile,' patiently waiting for the Age of Pisces to reach its inevitable end. And as the Fish Age passes, so St Peter's religious tyranny in Rome will crumble . . . and the Jewish Ark will lose its potency. Then, says Landig, the . . . banner of the Aryans will fly again . . .[37]

Added to the weird flights of fancy, *Götzen gegen Thule* contains several statements that mark it out as a work of pernicious historical revisionism, such as Juncker's claim that the bodies in the liberated concentration camps were actually those of Germans killed in Allied air raids on Munich.[38] Aside from this, the novel manages to weave together a wide variety of myths, all of which have come to be associated with the concept of Nazi survival: Nordic mythology, UFOs as man-made aircraft, the subterranean realms of Shambhala and Agartha, the Hollow Earth, the Holy Grail, and the international conspiracy to inaugurate a secret One-World Government. While it might be expected that such a ridiculous and (in its attempt at historical revisionism) morally reprehensible tale would sink into a merciful literary oblivion, it did nothing of the kind; instead, it entered the murky realm of the cultural underground, where it was discovered by certain interested parties who saw in it an opportunity to further their own agendas.

Ernst Zündel and 'Samisdat'

The articles in the neo-Nazi publication *Brisant* did not carry by-lines. Intrigued and unsettled by the strange information they contained, W. A. Harbinson embarked on a little detective work, checking the origins of the magazine and discovering that it had been published in West Germany by a company that had since disappeared, Lintec GmbH of Hamburg. According to Harbinson, the 'company was not listed with any of the West German press organizations, nor with any public relations bureau'.[39] Nevertheless, he realised that the information contained in the *Brisant* articles had been culled from two books: *UFOs: Nazi Secret Weapons?* by Mattern Friedrich and *Secret Nazi Polar Expeditions* by Christof Friedrich. Both books were published by a company called Samisdat Publishers Limited of Toronto, Canada.

As Harbinson notes, 'Mattern Friedrich' and 'Christof Friedrich' are actually pseudonyms for Ernst Zündel, a Canadian resident but German citizen and one of the most outspoken and active of those who deny that the Holocaust occurred. Through his many apparent links with surviving Nazis in South America and elsewhere, Zündel 'now runs Samisdat Publishers Limited as a mouthpiece of neo-Nazi propaganda and commercial enterprise, specializing in the sale of Nazi books, record albums, tape recordings, photographs, medals and other Nazi memorabilia'.[40] Zündel maintains in his books that UFOs are actually Nazi secret weapons, launched from their hidden base at or near the South Pole. He also is an advocate (apparently) of the Hollow Earth Theory, and in his *Samisdat* newsletter in 1978 advertised an expedition by chartered jet to the South Pole where, he claimed, the passengers would discover not only Hitler's Antarctic UFO base but also the entrance to the interior of the planet. A ticket for the chartered flight would cost $9,999.

The following selection from the *Samisdat* article will enable the reader to gain some idea of the nature of Zündel's claims:

ACHTUNG! SAMISDAT NEWS BULLETIN
SAMISDAT HOLLOW EARTH EXPEDITION $9999.00
IN SEARCH OF HOLES IN THE POLES
SEARCH FOR HITLER'S ANTARCTIC U.F.O. BASES . . .

Your response to our most recent mailout and activities has been most encouraging! We have received orders and enquiries from as far away as Noumea in the South Pacific, Easter Island, Chile, Argentina, Brazil, Venezuela, Panama, Mexico, Soviet Satellite countries, China, South Africa, Persia, the Congo, Australia, Japan, as well as from every country in Western Europe and almost every state in the U.S.A. Not only is this response extensive, it is massive – a clear indication on the part of knowledgeable UFO researchers and members of the public that they are tired of the 'Junk food' being served up by old-line UFO groups and publications who expound the official CIA-KGB alibi that all UFOs are extraterrestrial. What the UFO-watching world wants now is the real meat of the matter – a serious investigation of UFOs whose origins are terrestrial.

SAMISDAT is the only organization making such an effort, but we are not alone, for we have thousands of supporters like yourself who want to know the truth which the saucer-charlatans have for 30 years tried to cover up with fairy-tale fantasies of 'little green men'. It is people like yourself who have made SAMISDAT the most active UFO Organization and publisher on Planet Earth! . . .

Our discoveries have led us into the production of a number of currently suppressed and sometimes vilified books which are now underground bestsellers. "UFOs – NAZI SECRET WEAPON?" was our first title, now sold out in 5 complete editions. Our second book, "SECRET NAZI POLAR EXPEDITIONS", is coming up fast and has sold out 2 full editions. Foreign-language translations of these books are selling briskly, and it is becoming obvious to everyone that the media-enforced blockade of the truth has now been broken. Three additional books are currently under production and these will round out our Phase I Publishing Program: "THE CIA-KGB-UFO COVERUP", "THE ANTARCTICA THEORY" and "THE LAST BATTALION". . . .

We have also been able to establish research teams in Canada, the U.S.A. and in particular, Germany, whose task it is to rediscover basic wingless flight which brought the original Nazi UFOs into being. Already, these teams have designed and constructed small scale models, some using conventional power and others which have propulsion systems unprecedented in today's aerospace technology. With additional research, we hope to make available several different models in kit form for hobby-builders. Any contributions to these research projects, whether of ideas or money, will be very much appreciated. Checks should be made out to SAMISDAT with the notation "For SAMPROJ R-1" . . .

For the truly dedicated UFO researcher, SAMISDAT is embarking upon a magnificent and awe-inspiring experience! We are negotiating with several international airlines and chartered air carriers in regard to our planned investigation of the "Inner Earth Theory" coupled with our search for "Hitler's Flying Saucer Bases in Antarctica." Our 'launching pad' for which we are also negotiating will be located in Rio de Janeiro or Buenos Aires. This site will be the gathering place for an International UFO Convention which is scheduled to take place some time in 1979 or 1980. From this convention site, those who are interested and financially able may join Christof Friedrich and members of a specially-selected SAMISDAT research team on the Antarctic Expedition who will not only search for Hitler's Saucer Bases in German Antarctica, but who will further attempt to settle the controversy about Admiral Byrd's "Flight into the Polar Opening" by actually flying over the South Pole! Our tentative flight path is here shown. It is anticipated that a specially-prepared, long-range jet will be available for the Antarctic Expedition's polar flight . . .

SAMISDAT's Antarctic Expedition in Search of Hitler's Flying Saucer Bases and the South Polar Opening into Inner Earth will be the unique event of a lifetime. As only a very limited number of people can be accommodated, our selection standards are of necessity rigorous. The approximate cost per person on this expedition may be as high as $9,999.00. However, the cost could be reduced considerably, provided we are able to raise money from our SAMISDAT SERIES of lectures, tapes, conventions, UFO models and book sales in this interim period. You can help to realize this dream of a lifetime in several ways: (1) You can become one of our book distributors by buying SAMISDAT books and other items at wholesale dealers' prices and then retailing them to friends, colleagues, UFO conventioneers, and visitors to county fairs, psychic fairs and flea markets. By purchasing SAMISDAT titles in bulk, you could easily realize almost a 100% profit on each item sold. This money you could then apply toward your share in the Expedition or use as you see fit. (2) You can organize a UFO club and hold your own UFO conventions on a profit-sharing basis with SAMISDAT. (3) You can help us find sponsors for the Expedition. (4) If you are rich and conscientious, you can underwrite the whole or part of the Expedition and realize our goal of a lifetime much, much faster. But empty promises and other hot-air products from windbags and do-nothings, however well off, will not serve to waft the Expedition to Antarctica and back. The only thing capable of doing that is cold, hard cash up front. If you've got what it takes and want to put your money to work right away, then please contact us! (5) You can set up your own fund-raising campaign for the Expedition. For details and assistance in regard to these and other ideas, do not hesitate to contact us.

These are but a few of the ways in which we can hasten that glorious day when we board our sleek, silvery aircraft and wing our way to Antarctica and beyond – to our rendezvous with history. When we return, we shall have unearthed Inner Earth and/or found evidence of Hitler's UFO Bases – or we shall have gone a long way toward dispelling two of the most tenaciously persistent mysteries of our Scientific Era.[41]

The reader will note that Zündel's apparent intention to launch an expedition to Antarctica could only be realised if readers of *Samisdat* bought his products 'in bulk' (needless to say, the charter flight to the Antarctic never took place). Zündel's apparently nonsensical claims regarding Nazi UFOs, secret bases at the South Pole and the Hollow Earth hide an altogether more sinister revisionist agenda.

In fact, Zündel himself has admitted as much. According to Frank Miele, a member of the Skeptics Society in the United States, who wrote an article on Holocaust revisionism for that society's magazine in 1994, Zündel told him that his book *UFOs: Nazi Secret Weapons?* (which became an underground bestseller, going through seven printings) was nothing more than a ploy to attract readers. Said Zündel in a telephone conversation with Miele: 'I realized that North Americans were not interested in being educated. They want to be entertained. The book was for fun. With a picture of the Führer on the cover and flying saucers coming out of Antarctica it was a chance to get on radio and TV talk shows. For about 15 minutes of an hour program I'd talk about that esoteric stuff. Then I would start talking about all those Jewish scientists in concentration camps, working on these secret weapons. And that was my chance to talk about what I wanted to talk about.'[42]

As one might expect (and hope), Zündel's Holocaust revisionism has landed him in hot water with the Canadian authorities. In 1984, criminal proceedings were initiated against him by the Canadian Government, based on a private complaint made by a Holocaust survivor named Sabrina Citron. Zündel was charged under Section 177 of the Criminal Code of Canada, which makes it a criminal offence to publish wilfully a statement one knows is false and that causes, or is likely to cause, injury to the public interest. Zündel had published two books by other authors: *The West, War, and*

Islam and *Did Six Million Really Die?* He was convicted for publishing the latter title and sentenced to fifteen months in jail. The conviction, however, was overturned on appeal and a second trial was ordered.

The second trial received massive coverage in the Canadian media, with Zündel calling other leading revisionists as expert witnesses. He was again convicted, but the case was taken to the Canadian Supreme Court, which found that the statute on false statements was an unconstitutional violation of free speech. As Miele ironically remarks, Zündel the Holocaust revisionist found himself 'a civil libertarian hero of Canada'.[43] Notwithstanding this, several Canadian Jewish groups have initiated proceedings against him under Canadian anti-hate laws.

Miguel Serrano and the Glorification of Hitler

The strange and esoteric notions that seem so often to go hand in hand with Holocaust revisionism are most strikingly exemplified by the Chilean diplomat Miguel Serrano (b. 1917), who was Ambassador to India (1953–62), Yugoslavia (1962–64) and Austria (1964–70).[44] The possessor of a formidable intellect, Serrano wrote on a number of arcane subjects including Yoga, Tantra and other areas of mysticism, as well as a book on his friendships with Carl Jung and Hermann Hesse. He also travelled widely in search of wisdom in India, South America and Antarctica. In 1984 he published a long explication of his mystical and philosophical thought, entitled *Adolf Hitler, el Último Avatāra* (*Adolf Hitler, the Last Avatar*), which he dedicates 'To the glory of the Führer, Adolf Hitler'.[45]

According to Godwin:

> We are to understand the title quite literally: Serrano means that Hitler is the Tenth Avatar of Vishnu, the Kalki Avatar, who has incarnated to bring about the end of the Kali Yuga and usher in a New Age. In the terminology of Buddhism, Hitler is a Tulku or a

Bodhisattva, who having previously emancipated himself from bondage to the circles of this world has taken on voluntary birth for the sake of mankind. Therefore he is beyond criticism.[46]

Serrano believes that Hitler himself is still alive, having escaped from the ruins of Berlin in one of the Nazi disc-planes, and is continuing to direct an Esoteric War from the safety of a secret realm at the South Pole. The background to this scenario involves, once again, the legendary land of Hyperborea and its fabulous inhabitants, with further variations on the theme we have already discussed (see Chapter Two). According to Serrano, the Hyperboreans were originally from beyond our galaxy, arriving on Earth in remote antiquity. Their existence has been suppressed by a monumental conspiracy, which also seeks to misrepresent them as physical 'aliens'; in fact, we only perceive them as 'flying saucers' because we lack the perception to see them as they really are. They founded the First Hyperborea here on Earth, a realm that was not composed of mundane matter but which extended beyond the physical plane of existence created and controlled by the Demiurge, an inferior god whose first experiments in the creation of intelligent life resulted in Neanderthal Man.[47]

The Demiurge instituted a cosmic regime by which all creatures would take the Way of the Ancestors – in other words, they would be reincarnated on Earth indefinitely. This was unacceptable to the Hyperboreans who preferred to take the Way of the Gods, only being reincarnated if they chose. The Hyperboreans possessed the power of Vril (see Chapter Three), which they wielded in their battles with the mechanistic Demiurge.[48] The war between the Hyperboreans and the Demiurge resulted in the founding of a Second Hyperborea at the North Pole, taking the form of a physical, circular continent from which the Hyperboreans began to organise the spiritualisation of the Earth. This would be achieved through the instilling of a single particle of immortality in the Neanderthals and other proto-humans, which would raise them out of their semi-animal state.

The Hyperboreans' plans seemed to be going well enough, until they made the mistake of having sexual intercourse with the creations of the Demiurge. This miscegenation was associated with a catastrophic cometary impact that caused the North and South Poles to change position. From that moment on, the Earth became 'the battleground between the Demiurge and the Hyperboreans, the latter always in danger of diluting their blood'.[49] Godwin quotes Serrano thus: 'There is nothing more mysterious than blood. Paracelsus considered it a condensation of light. I believe that the Aryan, Hyperborean blood is that – but not the light of the Golden Sun, not of a galactic sun, but of the light of the Black Sun . . .',[50] the Black Sun being a symbol not only of the void inside the Hollow Earth but also of the ultimate void from which all creation flows.

Serrano claims to have met a certain Master who told him that at a certain point in the practice of Yoga one is able to leave one's body and go through mystical death to reach the Black Sun, the realm occupied by the Hyperboreans beyond the physical universe. However, such a spiritual voyage is not within the capabilities of all humanity – only those 'whose blood preserves the memory of the ancient White, Hyperborean race'.[51]

The Jewish people are seen by Serrano as the instruments of the Demiurge (whom he identifies with Jehovah). They constitute an 'anti-race' that is engaged in a gigantic conspiracy involving all the world's institutions, the undeclared enemies of Hyperborean ideals. These ideals gave rise to the Thule Society, which Serrano claims had links with the Hermetic Order of the Golden Dawn but 'was perverted by the degeneracy of Aleister Crowley and the Jewish Bergsons'.[52]

During the earlier part of Hitler's campaigns, according to Serrano, his intention had simply been to reconquer the ancient territories of the Aryans or Hyperboreans. Rudolf Hess's flight to England in 1941 was the last stage of this effort, intended through renewed contacts with the Golden Dawn to unite Germany with her Aryan cousins, the British, and encourage them also to purify their race. But after the apparent failure of this mission, Hitler took up his avataric destiny of total war on all fronts against international Jewry and the Demiurge, attacking them in their most powerful creation, the Communist Soviet Union.[53]

As with other revisionists, Serrano denies that the Holocaust took place (he calls it the 'Myth of the Six Million') on the grounds that the German is heroic but not cruel (cruelty being an attribute of mixed blood). Indeed, during the Second World War, the Nazis were allegedly concentrating on the perfection of 'magical realism', including the development of disc-planes, establishing contact with ascended Masters in Tibet and dematerialisation. Hitler himself did not commit suicide but escaped through an underground passage, designed by Albert Speer, connecting the Bunker with Tempelhof Airfield where he boarded one of the disc-planes and left the ruins of the Third Reich behind.[54]

As Godwin notes, quoting the Chilean writer thus, Serrano here enters realms usually identified with the bizarre fringes of ufology and cosmology:

Had the German submarines discovered at the North Pole or in John Dee's Greenland the exact point through which one penetrates, as through a black funnel, going to connect with the Other Pole, emerging in that paradisal land and sea that are no longer here, yet exist? An impregnable paradise, from which one can continue the war and win it – for when this war is lost, the other is won. The Golden Age, Ultima Thule, Hyperborea, the other side of things; so easy and so difficult to attain. The inner earth, the Other Earth, the counter-earth, the astral earth, to which one passes as it were with a 'click'; a bilocation, or trilocation of space.[55]

Serrano believes that the Hollow Earth is still inhabited by the First Hyperboreans and that the Nazis found a way through to their realm via the South Pole, a belief shared (apparently) by the French writer Jean Robin – although it must be added that Robin is no denier of the Holocaust. In 1989, Robin published his *Opération Orth*, which offers the account, supposedly given to Robin by a friend, of a journey to a subterranean complex made aboard a flying saucer that could pass through solid rock. The underground city was near the Chilean coastal city of Valparaiso, north of Santiago; it had a population of some 350,000, all of whom were members of the Black Order and some of whom were Jews who blamed 'their fellows for their "refusal to collaborate" with the evolutionary process'.[56] Robin's story differs from other Nazi-survival myths in that Hitler died in this new Agartha in 1953 and his body was placed in a transparent, hexagonal casket. Rather astonishingly, this casket also contained the body of the Swedish diplomat Raoul Wallenberg, who saved thousands of Jews from the concentration camps and who mysteriously disappeared at the end of the war. Godwin is justifiably nonplussed by this:

> *Opération Orth* poses every manner of problem . . . to the reader, who can only wonder what prompted Jean Robin to present the shocking images of Hitler and Wallenberg reconciled, and the casual dismissal of the Holocaust by the Jews of the Black Order. In the context of Guénonian attitudes, which are nothing if not respectful of the Jewish people and their tradition, there is nothing to be said, unless it be that Robin actually accepts his friend's account, and is warning us of the [evolutionary process's] final obscenity.[57]

Alternative 3

Anyone familiar with the above phrase will surely be wondering what possible significance it can have to the present study. I have decided to discuss it for two reasons: firstly, the terrifying conspiracy-to-end-all-conspiracies known as 'Alternative 3' has been implicated by more than one writer in the ongoing saga of ultra-secret Nazi activities;

and secondly because, since Alternative 3 was actually nothing more than a cleverly engineered hoax, it offers us a salutary lesson in how the public can be manipulated by fantasy and propaganda masquerading as fact. Since many readers may be unfamiliar with Alternative 3, we must review its principal elements before turning our attention to the Nazi connection and the reasons why, even today, it is still believed by many to be essentially true.

The tale begins on 20 June 1977, when the UK Independent Television Company Anglia transmitted a documentary programme in its highly regarded *Science Report* series. The programme was entitled *Alternative 3*, and the British TV guide *TV Times* had this to say about it: 'What this programme shows may be considered unethical, but this film is transmitted . . . as a challenge to those who know the answers to the questions raised to tell the truth.'[58] The programme finished at 10 p.m., and from then until midnight and throughout the following day Anglia Television was swamped with telephone calls (10,000, according to one estimate), some from people who had enjoyed the programme and wanted to know if there was any truth in it but many from viewers who were genuinely frightened by its 'revelations' and who wanted to know what was being done about them. Anglia hastily issued a statement assuring its viewers that *Alternative 3* had, in fact, originally been meant as an April Fool's Day joke – as evidenced by the closing credits, which included the copyright caption: 'Anglia Television – April 1, 1977'.

Shortly before the transmission, Anglia had issued a press release, stating:

A team of journalists investigating, among other topical subjects, the drought of 1976, and the changes in the world's atmospheric conditions, and also a disturbing rise in the statistics of disappearing people, follow a trail of information and scientific research through England and America.

A Cambridge scientist and an ex-astronaut living in unpublicised retirement following a nervous breakdown, are among the links in their investigations, which come together finally in some strange discoveries about the future of life on Earth and elsewhere in the Solar System.

As a result of our private screenings a few weeks ago, this programme has been acquired for simultaneous transmission in Australia, New Zealand, Canada, Denmark and Iceland and will be seen eventually in the majority of European and Asian markets.

The programme's theme may seem extraordinary, but it is scientifically possible. The question is, how far does it mirror the truth?

On the day of the transmission, journalist Kenneth Hughes, who had gained access to some of the material to be presented, wrote an article in the London *Daily Mirror* entitled 'WHAT ON EARTH IS GOING ON?'

A science programme is likely to keep millions of Britons glued to their armchairs.

ALTERNATIVE 3 . . . is an investigation into the disappearance of several scientists.

They seem simply to have vanished from the face of the Earth.

Chilling news is read by former ITV newscaster Simon Butler who gives a gloomy report on the future.

The programme will be screened in several other countries – but not in America. Network bosses there want to assess its effect on British viewers.

The programme's structure centred on a series of interviews with one Dr Carl Gerstein, who described the hideous nature of Alternative 3. Dr Gerstein claimed to have attended a secret conference in Huntsville, Alabama in 1957, at which it was agreed that industrial pollution and the accompanying greenhouse effect (caused by high levels of carbon dioxide trapping heat within the atmosphere) was destroying the Earth's biosphere, and that the decline in air quality was irreversible, so that by the year 2000 the Earth would undergo a complete environmental collapse, wiping out most life (including humanity).

Three alternatives for survival were suggested. Alternative 1 called for the deployment of a large number of nuclear bombs in the upper atmosphere. It was suggested that their detonation would blow holes in the carbon dioxide envelope, allowing the excess heat in the atmosphere to escape into space. This idea was rejected on the grounds that it would have replaced one problem with another – a massive amount of radiation in the atmosphere. Gerstein's description of Alternative 2 takes us right back to the subterranean realms discussed in Chapter Seven. In the book version of *Alternative 3*, Gerstein is quoted thus:

'Alternative 2, in my view, was even crazier than Alternative 1. I recognise, of course, that there is enough atmosphere locked in the soil to support life but . . . no, this was the most unrealistic of all the alternatives.

'There is good reason to believe that this world was once more civilised and far more scientifically advanced than it is today. Our really distant ancestors, living millennia before what we call Prehistoric Man, had progressed far beyond our present state of knowledge.

'Then, it is argued, there was some cataclysmic disaster – maybe one comparable with that facing us now – and these highly sophisticated people built completely new civilisations deep beneath the surface of the earth . . .

'There is evidence, quite considerable evidence, to suggest that there were once whole cities – linked by an elaborate complex of tunnels – far below the surface. Remains of them have been found under many parts of the world. Under South America . . . China . . . Russia . . . oh, all over the place. And in this subterranean world, so it is said, there is a green luminescence which replaces the sun as a source of energy – and which makes it possible for crops to be grown . . .

'Maybe there's some historical truth in the Biblical story of the great Flood. Maybe the disaster which drove

them there in the first place was followed by the Flood
– and they were all trapped and drowned down there.
Maybe that's how their civilisations ended . . .

'And it could follow that the people we think of as
prehistoric Men were merely the descendants of a
handful of survivors – the real children of Noah, if you
accept the Bible version – who had to start from scratch
in a world which had been utterly devastated. Is that
why they took so naturally – instinctively, if you like –
to living in caves? Then the agonisingly slow process of
rebuilding the world started all over again until now we
find ourselves in a similar position . . .'[59]

Thus, Alternative 2 called for the evacuation of the world's
elites (the rest would have to take their chances on the
surface) into these abandoned cities. However, this alternative was also discarded, since the heat from the greenhouse
effect would eventually permeate down through the Earth's
crust, making life equally impossible for those living
underground.

The only option left was Alternative 3, which called for the
evacuation (of the elites, once again) from Earth to Mars.
Gerstein reiterated the theory that the Red Planet was once
inhabited, and that its atmosphere might still be locked away
in the soil. He added that in 1959 a Russian rocket had
exploded on the launch pad, killing a large number of people
and devastating the surrounding area. The implication was
that the rocket had been carrying a nuclear device whose
detonation would have unlocked the atmosphere on Mars
and transformed it into a habitable planet once again.
Gerstein went on to suggest that another rocket might have
been sent to Mars, and that this mission might have been
successful.

The *Alternative 3* programme also contained some footage
of an alleged top secret unmanned mission to Mars,
undertaken by the United States and the Soviet Union in
1962. The film showed the rocky landscape of Mars, seen
from the approaching probe, accompanied by Russian and
American voices. Near the end of the footage, an American

voice said: 'That's it! We got it . . . we got it! Boy, if they ever take the wraps off this thing, it's going to be the biggest date in history! May 22, 1962. We're on the planet Mars – and we have *air*!' The presenter of the programme, Tim Brinton, commented that there must have been a very good reason why the true conditions on Mars were kept from the public, and why the mission had been jointly undertaken by the US and the USSR. The implication was of an ultra-secret interplanetary project which, Brinton claimed, could well be Gerstein's Alternative 3.[60]

By way of corroborative 'evidence', the makers of *Alternative 3* pointed to the large numbers of people who go missing throughout the world each year, suggesting that many are actually being abducted by the Alternative 3 controllers and transformed, through surgical and chemical means, into mindless slave labourers who are then transported as 'Batch Consignments' to the colony on Mars. These hapless victims are referred to as 'superfluous people' by the controllers, who see their barbaric treatment as perfectly acceptable.

The controllers were also interested in recruiting scientists and academics from a wide range of disciplines. These personnel were called 'Designated Movers', and apparently accounted for the so-called 'brain drain' of the 1960s and 1970s whereby many scientists left Britain, ostensibly to take up better-paid posts overseas. (It was claimed that an investigation of the brain drain had been the original impetus behind the *Science Report* programme.) The entire operation was headquartered in Geneva and was also controlled, in typical James Bond fashion, by a fleet of nuclear submarines stationed underneath the North Polar ice cap. Here the controllers ensured the conspiracy's continued secrecy by arranging 'hot jobs' (remote-controlled spontaneous human combustion) for those investigators who got too close to the truth.

The ingenious makers of *Alternative 3* also brought in the NASA Moon flights as more evidence of the conspiracy. The reader may be aware that the Apollo programme is a firm favourite of conspiratologists, some of whom maintain that

NASA is hiding the discovery of derelict alien cities on the Moon, while others claim that all of the Moon landings were actually hoaxed, with the astronauts bouncing around a sound stage somewhere in Nevada or California. In *Alternative 3*, it was suggested that the Apollo astronauts did not stumble upon a derelict alien city but a fully functioning man-made way station for flights en route to the Martian colony. The following transcript of a conversation between Mission Control in Houston, Texas and an astronaut named Bob Grodin was presented in the book:

MISSION CONTROL: Could you take a look out over that flat area there? Do you see anything beyond?

GRODIN: There's a kind of a ridge with a pretty spectacular . . . oh, my God! What is that there? That's all I want to know! What the hell is that?

MISSION CONTROL: Roger. Interesting. Go Tango . . . immediately . . . go Tango . . .

GRODIN: There's a kind of a light now . . .

MISSION CONTROL (hurriedly): Roger. We've got it, we've marked it. Lose a little communication, huh? Bravo Tango . . . Bravo Tango . . . select Jezebel, Jezebel . . .

GRODIN: Yeah . . . yeah . . . but this is unbelievable . . . recorder off . . .[61]

Another transcript, this time between astronauts Scott and Irwin and Mission Control during their Moonwalk in August 1971, runs thus:

SCOTT: Arrowhead really runs east to west.

MISSION CONTROL: Roger, we copy.

IRWIN: Tracks here as we go down slope.

MISSION CONTROL: Just follow the tracks, huh?

IRWIN: Right . . . we're (garble) . . . we know that's a fairly good run. We're bearing 320, hitting range for 413 . . . I can't get over those lineations, that layering on Mount Hadley.

SCOTT: I can't either. That's really spectacular.

IRWIN: They sure look beautiful.

SCOTT: Talk about organization!

IRWIN: That's the most organized structure I've ever seen!

SCOTT: It's (garble) . . . so uniform in width . . .

IRWIN: Nothing we've seen before this has shown such uniform thickness from the top of the tracks to the bottom.[62]

The book version of *Alternative 3* also contains an episode described by an inside source calling himself 'Trojan'. The events occurred in a base inside the crater Archimedes, which lies on the western border of the *Mare Imbrium*. The Archimedes Base is allegedly a large transit camp beneath a hermetically sealed transparent dome. Here one of the Designated Movers, a marine biologist named Matt Anderson, secretly visited a segregated area where the Batch Consignments of slaves were housed. In this slave village, Anderson encountered a childhood friend. Having yet to undergo the psychological conditioning that enabled the Designated Movers to accept the concept of slavery, Anderson was appalled and decided to escape with as many slaves as possible and expose the horror of Alternative 3.

Teaming up with a NASA-trained aerospace technician named Gowers, Anderson managed to get 84 slaves aboard a Moon ship and headed for one of the gigantic airlocks in the dome. However, a technician in the main control room saw what was happening and raised the alarm. The airlock was sealed shut and Gowers, who was flying the ship, panicked and lost control, sending it crashing into the dome. The resulting explosion tore a hole in the protective shell and the resultant cataclysmic depressurisation killed almost everyone at the base. As a result of this disaster, an earlier base in the crater Cassini was redeveloped, and Alternative 3 is going ahead as planned.

As mentioned, the huge number of telephone calls from concerned viewers resulted in a speedy statement from Anglia Television that *Alternative 3* had been an April Fool's Day jape and nothing more. Indeed, the participation of several quite well-known actors (one of whom appeared in a dog food commercial before the beginning of the programme!) could mean little else. In spite of this, Alternative 3 has taken on a life of its own, offering a kind of template for the suspicions of other writers and conspiracy researchers.

Most notable among these is the American conspiratologist Jim Keith (who sadly died in September 1999). In his *Casebook on Alternative 3* (1994), he lists more than 30 scientists connected with the Strategic Defence Initiative (SDI) 'Star Wars' anti-missile project who either committed suicide, disappeared or otherwise died in mysterious circumstances. This parallel with the missing scientists in the Alternative 3 scenario is an example of Keith's case as presented in his book. When the conspiracy is examined closely, its principal elements become recognisable aspects of other conspiracy theories. It is as if the creators of the Anglia Television programme had pre-empted the protagonists of Umberto Eco's novel *Foucault's Pendulum*, in which a small group of bored intellectuals working for a publisher of esoteric texts take all the information they can find on secret societies and historical conspiracies, and feed it into a computer nicknamed 'Abulafia' (after the cabalist). The computer then links all of the snippets it has been given into a cogent and internally consistent (although completely fictitious) scenario in which all the secret societies in history have handed down to each other the elements of a fantastic Secret that will give the holder incredible power. Through indiscretion, word of the protagonists' discovery spreads through the international network of contemporary secret occult groups, who then hound the intellectuals (literally) to death, thinking that they have the Secret. The book's hero, Casaubon, meets his death at the hands of occultists who wish the Secret to *remain* a secret.

With Alternative 3, we can see a similar process at work. The basic template of a secret power elite making plans to abandon a dying Earth and colonise Mars offers the basis for a wider and more elaborate scenario. It begins with the rise of human civilisation, which from its very inception contained the roots of a powerful and totally unscrupulous elite that has secretly directed the course of history for thousands of years. In the twentieth century (with which we are primarily concerned in this chapter), the most extreme and barbaric example of this power elite at work was Nazi ideology.

Jim Keith makes the interesting point that Hitler himself conceived of four 'alternatives' to deal with the coming world of scarcity that he envisaged. In *Mein Kampf* Hitler wrote:

> A clear examination of the premises for foreign activity on the part of German statecraft inevitably led to the following conviction:
>
> Germany has an annual increase in population of nearly nine hundred thousand souls. The difficulty of feeding this army of new citizens must grow greater from year to year and ultimately end in catastrophe, unless ways and means are found to forestall the danger of starvation and misery in time.
>
> There were four ways of avoiding so terrible a development for the future:
>
> 1. Following the French example, the increase of births could be artificially restricted, thus meeting the problem of over-population . . .
>
> 2. A second way would be one which today we, time and time again, see proposed and recommended: internal colonisation . . .
>
> 3. Either new soil could be acquired and the superfluous millions sent off each year, thus keeping the nation on a self-sustaining basis; or we could
>
> 4. Produce for foreign needs through industry and commerce, and defray the cost of living from the proceeds.[63]

Hitler rejected the first of these options on the grounds that the self-limitation of a population through birth control would necessarily result in a weakening of that population, since the natural laws of Darwinian survival of the fittest would be circumvented. 'For as soon as procreation as such is limited and the number of births diminished, the natural struggle for existence which leaves only the strongest and healthiest alive is obviously replaced by the obvious desire to 'save' even the weakest and most sickly at any price, and this plants the seed of a future generation which must inevitably grow more and more deplorable the longer this mockery of Nature and her will continues.'[64]

The second option – of 'internal colonisation' and the increase of resource-yield within Germany – he rejected on the grounds that it could not be sustained indefinitely: 'Without doubt the productivity of the soil can be increased up to a certain limit. But only up to a certain limit, and not continuously without end. For a certain time it will be possible to compensate for the increase of the German people without having to think of hunger, by increasing the productivity of our soil. But beside this, we must face the fact that our demands on life ordinarily rise even more rapidly than the number of the population.'[65]

The third option refers, of course, to the concept of *Lebensraum*:

> The acquisition of new soil for the settlement of the excess population possesses an infinite number of advantages, particularly if we turn from the present to the future. . . . We must . . . coolly and objectively adopt the standpoint that it can certainly not be the intention of Heaven to give one people fifty times as much land and soil in this world as another. In this case we must not let political boundaries obscure for us the boundaries of eternal justice. If this earth really has room for all to live in, let us be given the soil we need for our livelihood.
>
> True, they will not willingly do this. But then the law of self-preservation goes into effect; and what is refused to amicable methods, it is up to the fist to take.[66]

The fourth option, which relied on German interdependence with other nations through international commerce, Hitler rejected on the grounds that the survival of the Aryan race would necessarily depend on the activities of other nation states:

> If . . . Germany took this road, she should at least have clearly recognised that this development would some day . . . end in struggle. Only children could have thought that they could get their bananas in the 'peaceful contest of nations', by friendly and moral conduct and constant emphasis on their peaceful intentions, as they so high-soundingly and unctuously babbled; in other words, without ever having to take up arms.[67]

Having made the interesting but rather tenuous connection between Hitler's alternatives and the possible options stated in Alternative 3 (the former referring to Hitler's perception of the problems facing the German people; the latter referring to the problems facing humanity as a whole), Keith then quotes a passage from *Mein Kampf* in which Hitler writes:

> [T]he folkish philosophy finds the importance of mankind in its basic racial elements. In the state it sees on principle only a means to an end and construes its end as the preservation of the racial existence of man. . . . And so the folkish philosophy of life corresponds to the innermost will of Nature, since it restores that free play of forces which must lead to a continuous mutual higher breeding, until at last the best of humanity, having achieved possession of this earth, will have a free path for activity *in domains which will lie partly above it and partly outside it.*[68] [Keith's emphasis.]

Keith considers it highly significant that Hitler should have mentioned domains lying above and outside the Earth, in view of the events following the defeat of the Third Reich. He continues:

> Summing up ideas that seem to add up to . . . *Alternative 3*, we are familiar with the advanced disk aircraft

designs perfected by the Nazis during World War II, and also know that the American space program was run by prominent Nazis, or at least ex-Nazis. Nazi interests have also been entwined, since the emergence of the philosophy, with other totalitarian control mechanisms of the world, with the intelligence, police, and psychiatric establishments, with eugenics and genetic research, as well as with the plans of monied elites whose philosophies might better be defined in para-political, rather than political terms.[69]

We have already examined the theory of German flying discs in Chapter Eight, and noted at the beginning of this chapter that many prominent Nazis were transferred to the United States at the end of the war, under Project PAPERCLIP – including Wernher von Braun, who designed much of the hardware for NASA's Apollo programme. With regard to the continuation of Nazi objectives in the post-war years, mentioned earlier in this chapter, Keith offers the following quote from the Research and Analysis branch of the OSS from 1945:

The Nazi regime in Germany has developed well-arranged plans for the perpetuation of Nazi doctrines after the war. Some of these plans have already been put into operation and others are ready to be launched on a widespread scale immediately upon termination of hostilities in Europe . . . Nazi party members, German industrialists and the German military, realizing that victory can no longer be attained, are now developing post-war commercial projects, endeavouring to renew and cement friendships in foreign commercial circles and planning for renewals of pre-war cartel agreements.

German technicians, cultural experts and undercover agents have well-laid plans to infiltrate into foreign countries with the object of developing economic, cultural and political ties. German technicians and scientific research experts will be made available at low cost to industrial firms and technical schools in foreign countries. German capital and plans for the construction of ultra-modern technical schools and research laboratories will be offered at extremely favorable terms since they will afford the Germans an excellent opportunity to design and perfect new weapons.[70]

For conspiratologists such as Keith, the fabric of Alternative 3 can be unwoven to reveal its component strands, all of which seem to be supported by evidence of varying quality. As Keith himself states: 'One of the difficulties in researching Alternative 3 was that the evidence kept leading me in a direction I wasn't particularly happy to go in: toward the Nazis. ... A possibility, which I admit is wild speculation, yet at the same time comprises a startling alignment of facts, is that Alternative 3 is an expression of Nazi occult doctrine and that there is a long term elitist program to abandon Earth and to implement another step in Hitler's "Final Solution".'[71]

The component strands of Keith's vision of Alternative 3 can be summarised as follows: Towards the end of the Second World War, the Nazis developed radical aircraft designs, including the Foo Fighters and larger, manned flying discs. The plans for these machines, along with a number of components and scientific personnel, were transferred to a hidden colony in Neu Schwabenland, Antarctica in the closing stages of the war. The two operations known as 'Eagle Flight' and 'Paperclip' ensured that Nazi financial interests and espionage respectively were maintained after the war's end. Given that colonies of Nazis continue to exist in Antarctica and South America, it is probable that their own aerospace research has continued unabated, to the point where they have made manned spaceflight safe and routine. The discovery that life on Earth is doomed as a result of pollution and overpopulation led to the formulation of Alternative 3, whereby the monied elites of the world would effectively jump ship and establish a human colony on Mars. Far from being mortal enemies, the United States and the Soviet Union were actually the closest of allies: the Cold War was a monumental con on the rest of humanity, which unwittingly supplied the slave labour required for the gigantic construction projects. The Nazi survivors, one of the main players in this scenario of secret world history, saw this as a perfect opportunity to continue with the creation of a master race, with their *Lebensraum* relocated to Mars.

Keith continues:

My belief is that the Nazis have been major, but far from the only players in the game of world domination since the end of World War II: one among many heads of the Hydra. Influential Nazis (possibly including Hitler) have been behind the scenes since the end of the war, creating and implementing schemes for the ultimate triumph of *Die Neuordnung* [New Order]. Almost all of Hitler's cohorts survived Nuremberg and may have been involved in manipulations including international terrorism and the establishment of drug and arms markets, as well as in collaboration with other more 'respectable' networks of world influence.

While I cannot state with certainty that Nazis are creating the 'real' domination of *Alternative 3*, that they have constructed or are constructing bases on Mars or the moon to carry the ancient Grail of Aryan racial purity away from what they conceive as a cataclysm-doomed Earth, I do have to wonder at the logic and symmetry of detail.[72]

The complex, interconnected system of rumours – paranormal, historical and political – that has grown up around Alternative 3 is perhaps the most extreme expression of the post-war Nazi-survival idea. Indeed, its very extremeness provides a perfect example of the way in which seemingly unconnected mysteries, truths and half-truths can take on an independent life that quickly rages beyond control, spawning fantastically baroque conspiracy theories that bear scant resemblance to the components from which they arose.

Conclusion: the myth machine

The Reality and Fantasy of Nazi Occultism

O CCULTISM IS A CURIOUS and fecund beast. Beliefs, and the events to which they give rise, have a frequently unfortunate habit of generating additional beliefs. If, as in the case of Nazi occultism, the initial beliefs were little more than crypto-historical idiocies, there can be little hope of improvement in their ideological progeny. This book has been as much a history of belief about Nazi occultism as about Nazi occultism itself, and there is little doubt that the principal driving force behind the development of this belief is an attempt to explain the dreadful aberration that was the Third Reich.

Given that human beings have always been fascinated with the occult and the supernatural, precisely because they promise so much in offering the prospect of a higher meaning to the vagaries of existence, and given also our quest for an answer to the problem of evil, it is only to be expected that many should seek to explain Nazism in terms that transcend the merely human. We noted in the Introduction that some serious orthodox historians place Hitler outside the spectrum of human behaviour – a spectrum that includes the most barbarous of crimes. Hitler is seen by them as uniquely evil, wicked beyond even the human capacity for wickedness. Others, who are inclined to accept the reality of a cosmic evil originating beyond humanity, in some Outer Darkness eternally forsaken by God, see Hitler and the Nazis as examples of how, given the right circumstances, this Darkness can enter humanity, an 'eruption of demonism into history'.

Nevertheless, the demonic can easily be confused with insanity: one shudders to think of the number of unfortunates throughout history whose madness was mistaken by their fellows for possession by the forces of Darkness. We have seen that the origins of National Socialism can be traced to *völkisch* occultists who believed wholeheartedly not only in the existence of a prehistoric Germanic race of superhumans but also that their very superiority had been transmitted through the ages to modern Germans by means of a magically active, pure Aryan blood. The bizarre occult statements of Theosophists such as Madame Blavatsky, Rudolf Steiner and others seemed to offer evidence of the existence of a fabulous Aryan race that established great civilisations on the lost continents of Atlantis, Lemuria and the mythical island of Thule in the incredibly remote past.

The idea of genuine Nazi occult power (as opposed to Nazi *belief* in that power) seems to have arisen out of our own continuing fascination with the legends in which the *völkisch* and Pan-German occultists believed so fervently. Belief in all aspects of the paranormal is extremely prevalent, whether it be belief in alien visitation, the spirits of the dead, dark and demonic forces from beyond the realm of humanity, or technologically advanced prehistoric civilisations such as those of Atlantis and Lemuria; and it seems to me that this belief lies at the core of the mythological development of Nazi occultism that has occurred in the second half of the twentieth century. For if the supernatural really exists, might not the Nazis have discovered a way to harness its power to further their dreadful ambitions?

The answer to this question must be negative: we have already seen that the evidence for Hitler's intiation into the mysteries of the black arts is non-existent, while the evidence for his utter contempt for mysticism of any kind (particularly that practised by Himmler in Wewelsburg, his sick joke of a Grail castle) is documented time and again. Indeed, such was Hitler's lack of interest in these matters that he never deigned even to visit Wewelsburg. What of Himmler, then? Did he not practise dark rites with his SS Gruppenführers in their Order Castle, attempting to contact the souls of long-departed Teutons? The answer to this question is, of course, yes. However, occult-orientated writers have, over the years, continually made the same mistake in claiming that, because Himmler attempted to contact supernatural forces, *those forces exist to be contacted*. I consider myself a sceptic, rather than an incredulous doubter,* and so I cannot say that supernatural forces do *not* exist, any more than I can say that they *do* exist. In truth, no one can. But we must not allow ourselves to make any connection whatsoever between Himmler's ideas on the supernatural and the veracity of the supernatural itself.

Ken Anderson makes an interesting point in his *Hitler and the Occult*:

> From early in their rise to power Hitler and his Nazis were enveloped in an aura of mysticism almost despite themselves. This aura *appears* closer to the experience of occultism than any other major movement in the twentieth century. Hitler came to personify the invisible structure which became the occult myth dealt with here.
>
> With the help of contemporary occult writers, the illusion is today more pervasive. We find no such occult mystique surrounding other aberrations of civilisation . . .[1]

To this we might add that the aura of mysticism surrounding the Nazis was enhanced and disseminated throughout German society by means of photography and cinema, notably Leni Riefenstahl's virulently propagandist films, which include *Triumph of the Will* and *Olympia*, and which glorify German-ness and emphasise the inherent superiority of the Aryan race. The Nazis were nothing if not masters of self-promotion.

*See the quote from Umberto Eco at the front of this book.

Just as the early *völkisch* occultists took various elements of prehistoric mythology to construct a totally spurious history for the Germanic 'master race', so many occult-orientated writers have taken the image of the Nazi black magician and his diabolical allies and with it have attempted to create an equally spurious history of the Third Reich. The insubstantial edifice of their wild speculations is 'supported' by the incorporation of Eastern mysticism, with its tales of hidden cities inhabited by ascended masters who are the real controllers of humanity's destiny on Earth. Whatever their veracity, these myths are exquisitely beautiful and elaborate, and it is something of a tragedy that they should have been hijacked by Western writers in their quest to connect Nazism with a putative source of genuine occult power in the East.

We have also seen how Nazi cosmology, with its utterly insane notions of 'World Ice' and the Earth as a bubble in an infinity of rock, arose from the grandiose but untenable cosmological theories of previous centuries. Moreover, after the end of the Second World War they became part of the twentieth-century fascination with alternative cosmologies, including the Hollow Earth theory, which has stubbornly persisted to this day.

Another example of how the Third Reich generated strange rumours can be seen in the concept of the Nazi flying discs, which arose partly from admittedly intriguing (but still inconclusive) evidence, and partly from the *unassailable* evidence that Nazi scientists were indeed experimenting with radical aircraft designs and weapons systems. Thanks to clever manipulators of public opinion such as Ray Palmer, the quite possibly genuine mystery of the UFOs was 'explained' in terms of the rumours that the Nazis had actually perfected high-performance disc-shaped aircraft.

As we have seen, this in turn gave rise to the idea that these disc-planes were used by high-ranking Nazis to escape from the Allies during the fall of Berlin. Once again, it is clear that the various outlandish claims of Nazi hideouts in Antarctica owe their inception to genuinely puzzling events such as Admiral Byrd's apparently disastrous Operation Highjump, in addition to the indisputable fact that many Nazi war criminals did indeed escape from the ruins of the Third Reich to take up residence in various South American countries. All of this provides conspiracy theorists with a heady mixture of components with which to construct their nightmarish scenario of hideous clandestine forces maliciously pulling the strings on which we all dance. At the risk of offering a cliché, what we have here is a classic example of putting two and two together and getting five.

As we noted in the Introduction, with the passage of time and the deaths of important first-hand witnesses any chance of finding an adequate explanation of Nazism and the horrors it unleashed has now almost certainly been lost. We are left with the awful question that will continue to haunt us for as long as we remain human: why? The question is made more awful by the likelihood that the answer lies not in Outer Darkness, not in the 'Absolute Elsewhere', but much closer, in that most frightening and ill-explored of realms: the human mind.

Notes

Introduction: search for a map of hell

1. Rosenbaum 1999, p. xiii.
2. Ibid., p. xvi.
3. Davies 1997, p. 40.
4. Ibid.
5. Godwin 1993, p. 63.
6. Trevor-Roper 1995, p. xxviii.
7. Rosenbaum 1999, p. xv.
8. Ibid., p. xxi.
9. Ibid., p. xxii.
10. Ibid., p. xxii.
11. Ibid., p. xxiii.
12. Ibid., p. xxvii.
13. Ibid., p. xxxv.
14. Ibid., p. xliii.
15. Ibid., xliv.
16. Ibid., p. xlvi.

1 Ancestry, blood and nature

1. Goodrick-Clarke 1985, p. 7. Anyone attempting to examine the origins of Nazi occultism will necessarily owe a considerable debt to *The Occult Roots of Nazism*, a debt which the present author gratefully acknowledges. This is still by far the most level-headed, well-written and researched book covering this period; indeed, it remains the yardstick against which all writing on German occultism in the late nineteenth and early twentieth centuries should be judged.
2. *German Genealogy: Habsburg Empire*, from the German Genealogy Homepage at http://w3g.med.uni-giessen.de/gene/reg/ahe1814.html
3. Sowards, *Twenty-Five Lectures on Modern Balkan History*.

4. Davies 1997, p. 829.
5. Goodrick-Clarke 1985, p. 3.
6. Ibid., p. 4.
7. Ibid., p. 5.
8. Davidson 1997, p. 11.
9. Ibid.
10. Ibid., p. 13.
11. Ibid., p. 14.
12. Ibid.
13. Goodrick-Clarke 1985, p. 10.
14. Ibid.
15. Davidson 1997, p. 11.
16. Goodrick-Clarke 1985, p. 12.
17. Ibid., p. 12.
18. Ibid.
19. Ibid., p. 13.
20. Maser 1973, p. 170.
21. Cited in Maser 1973, p. 170.
22. Baigent and Leigh 1997, p. 24.
23. Ibid.
24. Guiley 1991, pp. 259–60; Baigent and Leigh 1997, p. 22.
25. Washington 1996, pp. 29–31.
26. Ibid., p. 27.
27. Ibid., p. 51.
28. Ibid., p. 32.
29. Ibid., p. 33.
30. Wilson 1996, p. 111.
31. Goodrick-Clarke 1985, p. 21.
32. Ibid., pp. 22–23.
33. Ibid., p. 23.
34. Ibid., p. 25.
35. Ibid., p. 28
36. Ibid., p. 56.
37. New Larousse Encyclopedia of Mythology 1985, p. 248.
38. Goodrick-Clarke 1985, pp. 49–50.
39. Ibid., p. 50.
40. Ibid.
41. Kershaw 1998, p. 50.
42. Goodrick-Clarke 1985, p. 53.
43. New Larousse Encyclopedia of Mythology 1985, pp. 248–9.
44. Goodrick-Clarke 1985, p. 54.
45. Kershaw 1998, p. 50.
46. Goodrick-Clarke 1985, p. 106.
47. Ibid., p. 108.
48. Runciman 1952, p. 127.
49. Daraul 1994, p. 40.

50. Guiley 1991, p. 416.
51. Daraul 1994, p. 40.
52. Guiley 1991, p. 416.
53. Ibid., p. 417.
54. Ibid.
55. Goodrick-Clarke 1985, p. 108.
56. Ibid., p. 109.
57. Ibid., p. 95.
58. Levenda 1995, p. 44.
59. Goodrick-Clarke 1985, p. 124.
60. Ibid.
61. Ibid., p. 125.
62. Payne 1995, p. 31.
63. Ibid.
64. Goodrick-Clarke 1985, p. 125.
65. Ibid., p. 126.
66. Ibid., p. 127.
67. Ibid., p. 128.
68. Ibid., p. 129.
69. Ibid., p. 130.
70. Ibid.
71. Ibid., p. 131.
72. Ibid., p. 133.
73. Davidson 1997, p. 137.
74. Godwin 1993, pp. 48–9.
75. Goodrick-Clarke 1985, p. 144.
76. Rudolf von Sebottendorff, *Bevor Hitler kam* (*Before Hitler Came*), 1934, p. 57. Quoted in Goodrick-Clarke 1985, p. 145.
77. Goodrick-Clarke 1985, p. 155.
78. Ibid., p. 157.
79. Ibid., p. 159.
80. Ibid., p. 161.
81. Ibid., pp. 161–2.
82. Ibid., p. 162.

2 *Fantastic prehistory*

1. Godwin 1993, p. 37.
2. Ibid., p. 38.
3. Ibid.
4. Ibid., p. 39.
5. Ibid., p. 40.
6. Ernest Renan, *Rêves* (*Dreams*), 1876, quoted in Godwin 1993, pp. 40–41.
7. Ibid., p. 27.
8. Ibid., p. 29.

9. Ibid., p. 30.
10. Ibid., p. 32.
11. Ibid., p. 33.
12. Ibid., p. 34.
13. Blavatsky II 1999, p. 7.
14. Ibid., p. 8.
15. Ibid., pp. 8–9.
16. Ibid., p. 404.
17. Godwin 1993, pp. 20–21.
18. Ibid., p. 22.
19. Ibid., pp. 22–23.
20. Ibid., pp. 23–24.
21. Levenda 1995, p. 14.
22. Ibid., p. 15.
23. Ibid.
24. Ibid., p. 23.
25. Rosenbaum 1999, p. 55.
26. Levenda 1995, p. 24.
27. Hitler 1998, p. 279.
28. Rosenbaum 1999, p. 57.
29. Levenda 1995, p. 15.
30. Washington 1996, p. 283.
31. Levenda 1995, p. 16.
32. Godwin 1993, pp. 47–48.
33. Levenda 1995, p. 168.
34. Quoted in Levenda 1995, p. 170.
35. Speer 1998, p. 150.
36. Quoted in Godwin 1993, pp. 56–57.
37. Quoted in Levenda 1995, pp. 171–2.
38. Harbinson 1996, p. 247.
39. Godwin 1993, p. 146.
40. Ibid., pp. 146–7.
41. Ibid., p. 147.
42. Ibid., p. 148.
43. Ibid.
44. Ibid.
45. Ibid., pp. 148–9.
46. King 1976, p. 116.
47. Anderson 1995, pp. 142–3.
48. Hitler 1998, pp. 451–2.
49. Anderson 1995, pp. 143–4.

3 *A hideous strength*

1. See *The Morning of the Magicians* by Louis Pauwels and Jacques Bergier, a fascinating, hugely entertaining (but not terribly reliable)

book, which more or less singlehandedly launched the European occult revival in the early 1960s. Part Two is entitled 'A Few Years in the Absolute Elsewhere', and deals extensively with the idea of genuine Nazi occult power. To the authors, the 'Absolute Elsewhere' denotes the realm of extreme notions, where we encounter the Hollow Earth Theory, Hörbiger's World Ice Theory, lost prehistoric civilisations, and so on.

2. Maclellan 1996, pp. 100–101.
3. See Julian Wolfreys's Introduction to the Alan Sutton edition of *The Coming Race.*
4. Bulwer-Lytton 1995, p. 20.
5. Ibid., p. 53.
6. Ibid., p. 26.
7. Ibid., p. 111.
8. Ibid., p. 120.
9. Maclellan 1996, p. 90.
10. Ibid., p. 84.
11. Ibid., p. 103.
12. Pauwels and Bergier 1971, p. 195.
13. Ibid., p. 193.
14. Goodrick-Clarke 1985, p. 221.
15. Kershaw 1998, p. 248.
16. Ibid., p. 240.
17. Pauwels and Bergier 1971, p. 198.
18. Maclellan 1996, p. 107.
19. Willy Ley 1947: 'Pseudoscience in Naziland', *Astounding Science Fiction* 39/3 (May), pp. 90–98. Quoted in Godwin 1993, p. 53.
20. Godwin 1993, p. 54.
21. Ibid.
22. Maclellan 1996, p. 109.
23. Ibid.
24. Ibid., pp. 109–110.
25. Quoted in Maclellan 1996, p. 111.
26. Kershaw 1998, p. xiv.
27. Quoted in Maclellan 1996, p. 113.
28. Ibid., pp. 113–14.
29. Levenda 1995, pp. 173–4.
30. Ibid., p. 175.
31. Ibid.
32. Quoted in Levenda 1995, pp. 176–7.

4 The phantom kingdom

1. Godwin 1993, p. 79.
2. Tomas 1977, p. 25.
3. Ibid., pp. 25–6.

4. Ibid., p. 32n.
5. Ibid., p. 32.
6. Le Page 1996, p. 4.
7. Ibid., p. 7.
8. Le Page 1996, p. 110.
9. Ibid., pp. 110–11.
10. Quoted in Maclellan 1996, p. 72.
11. Roerich 1930, p. 211.
12. Ibid.
13. Ibid., p. 212.
14. Ibid., p. 215.
15. Ibid.
16. Ibid., p. 222.
17. Tomas 1977, p. 42.
18. Ibid., pp. 42–3.
19. Godwin 1993, pp. 80–81.
20. Ibid., p. 81.
21. Ibid.
22. Childress 1999, p. 304.
23. Quoted in Maclellan 1996, pp. 63–4.
24. Quoted in Maclellan 1996, pp. 64–5.
25. Maclellan 1996, p. 69.
26. Ibid.
27. Godwin 1993, p. 83.
28. Ibid., pp. 83–4.
29. Godwin 1993, p. 87.
30. Childress 1999, p. 322.
31. Ibid., p. 323.
32. Ibid., p. 324.
33. Ibid.
34. Ibid., p. 325.
35. Ibid., p. 327.

5 *Talisman of conquest*

1. Ravenscroft 1982, p. xviii.
2. Ibid., pp. ix–x.
3. Ibid., p. xii.
4. Ibid., p. xv.
5. Ibid., p. 50. (See also Goodrick-Clarke 1985, pp. 221–2.)
6. Ibid., p. 40.
7. Ibid., p. 48.
8. Ibid., p. 49.
9. Anderson 1995, p. 47.
10. Ravenscroft 1982, p. 9.
11. Ibid., pp. 63–4.

12. Ibid., p. 64.
13. Anderson 1995, p. 147.
14. Ibid., p. 148.
15. Ravenscroft 1982, p. 318.
16. Godwin 1993, p. 99.
17. Anderson 1995, p. 49.
18. Ibid.
19. Ravenscroft 1982, pp. 11–12.
20. Anderson 1995, p. 52.
21. Ibid., pp. 78–9.
22. Ibid., p. 79.
23. Ibid., p. 80.
24. Ibid., pp. 80–81. See also Ravenscroft 1982, p. 13.
25. Ibid., p. 81. See also Smith 1971, p. 325.
26. Ibid., p. 85.
27. Ibid., p. 86.
28. Ibid.
29. Ibid., p. 88.
30. Ibid., p. 96.
31. Ibid., p. 97.
32. Ravenscroft 1982, pp. 315–16.
33. Fest 1974, pp. 548–9.
34. Ravenscroft 1982, p. 316.
35. Ibid.
36. Anderson 1995, p. 149.
37. Ibid., pp. 149–50.
38. Ibid., p. 151.
39. Ibid.
40. Ravenscroft 1982, pp. 103–5. See also Goodrick-Clarke's essay 'The Modern Mythology of Nazi Occultism' (Appendix E in *The Occult Roots of Nazism*); his demolition job on such lurid fantasies is as economical as it is eloquent.
41. Speer 1998, p. 147.
42. Ibid., p. 148.
43. Ibid., p. 183.
44. Langer 1972, p. 32, quoted in Anderson 1995, p. 224.

6 Ordinary madness

1. Goodrick-Clarke 1985, p. 177.
2. Ibid., p. 179.
3. Ibid., p. 180.
4. Ibid., p. 181.
5. Ibid., p. 182.
6. Levenda 1995, pp. 195–6.
7. Ibid., p. 196.

 8. Goodrick-Clarke 1985, p. 184.
 9. Ibid., p. 185.
10. Ibid.
11. Ibid., p. 186.
12. Ibid., p. 188.
13. Levenda 1995, p. 187.
14. Ibid., p. 189.
15. Ibid.
16. Ibid., pp. 189–90.
17. Goodrick-Clarke 1985, p. 189.
18. Ibid., p. 190.
19. Ibid., p. 191.
20. Fest 1979, p. 178.
21. Ibid.
22. Ibid., p. 179.
23. Payne 1995, p. 184.
24. Fest 1979, pp. 180–1.
25. Goodrick-Clarke 1985, p. 178.
26. Levenda 1995, p. 153.
27. Ibid.
28. Ibid., p. 154.
29. Ibid.
30. Ibid., p. 155.
31. Padfield 1990, p. 248, quoted in Levenda 1995, p. 156.
32. Fest 1979, p. 173.
33. Levenda 1995, p. 156.
34. Ibid., p. 157.
35. Quoted in Levenda 1995, pp. 158–9.
36. Quoted in Levenda 1995, pp. 159–60.
37. Levenda 1995, p. 160.
38. Payne 1995, p. 375.
39. Fest 1979, p. 189.
40. Ibid., p. 190.

7 *The secret at the heart of the world*

 1. Godwin 1993, p. 106.
 2. Ibid., p. 107.
 3. Ibid., p. 108.
 4. Childress 1999, p. 238.
 5. Michel Lamy: *Jules Verne, initié et initiateur. La clé du secret de Rennes-le-Château et le trésor des Rois de France*, Paris, Payot, 1984, p. 194. Cited in Godwin 1993, pp. 108–9.
 6. Godwin 1993, p. 109.
 7. Ibid.
 8. Quoted in Godwin 1993, pp. 109–110.

9. Gardner 1957, p. 20.
10. Ibid.
11. Ibid.
12. Quoted in Godwin 1993, p. 117.
13. Childress 1999, p. 239.
14. Ibid., pp. 239–40.
15. Gardner 1957, pp. 23–4.
16. Ibid., p. 24.
17. Quoted in Godwin 1993, pp. 116–7.
18. Gardner 1957, p. 25.
19. Godwin 1993, p. 117.
20. Gardner 1957, p. 26.
21. Quoted in Childress 1999, p. 240.
22. Childress 1999, p. 241.
23. Gardner 1957, p. 37.
24. Ibid.
25. Pauwels and Bergier 1971, p. 154.
26. Ibid., pp. 38–41.
27. Quoted in Gardner 1957, p. 41.
28. Ibid.
29. Pauwels and Bergier 1971, p. 185.
30. Quoted in Pauwels and Bergier 1971, pp. 185–6.
31. Pauwels and Bergier 1971, p. 186.
32. Ibid., p. 188.
33. Ibid., p. 189.
34. For a detailed description of Byrd's life and expeditions, see the polar explorers' Internet pages at http://www.south-pole.com/home-page.html, from which this account is borrowed.
35. Harbinson 1996, p. 209.
36. Giannini 1959, p. 14.
37. Harbinson 1996, p. 210.
38. Ibid.
39. Ibid., p. 211.
40. Ibid.
41. Quoted in Childress 1999, p. 258.
42. See Bruce Lanier Wright's piece, 'From Hero to Dero' in *Fortean Times* No. 127 (October 1999), pp. 36–41.
43. Childress 1999, p. 218.
44. Ibid.
45. Ibid., p. 219.
46. Ibid., p. 220.
47. Quoted in Childress 1999, pp. 221–2.
48. Quoted in Childress 1999, p. 214.
49. *Fortean Times* 127, p. 38.
50. Quoted in Childress 1999, pp. 222–3.

51. Childress 1999, p. 223.
52. Shaver, 'Thought Records of Lemuria', *Amazing Stories*, June 1945, quoted in Peebles 1995, p. 5.
53. *Fortean Times* 127, p. 39.
54. Ibid.
55. Ibid.
56. Quoted in Childress 1999, p. 224.
57. Peebles 1995, p. 6.
58. Childress 1999, p. 229.
59. *Fortean Times* 127, p. 40.
60. Quoted in Childress 1999, p. 229.
61. Childress 1999, pp. 232–3.
62. Quoted in Childress 1999, p. 233.
63. *Fortean Times* 127, p. 41.
64. Childress 1999, p. 244.
65. Ibid., p. 245.
66. Ibid.
67. Ibid., p. 246.
68. Ibid., p. 247.
69. Ibid.
70. Ibid., p. 249.
71. Ibid., p. 251.
72. Ibid.
73. Ibid., pp. 251–2.
74. Ibid., pp. 293–4.
75. Ibid., p. 295.

8 The cloud Reich

1. Brookesmith 1984, p. 202.
2. Cited in Sagan and Page 1996, pp. 207–8.
3. Cited in Harbinson 1996, pp. 45–6.
4. Cited in Vesco and Childress 1994, p. 79. The vast majority of this book is actually the work of Renato Vesco, with a small amount of additional material by David Hatcher Childress. The original work was entitled *Intercettateli Senza Sparare*, and was published in an English translation by Grove Press, New York in 1971 under the title *Intercept But Don't Shoot*.
5. Hough and Randles 1996, p. 46.
6. Ibid., p. 47.
7. Vesco and Childress 1994, p. 84.
8. Vesco and Childress 1994, pp. 80–81.
9. Ibid., p. 81.
10. Quoted in Vesco and Childress 1994, p. 82.
11. Hough and Randles 1996, p. 50.
12. Ibid., p. 83.

13. Vesco and Childress 1994, p. 82.
14. Ibid., p. 83.
15. Ibid., p. 84.
16. Good 1996, p. xxviii.
17. Ibid., pp. xxviii–xxix.
18. Jones 1998, p. 510.
19. Ibid., p. 511.
20. Ibid.
21. Ibid., p. 512.
22. Good 1996, p. xxxiii.
23. Ibid.
24. Harbinson 1996, p. 61.
25. Vesco and Childress 1994, p. 85.
26. Ibid., pp. 85–6.
27. Ibid., p. 86.
28. Ibid.
29. Ibid., p. 113n.
30. Ibid., p. 157.
31. Quoted in Harbinson 1996, p. 72.
32. Ibid., p. 73.
33. Vesco and Childress 1994, pp. 255–6.
34. Harbinson 1996, p. 74.
35. Ibid.
36. Vesco and Childress 1994, p. 244.
37. Ibid.
38. Hogg 1999, p. 52.
39. Marrs 1997, p. 69.
40. Ibid.
41. Ibid., p. 70.
42. Ibid.
43. Vesco and Childress 1994, p. 252.
44. Ibid., pp. 252–3.
45. Ibid., p. 253.
46. Ibid.
47. Ibid., p. 255.
48. Ibid., p. 258.
49. Ibid., pp. 259–60.
50. Ibid., p. 262.
51. Good 1996, p. 228.
52. Peebles 1995, p. 113.
53. Evans and Stacy 1997, p. 136.
54. See Jacobs 1994, pp. 49–236.
55. Quoted in Harbinson 1996, p. 172.
56. Ibid., p. 173.
57. Ibid., p. 175.

58. Ibid., p. 177.
59. Ibid.
60. Ibid., pp. 179–80.
61. Ibid., p. 180.
62. David Guyatt, 'Police State of Mind', *Fortean Times* No. 95, p. 35.
63. Ibid., p. 38.
64. Ibid., p. 36.
65. Quoted in Constantine 1995, pp. 2–3.
66. Guyatt, p. 36.
67. Ibid., pp. 36–7.
68. Constantine 1995, p. 4.
69. Guyatt, p. 36.
70. Defense Intelligence Agency (DIA) report, quoted in Guyatt, p. 37.
71. Constantine 1995, p. 9.
72. See Vallée 1993.
73. Constantine 1995, p. 18.
74. Ibid.
75. Ibid.
76. Ibid.
77. Ibid., p. 19.
78. Ibid., p. 26.
79. Sid Que, 'Radio Head', *Fortean Times* No. 113, p. 39.
80. Ibid., p. 37.
81. Ibid.
82. Constantine 1995, p. 40.

9 *Invisible Eagle*

1. Trevor-Roper 1995, p. 43.
2. Marrs 1997, p. 72.
3. Ibid.
4. Ibid., p. 73.
5. Quoted in Pool 1997, pp. 31–2.
6. Marrs 1997, p. 73.
7. Higham 1983, quoted in Marrs 1997, p. 73.
8. Ibid.
9. Quoted in Marrs 1997, p. 74.
10. Ibid.
11. *World Press Review*, vol. 41, no. 11, November 1996. Quoted in Marrs 1997, pp. 74–5.
12. Trevor-Roper 1995, pp. xxxvii–xxxviii.
13. Ibid., p. xxxviii.
14. Ibid., p. xi.
15. Ibid., p. xii.
16. Ibid.
17. Keith 1994, p. 30.

18. Ibid., p. 31.
19. Ibid., p. 33.
20. Harbinson 1996, p. 219.
21. Ibid.
22. Ibid., pp. 219–20.
23. Ibid., p. 220.
24. Ibid., p. 221.
25. Marrs 1997, p. 75.
26. Vesco and Childress 1994, pp. xv–xvi.
27. Ibid., p. xvi.
28. Godwin 1993, p. 105.
29. Ibid.
30. Ibid., p. 63.
31. Ibid., p. 64.
32. Ibid.
33. Ibid., p. 66.
34. Translated by Godwin, ibid., p. 65.
35. Ibid., p. 67.
36. Ibid.
37. Ibid., p. 68.
38. Ibid.
39. Harbinson 1996, p. 248.
40. Ibid., p. 249.
41. Quoted from a reproduction of the *Samisdat* newsletter, available on the Nizkor Website. Nizkor is an educational organisation dedicated to providing accurate information on the Holocaust and related Holocaust studies. One of its laudable objectives is to expose and dismantle the despicable arguments of Holocaust deniers such as Ernst Zündel. At the risk of patronising the reader (which is by no means my intention), I must state that anyone with the slightest suspicion that the Holocaust did not take place should visit this excellent Website, which will immediately set them straight. *The Nizkor Project: Remembering the Holocaust* can be reached at http://www.nizkor.org/
42. See 'Giving the Devil His Due: Holocaust Revisionism as a Test Case for Free Speech and the Skeptical Ethic' by Frank Miele, reproduced on the Nizkor Project website.
43. Ibid.
44. Godwin 1993, p. 70.
45. Ibid.
46. Ibid.
47. Ibid., pp. 70–71.
48. Ibid., p. 71.
49. Ibid.
50. Ibid.

51. Ibid., p. 72.
52. Ibid.
53. Ibid., p. 73.
54. Ibid.
55. Quoted in Godwin 1993, p. 73.
56. Ibid., p. 127.
57. Ibid.
58. *Fortean Times* No. 121 (April 1999), p. 29.
59. Watkins and Ambrose 1989, pp. 99–100.
60. Ibid., p. 207.
61. Ibid., p. 106.
62. Ibid., p. 214.
63. Hitler 1998, pp. 120–6.
64. Ibid., pp. 121–2.
65. Ibid., p. 122.
66. Ibid., pp. 126–7.
67. Ibid., p. 131.
68. Ibid., p. 348, quoted in Keith 1994, p. 152.
69. Keith 1994, pp. 152–3.
70. Quoted in Keith 1994, pp. 30–31.
71. Keith 1994, p. 148.
72. Ibid., p. 153.

Conclusion: the myth machine

1. Anderson 1995, p. 233.

Bibliography and suggested further reading

Anderson, Ken: *Hitler and the Occult*, Amherst, New York, Prometheus Books, 1995.

Baigent, Michael and Leigh, Richard: *The Elixir and the Stone: The Tradition of Magic and Alchemy*, London, Viking, 1997.

Baigent, Michael and Leigh, Richard: *Secret Germany: Stauffenberg and the Mystical Crusade Against Hitler*, London, Penguin Books, 1995.

Baigent, Michael; Leigh, Richard and Lincol, Henry: *The Holy Blood and the Holy Grail*, London, Arrow Books, 1996.

Baigent, Michael; Leigh, Richard and Lincol, Henry: *The Messianic Legacy*, London, Arrow Books, 1996.

Beckley, Timothy Green: *Subterranean Worlds Inside Earth*, New Brunswick, New Jersey, Inner Light Publications, 1992.

Beckley, Timothy Green: *The Smoky God and Other Inner Earth Mysteries*, New Brunswick, New Jersey, Inner Light Publications, 1993.

Blavatsky, Helena Petrovna: *The Secret Doctrine* (2 volumes), Pasadena, California, Theosophical University Press, 1999.

Blum, Howard: *Wanted! The Search for Nazis in America*, New York, Quadrangle, 1977.

Bower, Tom: *Nazi Gold*, New York, HarperPerennial, 1998.

Brookesmith, Peter (Editor): *The Age of the UFO*, London, Orbis Publishing, 1984.

Bullock, Alan: *Hitler, A Study in Tyranny*, London, Penguin Books, 1990.

Bullock, Alan: *Hitler and Stalin: Parallel Lives*, London, Fontana Press, 1998.

Bulwer-Lytton, Edward: *The Coming Race*, Stroud, Gloucestershire, Alan Sutton, 1995 (1st. ed. 1871).

Cavendish, Richard: *The Magical Arts*, London, Arkana, 1984 (originally published as *The Black Arts*).

Charroux, Robert: *The Mysterious Unknown*, London, Corgi Books, 1973.

Charroux, Robert: *One Hundred Thousand Years of Man's Unknown History*, London, Sphere Books, 1981.

Childress, David Hatcher: *Extraterrestrial Archaeology*, Stelle, Illinois, Adventures Unlimited Press, 1995.

Childress, David Hatcher and Shaver, Richard S.: *Lost Continents and the Hollow Earth*, Stelle, Illinois, Adventures Unlimited Press, 1999.

Condon, Dr Edward U. (Project Director): *Scientific Study of Unidentified Flying Objects*, New York, Bantam Books, 1969.

Constantine, Alex: *Psychic Dictatorship in the U.S.A.*, Portland, Oregon, Feral House, 1995.

Cookridge, E. H.: *Gehlen: Spy of the Century*, New York, Random House, 1972.

Daraul, Arkon: *A History of Secret Societies*, New York, Citadel Press, 1994.

Davidson, Eugene: *The Making of Adolf Hitler: The Birth and Rise of Nazism*, Columbia, Missouri, University of Missouri Press, 1997.

Davies, Norman: *Europe: A History*, London, Pimlico, 1997.

Evans, Hilary and Stacy, Dennis (Editors): *UFOs 1947–1997: Fifty Years of Flying Saucers*, London, John Brown Publishing, 1997.

Fest, Joachim C.: *Hitler*, New York, Harcourt Brace Jovanovich, 1974.

Fest, Joachim C.: *The Face of the Third Reich*, London, Penguin Books, 1979.

Freemantle, Brian: *CIA: The 'Honourable' Company*, London, Michael Joseph, 1983.

Gardner, Joseph L. (Editor): *Great Mysteries of the Past* (originally published as *Wie geschah es wirklich?*), Pleasantville, New York, Readers's Digest Association, Inc., 1991.

Gardner, Martin: *Fads & Fallacies in the Name of Science*, New York, Dover Publications, 1957.

Giannini, Amadeo: *Worlds Beyond the Pole*, New York, Vantage, 1959.

Godwin, Joscelyn: *Arktos: The Polar Myth in Science, Symbolism, and Nazi Survival*, London, Thames and Hudson, 1993.

Good, Timothy: *Beyond Top Secret: The Worldwide UFO Security Threat*, London, Sidgwick & Jackson, 1996.

Goodrick-Clarke, Nicholas: *The Occult Roots of Nazism: Secret Aryan Cults and Their Influence on Nazi Ideology*, New York, New York University Press, 1985.

Goodrick-Clarke, Nicholas: *Hitler's Priestess: Savitri Devi, the Hindu-Aryan Myth, and Neo-Nazism*, New York, New York University Press, 1998.

Guiley, Rosemary Ellen: *Harper's Encyclopedia of Mystical & Paranormal Experience*, Edison, New Jersey, Castle Books, 1991.

Harbinson, W. A.: *Projekt UFO: The Case for Man-Made Flying Saucers*, London, Boxtree, 1996.

Heideking, Jürgen and Mauch, Christof (Editors): *American Intelligence and the German Resistance to Hitler: A Documentary History*, Boulder, Colorado, Westview Press, 1998.

Heiden, Konrad: *Der Fuehrer*, Boston, Houghton Mifflin, 1944.

Hesemann, Michael: *UFOs The Secret History*, New York, Marlowe & Company, 1998.

Higham, Charles: *Trading with the Enemy: An Exposé of the Nazi-American Money Plot 1933–1949*, New York, Delacorte Press, 1983.

Hitler, Adolf: *Mein Kampf*, London, Pimlico, 1998.

Hogg, Ian V.: *German Secret Weapons of the Second World War*, London, Greenhill Books, 1999.

Hopkins, Budd: *Missing Time: A Documented Study of UFO Abductions*, New York, Richard Marek Publishers, 1981.

Hough, Peter and Randles, Jenny: *The Complete Book of UFOs: An Investigation into Alien Contacts and Encounters*, London, Judy Piatkus, 1996.

Howard, Michael: *The Occult Conspiracy: Secret Societies – Their Influence and Power in World History*, Rochester, Vermont, Destiny Books, 1989.

Hynek, J. Allen: *The UFO Experience*, London, Corgi Books, 1975.

Jacobs, David M.: *Alien Encounters: Firsthand Accounts of UFO Abductions*, London, Virgin Books, 1994.

Jones, R. V.: *Most Secret War*, Ware, Hertfordshire, Wordsworth Editions, 1998.

Keith, Jim: *Casebook on Alternative 3: UFOs, Secret Societies and World Control*, Lilburn, Georgia, IllumiNet Press, 1994.

Kershaw, Ian: *The 'Hitler Myth': Image and Reality in the Third Reich*, Oxford, Oxford University Press, 1989.

Kershaw, Ian: *Hitler 1889–1936: Hubris*, London, Allen Lane, 1998.

King, Francis: *Satan and Swastika*, St Albans, Herts., Mayflower Books, 1976.

Kolosimo, Peter: *Not of this World*, London, Sphere Books, 1977.

Langer, Walter: *The Mind of Adolf Hitler*, New York, Basic Books, 1972.

Le Page, Victoria: *Shambhala: The Fascinating Truth Behind the Myth of Shangri-la*, Wheaton, Illinois, Quest Books, 1996.

Levenda, Peter: *Unholy Alliance: A History of Nazi Involvement with the Occult*, New York, Avon Books, 1995.

Loftus, John and Aarons, Mark: *The Secret War Against the Jews*, New York, St. Martin's Griffin, 1994.

Loftus, John and Aarons, Mark: *Unholy Trinity: The Vatican, the Nazis, and the Swiss Banks*, New York, St. Martin's Griffin, 1998.

Maclellan, Alec: *The Lost World of Agharti: The Mystery of Vril Power*, London, Souvenir Press, 1996.

Marks, John: *The Search for the 'Manchurian Candidate': The CIA and Mind Control*, New York, Times Books, 1979.

Marrs, Jim: *Alien Agenda: The Untold Story of the Extraterrestrials Among Us*, London, HarperCollins, 1997.

Maser, Werner: *Hitler: Legend, Myth & Reality*, New York, Harper & Row, 1973.

Padfield, Peter: *Himmler: Reichsführer-SS*, New York, Henry Holt & Co., 1990.

Pauwels, Louis and Bergier, Jacques: *The Morning of the Magicians*, London, Mayflower Books, 1971.

Payne, Robert: *The Life and Death of Adolf Hitler*, New York, Praeger, 1973.

Payne, Stanley G.: *A History of Fascism, 1914–45*, University College London Press, 1995.

Peebles, Curtis: *Watch the Skies! A Chronicle of the Flying Saucer Myth*, New York, Berkley Books, 1995.

Poncé, Charles: *Kabbalah: An Introduction and Illumination for the World Today*, Wheaton, Illinois, Quest Books, 1995.

Pool, James: *Hitler and His Secret Partners: Contributions, Loot and Rewards, 1933–1945*, New York, Pocket Books, 1997.

Ravenscroft, Trevor: *The Spear of Destiny*, York Beach, Maine, Samuel Weiser, 1982.

Reed, William: *The Phantom of the Poles*, Mokelumne Hill, Health Research, 1964.

Roerich, Nicholas: *Shambhala*, New York, Nicholas Roerich Museum, 1978.

Rosenbaum, Ron: *Explaining Hitler: The Search For the Origins of His Evil*, London, Papermac, 1999.

Rosenfeld, Alvin: *Imagining Hitler*, Bloomington, Indiana University Press, 1985.

Runciman, Steven: *The Kingdom of Jerusalem and the Frankish East 1100–1187*, Cambridge, Cambridge University Press, 1952.

Russell, Jeffrey B.: *A History of Witchcraft: Sorcerers, Heretics and Pagans*, London, Thames and Hudson 1991.

Sagan, Carl and Page, Thornton (Editors): *UFOs: A Scientific Debate*, New York, Barnes & Noble, 1996.

Santillana, Giorgio de and Dechend, Hertha von: *Hamlet's Mill*, Boston, David R. Godine, 1998.

Serrano, Miguel: *Jung & Hesse: A Record of Two Friendships*, New York, Schocken Books, 1968.

Simpson, Christopher: *Blowback: America's Recruitment of Nazis and Its Effects on the Cold War*, New York, Weidenfeld & Nicholson, 1988.

Sklar, Dusty: *Gods and Beasts: The Nazis and the Occult*, New York, Thomas Y. Crowell, 1977.

Smith, John Holland: *Constantine the Great*, London, Hamish Hamilton, 1971.

Smith, Warren: *This Hollow Earth*, London, Sphere Books, 1977.

Speer, Albert: *Inside the Third Reich*, London, Phoenix, 1998.

Spence, Lewis: *An Encyclopaedia of Occultism*, New York, Citadel Press, 1996.

Stefansson, Vilhjalmur: *Ultima Thule*, New York, The MacMillan Company, 1940.

Steiger, Brad (Ed.): *Project Blue Book*, New York, Ballantine Books, 1990.

Strieber, Whitley: *Communion: A True Story*, New York, William Morrow & Company, 1987.

Thomas, Gordon: *Journey Into Madness: the True Story of Secret CIA Mind Control and Medical Abuse*, New York, Bantam Books, 1990.

Toland, John: *Adolf Hitler*, Garden City, Doubleday & Co., 1976.

Tomas, Andrew: *Shambhala: Oasis of Light*, London, Sphere Books, 1977.

Trevor-Roper, Hugh: *The Last Days of Hitler*, London, Macmillan, 1995.

Vallée, Jacques: *Revelations: Alien Contact and Human Deception*, New York, Ballantine Books, 1993.

Vesco, Renato and Childress, David Hatcher: *Man-Made UFOs 1944–1994: 50 Years of Suppression*, Stelle, Illinois, Adventures Unlimited Press, 1994. (Originally published as *Intercettateli Senza Sparare*, Milan, E. Mursia & Co., 1968.)

Waite, Robert G. L.: *The Psychopathic God: Adolf Hitler*, New York, Basic Books, 1977.

Washington, Peter: *Madame Blavatsky's Baboon: Theosophy and the Emergence of the Western Guru*, London, Secker & Warburg, 1996.

Watkins, Leslie and Ambrose, David: *Alternative 3*, London, Sphere Books, 1978.

Webb, James: *The Occult Establishment*, La Salle, Illinois, Open Court, 1976.

Wilson, Colin: *From Atlantis to the Sphinx*, London, Virgin Publishing, 1996.

Wilson, Don: *Our Mysterious Spaceship Moon*, London, Sphere Books, 1976.

Wilson, Robert Anton: *Cosmic Trigger: Final Secret of the Illuminati*, Phoenix, Arizona, New Falcon Publications, 1993.

Wilson, Robert Anton: *Everything is Under Control: Conspiracies, Cults, and Cover-ups*, New York, HarperPerennial, 1998.

USEFUL WEBPAGES:
Holocaust Studies:
http://www.nizkor.org/
German Genealogy:
http://w3g.med.uni-giessen.de/gene/reg/ahe1814.html
Antarctica:
http://www.south-pole.com/homepage.html
Comprehensive Links Page on Nazi Germany:
http://members.aol.com/AACTchrOz/Hitler-Holocaust.html

Index